Best of the Word for Today

Bob Gass

To "Auntie Roberta".

Thanks will never be enough
for everything you do for us!

All our love,
Gillian, Trevor & Hannah
xo

16

EasyRead Large

D1332753

Copyright Page from the Original Book

Bridge-Logos
Alachua, FL 32615 USA

Best of the Word for Today
by Bob Gass

Library of Congress Catalog Card Number: 96-78633
International Standard Book Number 978-0-88270-731-0

G351.318.FBM.m910.35220

A Word from the Author

This book contains the best of the first few years of *The Word for You Today.* Considering the insights God has given to me during the last few years, I can see how much I've grown personally. Those who began this program with me are experiencing this as well, and you can, too.

That's why I've put together a second, and more recent compilation of devotions which is called *A Fresh Word for Today.* It contains many of our most requested days. If you enjoy this book, you'll definitely want to get that one, too.

I thank God who does "exceedingly, abundantly, above all we are able to ask or think" for the way in which He has used these devotional writings. Over one million people now read them each day.

Every month we receive over 50,000 letters from readers around the world, whose lives have been touched through it. To God be all the glory!

Jesus

"...and thou shalt call his name Jesus: for he shall save his people from their sins."

(Matthew 1:21)

An anonymous author made this striking comparison. "Socrates taught for 40 years, Plato for 20, Aristotle for 40, and Jesus for only 3. Yet the influence of Christ's 3-year ministry infinitely transcends the impact left by the combined 130 years of teaching from these men who were among the greatest philosophers of all antiquity.

"He painted no pictures, yet some of the finest paintings of Raphael, Michelangelo, and Leonardo da Vinci received their inspirations from Him. Jesus wrote no poetry, but Dante, Milton, and scores of the world's greatest poets were inspired by Him.

"He composed no music, still Haydn, Handel, Beethoven, Bach, and Mendelssohn reached their highest perfection of melody in the hymns, symphonies, and oratorios they composed in His praise. Every sphere of human greatness has been enriched by this humble carpenter from Nazareth.

"His unique contribution to the race of men is the salvation of the soul! Philosophy could not accomplish that. Not art. Not literature. Not music. Only Jesus Christ can break the enslaving chains of sin and Satan. He alone can speak peace to the human heart, strengthen the weak, and give life to those who are spiritually dead."

Please let us introduce you to Jesus. He loves you, and you'll find Him very easy to love, too.

JANUARY 1

Never Out of His Sight!

The eyes of the Lord thy God are always upon [the land], from the beginning of the year even unto the end of the year.

(Deuteronomy 11:12)

As you look ahead to another year, God's Word gives you a glimpse into some of the wonderful things He has in store for you. Listen: "The land you are about to enter and possess is not like ... where you have come from.... It is a land of hills and valleys with plenty of rain—a land that the Lord your God personally cares for! His eyes are always upon it, day after day throughout the year!" (Deuteronomy 11:10-12 TLB).

You're about to enter a year when God promises you *everything* you need to succeed! No matter what you left behind in the old year, this new one offers you a fresh start. God says He will not remember your sins and shortcomings (see Isaiah 43:25), so close the door and move forward.

Note: The land ahead is not flat and monotonous. It's a land of hills and valleys; and you need both! This year you'll have to climb some mountains, and you'll need endurance to make it to the top. But when you do, the view will be breathtaking and the rewards will be greater than you ever dreamed.

You'll also go through some valleys, and deal with pain and loss, but there you'll drink from God's sweetest streams. There you'll understand the words, "He restoreth my soul." But most importantly, we're told that "His eyes are always upon it."

***

NO MATTER WHAT LIES AHEAD THIS YEAR,
HE'LL BE WITH YOU EVERY DAY.
NOW, THERE'S TRULY A REASON TO CELEBRATE!

JANUARY 2

Do You Have "Class"?

Demetrius is well spoken of by everyone—and even by the truth itself.

(3 John 12 NIV)

When others speak well of you, you've got acceptance; but when the truth speaks well of you, you've got class! Demetrius had it. Do you? Before you answer, listen to Paul's words to Timothy: "Set an example ... in speech, in life, in love, in faith and in purity ... give yourself wholly to them, so that everyone may see your progress" (1 Timothy 4:12-15 NIV). That's class!

Consider these words carefully. Class is just confidence dressed in humility. It keeps its word, its temper, and its friends. It has a steady eye, a steady nerve, a steady tongue, and steady habits. It's silent when it has nothing to say, is thoughtful when it judges, and is always first to make amends when it's wrong. Class doesn't run scared. It's sure-footed, committed, and handles whatever comes along. Class has a sense of humor. It knows that a good laugh is often the best lubricant for oiling the machinery of human relations.

Class never makes excuses. It takes its lumps, learns from its mistakes, and becomes wiser. Class knows that courtesy and good manners are nothing more than a series of small sacrifices. It bespeaks an aristocracy that is not dependent on ancestry or money. A blue-blood can be totally without it, while the son of a coal miner may ooze it out of every pore. Class walks with kings, yet still keeps its virtue; talks to crowds, yet still maintains the common touch.

***

EVERYONE IS COMFORTABLE WITH PEOPLE WHO HAVE CLASS—BECAUSE THEY ARE COMFORTABLE WITH THEMSELVES!

JANUARY 3

Stay on the Battlefield

**At the time when kings go forth to battle ...
David tarried still at Jerusalem.**

(2 Samuel 11:1)

David didn't get into trouble until he left the battlefield! When he stopped fighting, he suffered his greatest defeat. Your protection depends on being in the right place. Stay at your post—don't give the enemy an inch or he'll take a mile. Keep your sword drawn and your shield high. Of all the armor Paul speaks of in Ephesians 6, there's none for your back. If you think fighting is tough, wait till you see what happens when you *stop fighting.*

We read, "He saw a woman washing herself, and the woman was very beautiful to look upon." Even though she was someone's wife and David knew the consequences, he "sent messengers, and took her; and she came in unto him, and he lay with her" (2 Samuel 11:2-4). Before it was over, he committed murder in a vain attempt to cover up his sin, a baby was born and died, David's name was dragged through the mud, and, saddest of all, there was given "great occasion to the enemies of the Lord to blaspheme" (2 Samuel 12:14).

You need a goal so noble, and a cause so great, that you wouldn't dream of endangering it by laying down your sword and leaving the battlefield.

***

CHILD OF GOD, STAY ON THE BATTLEFIELD—IT'S THE ONLY SAFE PLACE TO BE.

JANUARY 4

Too Much to Lose

Then Jesus ... said unto him ... Take up the cross, and follow me. And he was sad at that saying, and went away grieved: for he had great possessions.

(Mark 10:21-22)

This man really wanted to follow Jesus, but he had too much to lose. He could have been another John or Mark, but instead that's the last we ever hear about him, because he had become accustomed to a life of privilege and couldn't live with less.

Imagine him years later as an old man. His grandson climbs up on his lap and says, "Granddad, who was the greatest man you ever met?" Without hesitating, he replies, "Jesus!" "What made Him so great?" the child asks. He replies, "Son, there's never been anyone like Him. He healed the sick and even raised the dead. I saw Him do it!" The little fellow says, "Granddad, did He ever talk to you?" "Yes," he replies. The child asks, "Well, Granddad, what did He say to you?" Looking at the child, he says, "He asked me to follow Him." Earnest eyes look up at the old man and ask, *"Did you do it, Granddad? Did you follow Him?"*

Fighting back tears of regret, he sets the little fellow down and walks out into the garden of his luxurious home, with the words ringing in his ears, "Did you do it, Granddad? Did you follow Him?"

***

WHEN YOUR LIFE IS OVER, WILL YOU BE ABLE TO LOOK BACK WITH JOY AND SAY, "I FOLLOWED JESUS"? WHAT ELSE MATTERS?

JANUARY 5

No Geographical Cures

Then Isaac sowed in that land, and received in the same year an hundred fold: and the Lord blessed him.

(Genesis 26:12)

Geographical cures don't work! Why? Because wherever you go, you take yourself with you! If God's dealing with you and you don't like the school, the teacher, or the tests, the worst thing you can do is run. Because when you get to your new destination, you'll find the school, the teacher, and the tests there are the same, or harder—and you'll be a grade behind.

Isaac was going through the worst time of his life. The Philistines were throwing rocks into his wells (the source of his livelihood). So he faced what we all face – fight or flight! Instead of running, he decided to stay and sow, even though he was in the middle of a famine. As a result, he received a 100 percent return. And that's not all. Listen: "[He] went forward, and grew until he became very great" (Genesis 26:13). The Philistines didn't determine Isaac's harvest—he did. And you, too, determine your own harvest.

The solution's not found in a different house, a new job, or a change of climate. The only question that matters is, "What's *God* saying to me in this?" Things may be rough where you are today, and "far-off fields" may be looking green.

***

BUT IF GOD'S TELLING YOU TO STAY WHERE YOU ARE, THEN START SOWING WHAT YOU'VE GOT – BECAUSE HE HAS A HARVEST IN STORE FOR YOU.

JANUARY 6

God Has a Purpose for Your Life

Ye have not chosen me, but I have chosen you.

(John 15:16)

It doesn't take a lot of people to bring about change. In fact, too many can get in the way. Gideon chose 32,000 men to fight, but God only needed 300. He doesn't care how many can be *counted*—He only cares how many can be *counted on.* The truth is, your life could be messed up because too many people are telling you what to do. Don't listen to them. Get down before God and ask *Him* to speak to you. He'll give you the word you need.

God doesn't need a crowd—He just needs someone who will listen and obey. If He wants to start a nation, He'll give hope and vision to an Abraham. If He wants to bring down an Egyptian Pharaoh, He'll reach into the bulrushes and pull out a Moses. When He wants a lineage for His Son, He'll go to the "red light district" and find a Rahab. He's just looking for a willing heart!

Ethel Waters loved to say, "My God don't sponsor no flops!" Her grammar was slightly off, but her theology was right on. Don't spend your life trying to be *ordinary.* Don't try to fit somebody else's expectations. *God has an agenda just for you!*

✳✳✳

THE REASON GOD HAS BROUGHT YOU THROUGH SO MUCH IS BECAUSE HE HAS A HIGHER PLAN AND PURPOSE FOR YOUR LIFE. GET INTO HIS PRESENCE TODAY AND ASK HIM ALL ABOUT IT.

JANUARY 7

Corrected, but not Discarded

Out of weakness were made strong ... (Hebrews 11:34)

The heroes of the Bible were powerful, but not perfect. They were corrected but not discarded, and their human frailties encourage the rest of us that God can use us, too. The contrast between God and the people He uses reminds us who is to be worshiped.

Paul readily admitted he fell far short of his goal. Yet, the light of revelation that shone from his earthen vessel illuminates our walk today. A perfect word from imperfect vessels—that's "the high calling of God," and it's through ordinary people like you and me that He chooses to bring it. Amazing!

In Hebrews 11, God lists some of His heroes. But notice what He said about them: "Out of weakness were made strong." *They were strengthened through struggle, and that's still God's way.* Look at them, but don't judge them because of a weak moment – judge them on the entirety of their lives! The dents in their armor didn't affect their performance on the battlefield. They're remembered for their faith—not their flawlessness!

Samson shone on the battlefield, but struggled in the bedroom. Samuel judged the sins of Eli's children, but failed to keep his *own* sons on the right track. You ask, "Why does God use such people?" For three reasons:

(1)   Because His strength is made perfect in our weakness (see 2 Corinthians 12:9).

(2)   Because our limitations are not His (see Ephesians 3:20).

(3)   Because He uses what's available (see 1 Corinthians 1:27).

***

NOW, AREN'T YOU GLAD FOR THAT TODAY?

JANUARY 8

Kindness Aforehand

There came a woman having an alabaster box of ointment of spikenard very precious ... and poured it on his head.

(Mark 14:3)

Don't keep the alabaster box of your love sealed up until your friends are dead! Break it open now, pour it out, and fill their lives with joy while you can. Those words of kindness you've thought of saying a thousand times—say them now, while their ears can hear them and their hearts can still be touched. Those flowers you keep meaning to send—do it this week and brighten their home *before they leave it!*

It's amazing! The crowd in the house saw her do it, argued about it, and *missed the whole point.* That very night, following this woman's act of devotion, Judas would go out and set wheels in motion that would lead Jesus to the Cross. Somehow she sensed that time and opportunity were running out. If she was ever going to show Him her love, this was it! Listen to what Jesus said: "She is come aforehand to anoint my body" (Mark 14:8). There it is—*kindness aforehand.*

Joseph of Arimathea brought 100 pounds of precious ointment to anoint Jesus after He was dead, but not a word of praise is spoken about his "post-mortem" kindness. She brought only one pound of ointment and poured it on Him—*while He was still living*—and Jesus said, "Wherever the gospel is preached throughout the world, what she has done will also be told, in memory of her" (Mark 14:9 NIV). Are you getting the message?

***

IF MY FRIENDS HAVE ANY ALABASTER BOXES LAID AWAY FOR ME, I WOULD RATHER THEY BRING THEM OUT NOW.

JANUARY 9

Walking Through the Fire

The One who called you is completely dependable. If He said it, he'll do it!

(1 Thessalonians 5:24 TM)

Did you hear that? *If He said it, He'll do it!* He's completely dependable. No matter what you're going through today, you can count on Him to be with you—and when *He's* with you, you can be sure He'll bring you through.

Remember the three Hebrew children? They refused to bow to the king's idols, so he threw them into a furnace heated seven times over. Maybe you feel like you're walking through the fire, and it's seven times worse than anything you've ever experienced. But look what happened. When the king looked into the fire, he said, "Did not we cast three men bound into the midst of the fire? Lo, I see four men loose, walking in the midst of the fire, and they have no hurt; and the form of the fourth is like the Son of God" (Daniel 3:24-25). In the midst of the furnace the three Hebrew children were *"loose,"* they had *"no hurt,"* and they were *"walking with the Son of God."*

Today, if He allows you to go through the fire. He'll be with you; it won't hurt you; *and the very thing the enemy meant to destroy you, will set you free.* The One who called you is *completely dependable.*

***

REMEMBER, YOU ARE NOT THE ONLY CONSIDERATION HERE. LIKE THE HEBREW CHILDREN, YOUR FAITH IN THE FIRE WILL TOUCH THE LIVES OF OTHERS AND TURN THEM TO GOD.

JANUARY 10

Your Attitude Determines Everything

My servant Caleb has a different attitude, and has wholeheartedly followed me.

(Numbers 14:24, Berkeley)

Caleb went against the crowd and popular opinion. While the majority thought the giants were too big and God's people were too small, Caleb never doubted God for a minute. The *miracles* proved that nothing was too big for God to handle. The *manna* proved He cared and that *every need* would be supplied. So with a God like this, how can you fail?

Listen: "Caleb stilled the people before Moses, and said, Let us go up at once, and possess it; for we are well able to overcome it" (Numbers 13:30). What an attitude! If only they'd listened. But no; their negative attitude landed them in the wilderness – for forty years! Doubt and unbelief will always lead you into the wilderness. Grumbling and complaining will fill your life with barrenness. John Mason says, "It's your *attitude* that determines your *altitude.* You'll never rise any higher than it." Caleb had a different attitude and look at the results he got: "Hebron therefore became the inheritance of Caleb ... because that he wholly followed the Lord God of Israel" (Joshua 14:13).

***

HOW'S YOUR ATTITUDE AND YOUR OUTLOOK TODAY?

JANUARY 11

Go for the Gold!

**I'm running hard for the finish line.
I'm giving it everything I've got. No sloppy living
for me!
I'm staying alert and in top condition.**

(1 Corinthians 9:26 TM)

In Atlanta when they held the 1996 Olympics, you should have seen the place! Three billion dollars worth of new construction, half a million visitors, and thousands of athletes and their trainers from all over the world competing for Olympic Gold. No hour was too early to rise; no distance too great to run; no sacrifice too great in order to win.

Listen to how Paul describes it: "You've all been to the stadium and seen the athletes race. Everyone runs; one wins. Run to win" (1 Corinthians 9:24 TM). Mom, use today to sow the seeds of Christian character into the lives of your children. Sir, strive for excellence, whether you sweep streets or build skyscrapers. Reach out in love and touch someone with kindness, expecting nothing in return, and be assured that every thought, *every* word, and *every* deed will be rewarded at the end of the race. Don't let *anything* keep you from reaching the finish line.

Paul said, "I'm not going to get caught napping, telling everyone else all about it and then missing out myself (1 Corinthians 9:27 TM). Come on, child of God, this calls for discipline! It calls for endurance! It calls you to sacrifice lesser things in order to win a crown of glory.

***

THE WORD FOR YOU TODAY IS, "GO FOR THE GOLD!"

JANUARY 12

Look for the Best in Others

Be careful not to stir up discontent.

(1 Corinthians 10:10 TM)

Have you ever been around someone who loved to stir things up? It may seem harmless to us, but God has a different view of it. Twenty-three thousand of His people died in one day because they murmured against Moses, the manna, the direction God was leading them, and all sorts of things. Never had a people been more protected, privileged, or prosperous, but you couldn't tell it by what they were saying. These murmurers never made it into the Promised Land. Murmurers never do!

Do you know which church Paul was speaking to when he wrote, "I have confidence in you"? The Corinthians. Amazing! Some of them got drunk at communion, tolerated fornication, doubted the resurrection, and these were only a *few* of their problems. One man said, "I read the Book of Corinthians just to get encouraged. I know at least I'm not doing *that* badly." But along comes Paul and says, "I have confidence in you. You're full of faith. You come behind in no gift." He focuses on the positive; he builds on their strengths. A mature Christian always focuses on the strengths and good things in others.

So today, look for the best in others. Listen: "You'll do best by filling your minds and meditating on ... the best, not the worst; the beautiful, not the ugly; things to praise, not things to curse" (Philippians 4:8 TM).

***

WHEN YOU LOOK FOR THE GOOD IN OTHERS—YOU'LL FIND IT!

JANUARY 13

God Wants to Bless Your Work

Put God in charge of your work, then what you've planned will take place. (Proverbs 16:3 TM)

God wants to be *included* in all your plans, *consulted* in all your decisions, and *honored* in *every area* of your life. If you do, what you plan will prosper, and what you plant will produce fruit.

If you've been taught that He is only interested in church matters, or the spiritual side of your life, then listen: "In all thy ways acknowledge him, and he shall direct thy paths" (Proverbs 3:6). Did you hear that? *All* thy ways!

Moses told the people, "Remember the Lord thy God: for it is he that giveth thee power [ability, insights, ideas, and skill] to get wealth" (Deuteronomy 8:18). Imagine having one of God's ideas for your business, your career, or your life! He has ideas nobody has ever thought of. Imagine, the God who gave Edison incandescent light, and showed Fleming how to turn a piece of molding bread into the miracle of penicillin, being your God, your source of inspiration.

Today He wants to talk to you, if you'll just take time to listen.

***

HAVE YOU TALKED WITH HIM TODAY!

JANUARY 14

Getting Over the Past

My heart is fixed, O God, my heart is fixed: I will sing and give praise. (Psalm 57:7)

There are people who've had things worse than you and done better, and some who've had it better than you and done worse. Your circumstances have little to do with getting over your past ... However, these four things can keep you stuck:

1. *Resentment.* Are you busy trying to "keep up with the Joneses," or are you trying to bring them down to your level? If so, then listen: "In honour preferring one another" (Romans 12:10).

2. *Regret.* Paul said, "Forgetting those things which are behind, and reaching forth unto those things which are before" (Philippians 3:13). You'll never reach ahead until you forget what's behind. We all have things we wish we'd done differently. Learn from them, forgive yourself, and move on.

3. *Self-pity.* After his greatest victory, Elijah wallowed in it. Listen: "I've had enough ... take away my life ... the people of Israel have ... killed your prophets, and only I am left; and now they are trying to kill me too" (1 Kings 19:4-10). That's self-pity in the raw, and if you let it in, it'll take over your life.

4. *An unteachable spirit!* Listen: "My people are destroyed from lack of knowledge" (Hosea 4:6 NIV). The only thing that's worse than ignorance is the prejudice that defends it, and the pride that refuses to acknowledge it or rise above it. God has surrounded you with opportunities to learn. Take advantage of them.

***

REMEMBER, WHAT YOU LEARN TODAY WILL DETERMINE WHAT YOU BECOME TOMORROW.

JANUARY 15

It Rubs Off

His face glowed from being in the presence of God.

(Exodus 34:29 TLB)

You can only talk convincingly about the God you know—the One you've spent time with. Any other God belongs in a theology book, and you'll have a hard time selling Him. When Moses came down the mountain, his face shone. He had been in God's presence, and when you've been there it shows. It shows in the way you look, the way you walk and talk, the way you treat your family, the way you spend your money, and the way you respond to hurting people. It rubs off!

Paul Cain says, "Most of us are as close to God as we want to be." Think about it. "Draw nigh to God, and he will draw nigh to you" (James 4:8). How could you possibly be the same when you've been with Him? He transforms everything He touches. Listen: "He that dwelleth in the secret place of the most High shall abide under the shadow of the Almighty" (Psalm 91:1). He didn't say "visit" or "drop in if you have time"; He said "dwell." Take up residence. Move in and set up house. It's all got to do with your desire.

David said, "One thing have I desired of the Lord, that will I seek after" (Psalm 27:4).

***

TODAY, MAKE UP YOUR MIND TO REARRANGE THINGS IN YOUR LIFE SO THAT YOU CAN SPEND MORE TIME IN HIS PRESENCE. IF YOU DO, IT WILL SHOW, BECAUSE IT RUBS OFF!

JANUARY 16

In the Presence of Mine Enemies

Thou preparest a table before me in the presence of mine enemies: thou anointest my head with oil; my cup runneth over.

(Psalm 23:5)

When does God make your cup overflow? In the presence of your enemies. *When does God anoint your head with oil?* In the presence of your enemies. *When do you need goodness and mercy the most?* In the presence of your enemies. *When do you need the rod and staff of His comfort and protection?* In the presence of your enemies. Can you see this? The very fact that you've made it this far proves His goodness and mercy have been with you all—not just some, but all—the days of your life.

You may say, "But I'm still struggling." Wonderful; struggle is proof that you refuse to surrender, and that you haven't been conquered. As long as you hold that position, God can do something for you. He can send His Spirit; He can send His Word; He can send friends who've been where you are, and who are strong where you're weak. If you're teachable, you're reachable. Just keep an open heart and listen. His promise to you today is, "Thou preparest a table before me in the presence of mine enemies: thou anointest my head with oil; my cup runneth over. Surely goodness and mercy shall follow me all the days of my life" (Psalm 23:5-6).

***

TODAY IS ONE OF THOSE DAYS.

JANUARY 17

Have You Prepared Your Will Yet?

A good man leaveth an inheritance to his children's children.

(Proverbs 13:22)

Most people—about 99 percent—hate to make a will because they're afraid that as soon as they do, they'll "cash in their chips." What nonsense! *Long life is one of God's promises to you* (see Proverbs 10:27).

I pose a question to every person reading these words. If you died tomorrow, would your money, your home, your furnishings, your clothing, your jewelry, and your valuables, go to the people you want them to? Are you sure?

The best way to be certain that your wishes are respected is to sit down now with a pencil and pad, and write down what you want to leave to whom. Think also of your liquid assets; do you want to leave a certain amount to your church, or a ministry, or a charity you believe in?

Then, call a lawyer right away, and have it put in a legal document. Don't leave a mess that will mean work for the courts, more taxes for the government, and a legacy of bitterness and confusion for your loved ones.

Your stewardship doesn't end at the grave. (See 2 Kings 20:1.) If the parable of the talents means anything, then you'll be rewarded by one standard—what you did with what you had!

***

THINK ABOUT IT!

JANUARY 18

Don't Quit—Just Keep Playing

My grace is sufficient for thee: for my strength is made perfect in [your] weakness.

(2 Corinthians 12:9)

One day a mom who wanted to encourage her little boy to keep practicing the piano, took him to hear Paderewski play. They sat near the front, and the boy was fascinated by the big grand piano on the stage. While his mother was talking to a friend, she didn't notice her son slip away. As the house lights dimmed and the spotlight hit the piano, she gasped as she saw her son on the piano bench, playing, "Twinkle, Twinkle, Little Star." Before she could get to him, Paderewski walked over to the keyboard and sat down beside the boy. "Don't quit, keep playing," he whispered. Then he reached down with his left hand and began filling in the bass part, and with his right arm he reached around the other side encircling the child, and added a running obligate. Together the old master and the child brought the crowd to its feet.

Child of God, no matter how ill-equipped you may feel, the Master has a word for you: *"Don't quit, keep playing."* No matter what you're doing today—raising those children, running that business, pastoring that church, or just trying to be a better Christian—*don't quit, keep playing.* He will add whatever is needed to turn your efforts into a masterpiece.

***

REMEMBER, HIS GRACE IS SUFFICIENT FOR THEE.

JANUARY 19

Free to "Keep Quiet"

Self-control means controlling the tongue! A quick retort can ruin everything.

(Proverbs 13:3 TLB)

Don't let the need to rescue someone push you into answering before you have heard the whole story, and taken time to pray about it. You'll be amazed how differently you feel about something a few hours, a few days, and in some cases, a few years later. Hindsight truly has 20/20.

Pride says, "Don't just stand there; *say* something!" Wisdom says, "Don't just say something; stand there!" Quietly ask God for insight. One word from Him can turn things around in a hurry. In this age of instant tea and instant potatoes, we look for *instant answers.* When tragedy strikes, not only do we get the news immediately, but within minutes experts appear on television to tell us *why* it all happened. But sometimes wisdom is silent.

Jesus had the power to summon twelve legions of angels to defend Him, yet "He opened not His mouth" (see Isaiah 53:7). Pilate did all the talking. Jesus just stood there quietly, for *He* was not on trial; Pilate and the religious system were. He knew His destiny, and most of all, He knew His Father intimately.

***

WHEN YOU KNOW GOD, YOU CAN FACE ANYTHING WITH CONFIDENCE—AND STILL BE FREE TO KEEP QUIET. WHAT A WONDERFUL PLACE TO BE!

JANUARY 20

Decisions

Choose for yourselves this day whom you will serve.

(Joshua 24:15 NIV)

What you are *today* was determined by the decisions you made *yesterday.* If you want to change your future, learn how to make better decisions today. Here are a few principles to guide you:

(1) Never make a permanent decision about a temporary situation. When the smoke clears, you'll regret it. (2) Never let your emotions blind you to reason. Weigh things prayerfully, and base your decisions on mature judgment. (3) Surround yourself with wise people and draw on their gifts, without being intimidated by their expertise. (4) Take the time to consider all options. What looks good today may not look so good tomorrow. (5) You can't fight successfully on every front, so choose your battles carefully. Don't go into a battle where there are no spoils. (6) Get all the facts; conjecture leads to crisis. (7) Consider the consequences of each option, and ask yourself, *Am I ready to handle them right now?* (8) Make sure your expectations don't exceed your potential and resources. Be realistic. If you can't sing, don't cut an

album. (9) Time is your most limited and valuable resource. Don't waste it. (10) Allow yourself a 10 percent risk of being wrong, a 50 percent likelihood of betrayal, and a 100 percent commitment to survive it all.

***

SO TODAY, WHOM WILL YOU CHOOSE TO SERVE?

JANUARY 21

A Discerning Heart

Give therefore thy servant an understanding heart.

(1 Kings 3:9-10)

God guides us by *revelation* and by *relationships.* That means you need *discernment* about the people who come into your life. For example, when trouble hits, you'll discover who your friends really are. You can't lose a *real* friend, for the Word says, "A friend loveth at all times, and a brother is born for adversity" (Proverbs 17:17). But a lot of us get hurt by discovering that some people weren't true friends at all.

A man who was going through some difficulties reached out to a pastor he thought would stand by him. The pastor said, "I'm sorry you're going through this and I'll pray for you, but it would hurt me to associate with you at the moment. People might think I was being soft on sin." How sad. But would you have acted any differently?

Discernment is not to be used for judging people. It's for discerning *their spirit.* Have you ever been around someone with a critical spirit? A competitive spirit? A controlling spirit? Jesus once said to His disciples, "Ye know not what manner of spirit ye are of"

(Luke 9:55). Amazing! Even the disciples couldn't discern the spirit that was at work in their own ranks. Can you?

***

TODAY, WHEN YOU ASK GOD FOR A DISCERNING HEART, HE'LL GIVE YOU ONE.

JANUARY 22

Hungry for God

O God, thou art my God; early will I seek thee: my soul thirsteth for thee.

(Psalm 63:1)

Talk about lifestyles of the rich and famous! David had the world's most beautiful women, but sex could not fill the void. If fame could satisfy, he was in a class of his own. If looks could do it, he was an Old Testament version of Sean Connery. But you can eat lobster every night, own resort homes in paradise, and yet still have an emptiness in your heart as big as the Grand Canyon. *You see, there's a God-shaped blank inside of you.* He made you that way.

Ever since Adam walked with God, there has been a longing—akin to a *primal scream*—for God's presence in our lives. David speaks for all of us: "My soul thirsteth for thee, my flesh longeth for thee in a dry and thirsty land, where no water is" (Psalm 63:1). He's saying, "I've seen man's best—and it's fleeting." It's a seat on the board, a trophy from the field of athletics, or a crowd applauding. Then it's all gone and the emptiness remains.

There's only one place to go, and that's to *Him.* Listen to the rest of the psalm: "Because thy lovingkindness is better than life, my lips shall praise thee. Thus will I bless thee while I live" (Psalm 63:3-4).

***

TODAY, LET YOUR HUNGER LEAD YOU INTO HIS PRESENCE.

JANUARY 23

The Habit of Lying

Lie not one to another, seeing that ye have put off the old man with his deeds.

(Colossians 3:9)

Rick Pitino says, "Lying makes a problem part of the future; truth makes it a part of the past." You see, when you tell the truth, you never have to remember what you said; no one has a good enough memory to be a successful liar!

A lie may seem to be the easy way out. But even if it solves your *present* problem, it *creates future* ones that blur your vision, cause you to lose confidence before God in prayer, and eventually cost you the respect of others. Even worse—your present lies can only be defended by future lies.

The Ninth Commandment summarized says, "Thou shalt not lie" (see Exodus 20:16), and it is often the most difficult to keep. Have you ever told a lie to spare someone's feelings, avoid confrontation, or make yourself look better?

One writer says it this way: "Hope built on a lie is always the beginning of loss. Never attempt to build anything on a foundation of lies and half-truths. It will not stand." If you want to walk with confidence toward God, ask Him to give you the courage to always walk in truth.

***

REMEMBER, ANYTHING LESS DISTORTS GOD'S PLAN AND LEADS YOU INTO PLACES WHERE HE NEVER MEANT YOU TO BE.

JANUARY 24

Are You Anxious Today?

What time I am afraid, I will trust in thee.

(Psalm 56:3)

Anxiety can be like a big wave that washes over you and stops you dead in your tracks. It can paralyze you and take away everything good in your life. If you let it take control, you'll *do* nothing, *say* nothing, and end up *feeling* like nothing.

When you think about it, worry is silly! (And dangerous.) It means you're *not* trusting God to carry out the promises He has made to you. Yes, He's given you responsibilities, and it's important to take them seriously; but He has commanded you to trust Him (see Proverbs 3:5).

Paul says, "Do not be anxious about anything, but in everything, by prayer and petition, with thanksgiving, present your requests to God. And the peace of God, which transcends all understanding, will guard your hearts and your minds..." (Philippians 4:6-7 NIV).

You are special in the eyes of the Lord. Let that sink in! He loves you and cherishes you. What are you afraid of? Don't you know your Father is with you? Every step you take He accompanies you! If you stumble, He'll catch you. If you fall, He'll lift you up.

If you walk with Him, He guarantees that you'll reach your destination.

**

TODAY, REST IN HIS LOVE, FEEL HIS STRENGTH, AND BEGIN TO MOVE AHEAD WITHOUT FEAR.

The Wisdom to Win Souls

He that winneth souls is wise.

(Proverbs 11:30)

If you want to win someone to Christ today, use wisdom, especially in these three areas:

1. Don't assume because they were raised in church that they understand; or because you've "lived the life" before them, that they'll get it by osmosis. Listen: "How can they believe in the one of whom they have not heard?" (Romans 10:14 NIV). Share your testimony—the short version. Forget the good advice; just give them the good news!

2. As much as you'd like to close the deal right then, sometimes you have to sow the seed, and leave the rest to the Lord of the Harvest. Don't try to corner them into praying the sinner's prayer. Share the Word, leave the door open, and trust the God who said, "I am watching over My word to perform it" (Jeremiah 1:12 NAS).

3. When God speaks to you, don't put it off. R.A. Torrey had an experience that totally changed his attitude toward "soul-winning." While eating in a restaurant with some friends, God impressed him

to talk to the waiter about his soul. But he ignored it. An hour later when the waiter didn't return, Torrey inquired about him. The manager replied, "We just found him dead in the back of the restaurant. He hanged himself." He'd committed suicide during the meal!

***

REMEMBER, WHEN GOD LEADS YOU TO SPEAK TO SOMEONE—DO IT! YOU MAY NOT GET ANOTHER OPPORTUNITY.

JANUARY 26

The Unheard Cry

There met him out of the tombs a man with an unclean spirit.

(Mark 5:2)

Jesus heard a cry nobody else heard, from a place nobody else wanted to go, from a man nobody else wanted to associate with. *And when Jesus lives in your heart, you will hear that cry, too. It will touch your spirit.*

It came from a madman living in a graveyard, whose very appearance was enough to make any normal person avoid him. But something deep inside him longed to be free, and that longing touched Jesus. To get to him, Jesus had to go through a storm. He also had to overcome the objections of His disciples, who probably said, "Why risk it? He's not worth it."

If you want to follow Jesus, you'll have to open your heart to a cry that nobody else is listening to. You can't listen to the crowd around you. You've got to listen to the Spirit within you. He'll tell you where to go and He'll tell you whom to minister to. You can't be put off by lifestyle or appearance. All that matters is getting them to Jesus.

***

JUST GET THEM TO HIM, AND HE'LL TAKE CARE OF THE REST.

JANUARY 27

When You Can't Understand—Trust!

The secret things belong unto the Lord our God.

(Deuteronomy 29:29)

Listen to this letter from a missionary couple who lost their child: "Last summer our younger son, aged 14, came down with a very severe strain of meningitis. Many prayed for his healing, but we lost him. Our hearts are broken. We cannot understand why God would send or allow us such a sorrow and burden to carry. Can you help us?"

One thing is sure. God is too good to do wrong, and too wise to make a mistake. When we have to know all the details, we're walking by sight, but when we can trust Him in the dark, we're walking by faith.

"Without faith it is impossible to please God" (Hebrews 11:6 NIV). Note that it doesn't say, "without understanding." When we walk by faith, we don't necessarily gain understanding, but rather acceptance. Confidence in God is His highest purpose for our lives. When we can trust and accept without question, we move into a dimension of greater peace and intimacy with Him.

Someone is probably watching you as you walk through this storm to see how your faith works, and if your relationship with God will sustain you. It will!

***

THESE DAYS OF QUESTIONING AND GRIEVING WILL PASS; EVENTUALLY YOU WILL SAY, LIKE JOB, "WHEN I AM TRIED I SHALL COME FORTH AS GOLD" (JOB 23:10).

JANUARY 28

Then Jesus Comes

Then they went out ... and found the man ... sitting at the feet of Jesus, clothed, and in his right mind.

(Luke 8:35)

The man in the tombs was bound by evil spirits, filled with fear, and separated from his family. Society said he was hopeless. That's when Jesus loves to step in! When human wisdom says, "It can't be done," *Jesus comes!* Look at this man now; he's "clothed, and in his right mind."

But the locals couldn't handle it, so they asked Jesus to go back to where He came from. The world hasn't changed much. When you meet Jesus, and they see you clothed and in your right mind, they won't know what to do with you either. Have they noticed the difference yet? If none of your old friends are shaken up, then you're not doing something right. Listen: "If any man be in Christ, he is a new creature" (2 Corinthians 5:17).

This man wanted to join Jesus and His disciples, but Jesus said no. Most of us are not called to full-time ministry, but we've *all* been called to do one thing: "Return to thine own house, and shew how great things God hath done unto thee" (Luke 8:39). The first place you need to start today is among the people you love and live with. Tell *them* how great Jesus is. Tell *them* what He's done for you. Tell *them* what He can do for them.

***

DON'T PUT IF OFF UNTIL TOMORROW—DO IT TODAY.

JANUARY 29

Waiting for Jesus

When Jesus was returned, the people gladly received him: for they were all waiting for him.

(Luke 8:40)

That's what your friends and loved ones are doing today—waiting for Jesus. Don't leave Him in church or confine Him to your Sunday activities.

The miracles Jesus and the apostles did were not done in church; they did them *on their way* to wherever they were going. *With them it wasn't an event—it was a lifestyle.* The very shadow of Peter touching the sick as he walked by would bring healing. (See Acts 5:15.)

Today, we try to reproduce it in *a controlled environment,* and look at the results. If all our churches were filled tomorrow, they would hold less than 10 percent of the population. Something's got to happen! We've got to start praying for boldness and compassion to take the Gospel to the neighborhood, instead of trying to bring the neighborhood to us.

They've been to church, and most of them didn't like it because they didn't see Jesus there. And they're still waiting for Him!

***

INTRODUCE HIM TODAY TO SOMEBODY YOU LOVE.
THEY'LL BE ETERNALLY GRATEFUL.

JANUARY 30

Listening Prayer

Be still, and know that I am God.

(Psalm 46:10)

Jesus did a lot of praying. On more than one occasion He prayed all night, yet few of His words were recorded. Could it be that He did more listening than talking? And when His prayer was recorded, what was it? "Father ... not my will, but thine, be done" (Luke 22:42).

When Jesus prayed He surrendered totally to the will of God. He believed He would automatically be given two things for which we all keep asking—*direction* and the *ability to deal with things*.

Thank God for the revelation of who we are in Christ, and our authority as believers before God and before men. But recently God's been letting me know that there's *more* to prayer than coming "boldly unto the throne" (Hebrews 4:16). That kind of praying is about what *you* want, but this kind is about what *He* wants. Now, since He sees the whole picture clearly, and since He designed the plan to begin with, don't you think it's time to get quiet before Him, so that He can *tell* you all about it?

***

THE WORD FOR YOU TODAY IS, BE STILL AND LET
GOD BE GOD IN YOUR LIFE.

JANUARY 31

It's a Daily Walk

Noah walked with God.

(Genesis 6:9)

To walk with God means to be attentive to His Word and yielded to His presence. Though we do not see Him, we know Him. We find our security not in people, places, or things—but in Him alone!

The name *Noah* means "rest." Noah not only knew his mission in life, but he also knew his source, and when you know that you don't have to worry any more.

But knowing God deeply doesn't happen quickly; it takes time. Time spent with Him on the mountaintop and in the valley; time spent with Him in joy and in adversity. Time will test the quality of any relationship! Prisons, shipwrecks, betrayals, beatings, hunger, and disappointment didn't shake Paul's confidence in God. Listen: "None of these things move me" (Acts 20:24).

Another man who walked with God was Enoch. Listen: "Enoch walked with God: and he was not; for God took him" (Genesis 5:24). Every day he rose and sought the Lord, walking with Him and seeking to please Him in all that he did. Their relationship was intimate. The Bible says, "He obtained the witness that before his being taken up he was pleasing to God" (Hebrews 11:5 NAS). Imagine living in such a way that you have a "witness" in your spirit that God is truly pleased with you!

***

NOT ONLY IS SUCH A LIFE POSSIBLE, BUT IT CAN BE YOURS, STARTING TODAY.

FEBRUARY 1

Ten Reasons Why I Never Wash!

I was glad when they said unto me, Let us go into the house of the Lord.

(Psalm 122:1)

Before you tell me why you never go to church, please read *Ten Reasons Why I Never Wash!*

(1) I was forced to wash as a child. (2) People who wash are all hypocrites; they think they are cleaner than everybody else. (3) There are so many different kinds of soap; I just can't decide which one is best for me. (4) I used to wash, but I got bored and stopped doing it. (5) I wash only on special occasions like Christmas and Easter. (6) None of my friends wash. (7) I'll start washing when I get older and dirtier. (8) I don't have time to wash. (9) The bathroom is never warm enough in winter or cool enough in summer. (10) The people who make soap are only after your money! *Are you getting the message?*

There are principles you'll hear in God's house that you won't hear anywhere else. Can you afford to live without knowing them? Everybody who was anybody in the Bible went to church. Why? Because that's where you'll find a family to belong to and insights to live by, that will make this life better—and eternity wonderful!

**

SEE YOU IN CHURCH THIS SUNDAY!

FEBRUARY 2

The Call of God

Before I formed thee in the belly I knew thee; ... and I ordained thee a prophet unto the nations.

(Jeremiah 1:5)

Before Jeremiah was born, God already saw him ministering to nations.

That's why discernment is so important. You don't *decide* your calling—you *discern* it. Have you discerned yours yet? If you haven't, then get into God's presence and stay there until He reveals it to you.

Listen to what Jeremiah told God: "Ah, Lord God! Behold, I cannot" (Jeremiah 1:6). Is that what you've been saying? "I cannot—I'm too young. I'm too poor. I don't have the training. I'm the wrong nationality. I'm too old. I don't have the right connections." The first thing God did was to change what was coming out of Jeremiah's mouth. But listen to God's reply: "Say not I am a child" (Jeremiah 1:7). Did you hear that: "Say not"? If you keep contradicting what God says, you're pulling the plug on everything He wants to do for you. "Be not afraid of their faces: for I am with thee to deliver thee.... I have put my words in thy mouth.... I will hasten my word to perform it"

(Jeremiah 1:8-9, 12). When God guides, He provides. Don't listen to the wrong voices.

***

TODAY, START LISTENING TO THE WORD OF GOD; RECEIVE IT BY FAITH; STEP OUT AND OBEY IT. FOR HIS PROMISE TO YOU TODAY IS, "I AM WITH THEE."

FEBRUARY 3

Perfect Love

His perfect love for us eliminates all dread.... If we are afraid, it ... shows that we are not fully convinced that he really loves us.

(1 John 4:18 TLB)

God couldn't love you any more than He does right now! Take a moment and let that sink in!

You say, "What does God's love look like?" Look at the Cross. If you were the only person who needed forgiveness, Jesus would have gone to the Cross just for you. You ask, "What does God's love cost me?" It comes with *no strings attached.* You can't do anything to deserve it—so when you fail, you don't forfeit it. He'll never stop loving you. (See Romans 8:38-39.)

John says that since God's love is the only "perfect" love, it casts out all your fear (see 1 John 4:18). What are you afraid of today? Afraid you won't get something you need, or that you'll lose something you already have? You need to ask God to give you a fresh understanding of how much He loves you, for what He loves He protects!

We're attracted to people who love us and show it, so why is it so difficult for us to go to God in prayer? It's because we need a fresh revelation of His love. Listen to Paul: "[I pray that] you'll be able to take in ... the extravagant dimensions of Christ's love. Reach out and experience the breadth! Test its length! Plumb the depths! Rise to the heights!" (Ephesians 3:18-19 TM).

***

MAY GOD HELP YOU TO EXPERIENCE HIS LOVE TODAY!

FEBRUARY 4

The Orphan Heart

God's Spirit touches our spirits and confirms who we really are.

(Romans 8:16 TM)

Do you have an orphan heart? It's a heart that needs everybody to love it. Ten thousand people may, but that's not enough—it will always focus on the one who doesn't, and obsess over that. Have you ever held arguments in your mind with people who criticized you, or worse, snubbed you? That's the orphan heart, and no amount of human love can ever satisfy it.

But there's something that can: the Spirit of adoption. Listen: "Ye have received the Spirit of adoption, whereby we cry, Abba, Father" (Romans 8:15). The Message says, "God's Spirit ... confirms who we really are" (Romans 8:16). That's what the Spirit of God wants to do for you; let you know who you really are. You're God's child! You're an heir to all He owns! You're protected day and night by His love! You're directed step-by-step by His Spirit! You're given favor even in the midst of adversity! You're His!

Adoption is an act of premeditated love. It says, "Before you saw Me, I saw you. I adopted you. I gave you My name, My nature, My family, and My inheritance. Now you can call Me "Abba," which literally means "my daddy." How wonderful!

***

YOU CAN RUN TO HIM TODAY, CURL UP IN HIS ARMS, AND SAY, "MY DADDY."

FEBRUARY 5

Patience Is the Bridge

For ye have need of patience, that, after ye have done the will of God, ye might receive the promise.

(Hebrews 10:36)

Patience is the bridge that carries you from the will of God to the promises of God. If you do the will of God on this side, the promises are waiting for you on the other side; but patience is the bridge that gets you from one side to the other! The key is—*bridges come in different lengths, and only God knows the length of yours!* Sometimes you'll get to the promise in just a few steps, and other times it may feel like you'll never get there. Maybe that's where you are today.

If so, there are two questions you need to answer. First, have you done the will of God yet? Be honest with yourself, for you only receive the promise after you've done the will of God. Next, are you walking patiently and confidently before the Lord in this matter? You may ask, "How does patience walk? How does it act?" Look at Abraham; even though he was 100 years old when God told him he was to be a father, we read, "He considered not his own body"

(Romans 4:19). Did you hear that? Don't even consider your limitations; they mean nothing to God. Abraham waited twenty years before Isaac was born, but he "was strong in faith, giving glory to God" (Romans 4:18-21). Stay in the Word! Keep strengthening your faith daily, and whatever you do, keep giving glory to God for what He is going to do.

***

STAND ON THE WORD, AND WHEN THE PROMISE ARRIVES, MAKE SURE YOU'RE AT THE RIGHT ADDRESS.

FEBRUARY 6

Self-Acceptance

May you be ... founded securely on love.

(Ephesians 3:17 AMP)

Many people really don't like themselves. Now the trouble is, if you don't like yourself you'll be convinced that others don't like you either—and you'll act accordingly. I know; I did it! I thought, *If people knew the struggles I had and the failures I've experienced, they wouldn't listen to me for a minute!* It's agony being with people, and feeling deep down that they don't like you; or wanting to do things, but not feeling free enough to step out and try them. Sound familiar?

My healing began when I read the Bible and discovered that God chose to love me—just as I am! Imagine that! I didn't have to earn it! That set me free to stop trying and start trusting what God said about me. It took a while, because I'd spent a lifetime putting myself down.

God had a special destiny for me, but I couldn't fulfill it as long as I was insecure and had a poor self-image. So I began confessing His Word over my life each day. One verse that helped me greatly was: "Before I formed you in the womb I knew [and] approved of you [as My chosen instrument]" (Jeremiah 1:5 AMP).

Next, I learned the difference between my *who* and my *do.* God doesn't love everything I do, but He loves me! He sees my heart, not just my flesh. Now if He can keep the two separated, then He can teach you to do the same. His unconditional love enables you to accept yourself as you are, and then see yourself as you're going to be.

***

WHAT AN ASSURANCE!

FEBRUARY 7

Friends

I have called you friends; for all things that I have heard of my Father I have made known unto you.

(John 15:15)

If Jesus walked into your home today, He'd probably say, "Hello, friend!" What a privilege! It means, "My door is always open to you. There's nothing you can't talk to Me about. I'll never betray you. I'll always listen. If you're restless and can't sleep, I'll sit up with you. I'll go with you wherever you go—My love for you isn't performance-based. Whether you're comforting a crying child, working at a computer, or driving a bus, your spirit can commune with Me."

Flesh will fail you—even well-intentioned flesh—but not Jesus. Listen: "I will not leave you comfortless: I will come to you" (John 14:18). The precious Holy Spirit, who is living in you right now, is how Jesus keeps His promise never to leave you.

But remember, His friendship is connected to obedience. Jesus said, "Ye are my friends, if ye do whatsoever I command you" (John 15:14). The Holy Spirit is pictured in the Bible as a dove, and when a dove returns to its nest, it is so sensitive that if it finds one thing out of place, it will not land. Are you getting the message?

***

ALWAYS MAKE JESUS FEEL AT HOME, AND PROTECT HIS FRIENDSHIP. IT'S THE MOST WONDERFUL RELATIONSHIP YOU'VE GOT.

FEBRUARY 8

An Anti-Gossip Pact

A gossip betrays a confidence, but a trustworthy man keeps a secret.

(Proverbs 11:13 NIV)

In 1752 a group of Methodist men, including John Wesley, signed a covenant that every man agreed to hang on his study wall. The six articles of this agreement were as follows:

That we will not listen to, or willingly inquire after ill concerning one another;

That if we do hear any ill of each other, we will not believe it;

That as soon as possible, we will communicate what we hear by speaking or writing to the person concerned;

That until we have done this, we will not write or speak a syllable of it to any other person;

That neither will we mention it after we have done this, to any other person;

That we will not make any exception to any of these rules, unless we think ourselves absolutely obliged, and then only in conference.

Always remember, the person who says to you, "Don't tell this to a soul," has probably told all the souls he knows! Confront him in love, and don't carry it one step further.

***

DON'T YOU THINK WE OWE THAT TO ONE ANOTHER?

FEBRUARY 9

The Business of Loving Others

For I have given you an example, that ye should do as I have done to you.

(John 13:15)

Armand Hammer, the great humanitarian and chairman of Occidental Petroleum, tells the following story:

My father had become a prominent and greatly loved figure in the area.... It was an almost ecstatic experience for me to ride with him when he went on his doctor's rounds. Patients at their doors greeted him with such warmth that waves of pride would surge in me to find myself the son of such a father, a man so obviously good, so obviously deserving of the affection he received.

He could have made himself many times richer, however, if he had insisted on collecting all his bills; or if he could have restrained himself from giving money away; but then he would not have been the man he was. I have seen in his office drawers full of unpaid bills for which he refused to demand payment, because he knew the difficult circumstances of his patients. And I heard innumerable stories from patients about his leaving money behind to pay for the prescriptions he had written, when he visited people who were too poor to eat, let alone pay the doctor. What a wonderful legacy to leave your child—the business of loving and giving to others.

***

TODAY, YOU'LL HAVE OPPORTUNITIES TO SHOW GOD'S LOVE; DON'T MISS ONE OF THEM.

FEBRUARY 10

He's Watching Over You Today

Let him have all your worries and cares, for he is always thinking about you and watching everything that concerns you.

(1 Peter 5:7 TLB)

What a source of strength! Not only is He watching over you. He's watching over those you love, including the ones you've been so worried about lately.

God's love and care followed the Prodigal Son all the way to the hog pen, and brought him safely home again. When others give up, God doesn't! Every day for forty years He fed the Israelites, clothed them, protected them, and directed each step they took. He never missed a day! Listen: "Thou shalt remember all the way which the Lord thy God led thee" (Deuteronomy 8:2). What a God!

Do you remember the poem "Footprints"? First there were two sets of footprints; then there was only one set. When the Lord was asked, "Why? Didn't you promise you'd never leave me?" He answered, "Yes, My child. The two sets of footprints were the times when we walked together side-by-side. But when you saw only one set, they were not yours but Mine. Those were the times when you didn't have the strength to go on—so I carried you."

***

YOU'RE NOT HERE TODAY BECAUSE YOU'RE LUCKY. YOU'RE HERE BECAUSE YOU'RE BLESSED! TAKE A MOMENT TO THANK HIM!

FEBRUARY 11

An Attitude of Gratitude

Freely ye have received, freely give.

(Matthew 10:8)

The Bible teaches sowing in order to reap, or giving for a desired result. In salvation, you gave your heart to Jesus expecting something in return—eternal life. And He didn't disappoint you. It also says about Jesus, "Who for the joy that was set before him endured the cross, despising the shame, and is set down at the right hand of the throne of God" (Hebrews 12:2). He looked beyond the Cross to the throne; that was His reward.

But there's another perspective to consider. Instead of giving to receive, why don't you give because of what you've *already* received? If God never did one more thing for you, wouldn't it take eternity to praise Him for the love He has *already* shown you? Do you remember what your life was like before you met Jesus? The habits that bound you? The awful emptiness you could never fill? Where would the road you were on have ended?

In those times when I'm tempted to pass judgment on someone, I pray, "God, help me to be quiet, look up, and remember with David, 'He brought me up also out of an horrible pit, out of the miry clay, and set my feet upon a rock.... He hath put a new song in my mouth, even praise unto our God'" (Psalm 40:2-3).

***

TODAY, ASK GOD TO GIVE YOU AN ATTITUDE OF GRATITUDE!

FEBRUARY 12

You Taught Me How to Love

Love comes from God. (1 John 4:7 NIV)

James Dobson shares this "letter of tribute" to a little girl called Bristol, from her dad.

My dear Bristol, before you were born I prayed for you. In my heart I knew that you would be a little angel—and so you were. You taught me how to love. I loved you when you were cuddly and cute. I also loved you when the realization took hold that something was wrong; that you weren't developing as quickly as your peers. I loved you when we went from hospital to hospital looking for hope; and of course, we prayed for you—and prayed, and prayed.

I loved you when you'd bite your fingers or your lips by accident; and when your eyes crossed and finally went blind. I loved you when scoliosis wrenched your body like a pretzel, and we had to put a tube into your stomach to feed you. I loved you when your contorted limbs made it so hard to change your messy diapers—so many diapers, ten years of diapers. I loved you when you couldn't say the one thing I longed to hear back—"Daddy, I love you." I loved you when I was close to God, and when He seemed far away; when I was full of faith, and also when I was angry at Him.

The reason I loved you, Bristol, is that God put this love in my heart. The wondrous thing about God's love is He loves us when we're blind, deaf, or twisted—in body or in spirit. He loves us even when we can't tell Him that we love him back. My dear Bristol, now you're free! I'm so happy that you have your crown first. We will follow you someday—in His time. Before you were born, I prayed for you; I knew that you would be an angel, and so you were! Love, Daddy.

***

WHAT A WONDERFUL LESSON!

FEBRUARY 13

Importunity

Many tried to hush him up, but he yelled all the louder ... [and] Jesus stopped in his tracks.

(Mark 10:46 TM)

His *deliverance* meant more to blind Bartimaeus than his dignity, and *seeing* meant more to him than looking good. If what you've done so far hasn't worked, be willing to try something different. Don't give up until you get God's attention.

Most of the crowd that day would have been happy to see Bartimaeus remain blind and begging for the rest of his life. Note the words, "Many tried to hush him up." You'll have to overcome some of those same voices to get to Jesus, too. Like the sincere Christian who'll tell you that "the day of miracles is over." Please understand that there never was a *day* of miracles. There's only a *God* of miracles, and He never changes.

Others will try to lower your expectations, to keep you from reaching out and being disappointed. Some will even say, "You got yourself into this mess; don't expect God to get you out of it." Don't listen to those voices.

Zacchaeus climbed up a tree to get to Jesus. Others raised the roof. If you can think—pray! If you can breathe—call on His name! As long as you're living, keep reaching for Him!

***

NEVER! NEVER! NEVER GIVE UP!

FEBRUARY 14

Love and Answered Prayer

Giving honour unto the wife ... that your prayers be not hindered.

(1 Peter 3:7)

When preachers talk about hindrances to prayer, they usually talk about things like lack of faith, disobedience, or unforgiveness. But Peter says a big one is—*how you treat your partner!*

I have a wonderful wife, but, like anyone else, when she gets tired she gets touchy. Now knowing this, you'd think that when she says something that bothers me I'd be mature enough to let it pass. But not me! More times than I'd like to admit—I'm carnal. So I *straighten her out!* Usually the issue is so insignificant that later neither of us can even remember it, yet at the time it generated a lot more heat than light!

Listen: "Love suffers long and is kind" (1 Corinthians 13:4 NKJV). Sometimes I wonder why God put this stuff into the Bible, because it's so hard to live up to it.

So, I apologize to my wife, ask God to help me do it better next time, and that makes for a happy home.

***

I ALSO DO IT FOR ANOTHER REASON: "THAT [MY] PRAYERS BE NOT HINDERED."

FEBRUARY 15

No One Has the Right to Do Less Than His Best

Whatever your hand finds to do, do it with all your might.

(Ecclesiastes 9:10 NIV)

The area I live in recently had the lowest voter turn-out in the state. That may not seem significant, until you start listening to some of the people around here complaining. Do we really have the right to complain about what we permit?

We march against abortion, but how about providing a home for the single mother and her baby?

We give a lot of attention to the plight of the elderly, who often have to choose between prescriptions to keep them healthy, or food to keep them alive. So many live in despair and loneliness. But have you visited any of them lately? James says that pure religion will cause us to reach out to those who hurt. (See James 1:27.)

When Jesus told the rich young ruler how much it would cost to follow Him, "he went away sorrowful," wishing it could have been easier (Matthew 19:22).

Salvation may be free, but discipleship will cost you everything you've got. It's literally signing your name at the bottom of a blank check, and saying, "Lord, You fill in the amount."

***

REMEMBER YESTERDAY? THERE'S NOT A THING YOU CAN DO ABOUT IT, EXCEPT LEARN FROM IT, AND GO OUT TODAY ASKING GOD TO GIVE YOU THE GRACE TO MAKE IT COUNT FOR HIM.

FEBRUARY 16

Perfect Peace

Thou wilt keep him in perfect peace, whose mind is stayed on thee: because he trusteth in thee.

(Isaiah 26:3)

My friend, Sarah Utterbach, called me today with a great insight. She was singing the little chorus, "He is our peace who has broken down the middle wall," when suddenly it dawned on her that *He can't be your peace until He first becomes your focus.* Think about it! Did you notice the words, "whose mind is stayed on thee"? An athlete has only one thing in mind—the prize. Paul says that as we focus on Jesus, we're changed into His likeness. (See 2 Corinthians 3:18.) For us the only questions that matter are: "Where is *He* in it?" and "What does *He* want me to do?"

The disciples failed to see Jesus in the worst storm of their lives, and yet He was right there beside them. Mark says, "And about the fourth watch of the night he cometh unto them, walking upon the sea, and would have passed by them" (Mark 6:48). He was in control of their circumstances. He was watching over them every moment. He was right there beside them. But they almost missed Him. Sound familiar? Don't leave Him in church. Don't confine Him to your morning devotions. Today, look for Him constantly in every storm and every circumstance of your life.

***

FOR WHEN YOUR EYES ARE ON HIM, HIS PEACE WILL FLOOD YOUR SOUL.

FEBRUARY 17

How to Treat One Another

Make a clean break with all cutting, backbiting, profane talk. Be gentle with one another, sensitive. Forgive one another as quickly and thoroughly as God in Christ forgave you.

(Ephesians 4:31-32 TM)

G. Le Tourneau, an outstanding Christian business-man, made a fortune manufacturing earth-moving equipment. He made a scraper known as "Model G." One day someone asked one of his salesmen what the "G" stood for. The man, who was quick-witted, replied, "I'll tell you, the G stands for *gossip,* because this machine can move a lot of dirt and move it fast." *The trouble with gossip is not so much that it is spoken as an intended lie, but that it is heard as the absolute truth.*

Abraham Lincoln had a favorite riddle he used to ask people: "If a man were to call the tail of a dog a leg, how many legs would the dog have?" The usual reply was "five." "Wrong!" Lincoln would say with his wry smile. "The dog still has four legs. Calling the tail a leg doesn't make it one."

Because a story has been repeated many times by so-called reliable sources doesn't make it true. And if it is true, it should be put under the blood and not into your conversation.

***

ASK GOD TODAY TO HELP YOU TALK LIKE A CHRISTIAN.

FEBRUARY 18

President Kennedy's Question

Then we which are alive and remain, shall be caught up ... to meet the Lord in the air.

(1 Thessalonians 4:17)

Billy Graham says: "A few days before John F. Kennedy was inaugurated, I was invited to join him for golf, and afterwards to visit the Kennedy compound in Palm Beach, Florida. As we were driving back from the game, the president turned to me and asked, 'Do you *really* believe that Jesus Christ is coming back to earth again?' I was dumbfounded! I never dreamed that he would ask a question like that. I replied, 'Yes, sir, I do!' 'Alright,' he said, 'Explain it to me.' So for the next several minutes I had the opportunity to talk to him about the Second Coming of Christ. I've often wondered *why* he asked that question.

"I think part of the answer came 1,000 days later—when he was assassinated! Remarkably, at his funeral, while millions around the world watched and listened, these words were spoken over his casket: 'For the Lord himself shall descend from heaven with a shout ... and the dead in Christ shall rise first: then we which are alive and remain shall be caught up ... to meet the Lord in the air: and so shall we ever be with the Lord. Wherefore comfort one another with these words' (1 Thessalonians 4:17-18)."

***

WHEN CHRIST RETURNS, SOME OF US WILL BE CAUGHT UP—OTHERS WILL BE CAUGHT OUT! WHICH GROUP WILL YOU BE IN?

FEBRUARY 19

Things That Never Change

Remove not the old landmark.

(Proverbs 23:10)

Thank God for "Big Ben." It has kept us on time for generations. Thank God for the compass that always points toward the magnetic north—without it no one would be able to get anywhere. Thank God for "seedtime and harvest," for the Word says, "While the earth remaineth, seedtime and harvest ... shall not cease" (Genesis 8:22). That reassures me that the seeds I've sown will produce a harvest.

Recently on the national news, some people were trying to stop the sale of a hot-selling video protected under The Freedom of Speech Act. The video shows how to professionally assassinate someone. Dear God! I never thought I'd get this old this fast. But today I thank God for values that don't change, and principles that *still* guarantee the more abundant life that Jesus talked about. (See John 10:10.)

Prayer *still* changes things. But more importantly, it changes you. Bible reading *still* strengthens and gives you peace and joy like nothing else. Most of all I'm glad He said, "I am the Lord, I change not"

(Malachi 3:6). What He was, He still is. *What He said, He still says. What He did, He still does.*

***

I'M SO GLAD HE'S THE UNCHANGING ONE, AREN'T YOU?

FEBRUARY 20

The Open Door Policy

Behold, I have set before thee an open door, and no man can shut it.

(Revelation 3:8)

God guides us in many ways, and one of them is what I call "the open door policy." I'm stubborn, and it's taken me a long time to learn not to keep knocking on doors that are closed, and instead to walk through the ones He has opened. Are you like that? Remember, don't stay where you're tolerated; go where you're celebrated. God says no man can close the door. So if it's closed, He may have a hand in it, and you need to pay attention.

The mighty Mississippi is two miles wide at one point, but so narrow at another that you can jump across it. Now, when you first walk through a door, things may look small, but as you remain faithful and keep walking, you'll discover that you're connected to something deeper, wider, and bigger than you ever conceived.

Years ago I thought my life was over, but today I have more joy and greater purpose than ever. *When God closes one door, He opens another.* Walking through it can be fearful, especially when you don't know what's on the other side. But it shouldn't be, for Jesus said, *"He goes on ahead of them, and his sheep follow him because they know his voice"* (John 10:4 NIV).

***

WHEN YOU WALK THROUGH THIS DOOR, HE'LL BE WAITING THERE FOR YOU, SO DON'T BE AFRAID.

FEBRUARY 21

Friends With God

...I have called you friends...

(John 15:15)

The difference between a friend and a servant lies in what they *know.* Jesus was telling His disciples, "I'm bringing you from the place of obedience to the place of intimacy; from functioning without insight, to knowing My mind and My purposes. I had to see if you could (1) take bad news and still keep a good attitude; (2) trust Me and not try to manipulate things; and (3) follow My plan, even when you couldn't see the big picture. And you did, so now I no longer call you servants, but friends."

Before God destroyed Sodom He discussed it with Abraham, because Abraham was "the Friend of God" (James 2:23). Before He gave Israel His Law, He talked it over with Moses. Listen: "And the Lord spake unto Moses face to face, as a man speaketh unto his friend" (Exodus 33:11). "Is such a relationship possible?" you ask. Yes, but check the price tag!

David said, "The secret of the Lord is with them that fear him" (Psalm 25:14). God will share things with His friends that He won't with others! Do you know somebody who's clear-headed in the midst of confusion, and cool when the heat's on?

***

IT COULD BE THAT THEY KNOW A SECRET—SHARED WITH THEM BY A FRIEND!

Things I've Noticed About Jesus

This is my beloved Son, in whom I am well pleased.

(Matthew 3:17)

Jesus didn't care about His reputation, or He wouldn't have eaten dinner with Zacchaeus. Tax collectors were despised Jews who worked for the Romans, extorting taxes from their own people. But Jesus wasn't concerned with what people thought of Zacchaeus, for He sees us not as we *are,* but as we *will* be when He gets through with us. After he met Jesus, Zacchaeus was so changed that he said, "If I have taken any thing from any man ... I restore him fourfold" (Luke 19:8). That's real conversion.

I've noticed, too, that Jesus always went to bat for losers, like the woman caught in the act of adultery. He listened to her self-righteous judges, and then wiped them out with one last sentence: "He that is without sin among you, let him first cast a stone at her" (John 8:7). To fully appreciate this story, you have to know what it's like to be personally lifted by Christ from your own gutter. Listen: "Neither do I condemn thee: go, and sin no more" (John 8:11). Is He serious? This woman could no more stop sinning than you could pull yourself up by your own bootstraps. Ah, but what He meant was, *"Because you've met Me, you'll never have to go back to your old life anymore."*

***

HE'S THE "LIFTING CHRIST," AND HE CAN LIFT YOU TODAY FROM WHERE YOU ARE. JUST REACH FOR HIM.

FEBRUARY 23

So You Planned to Go to Spain?

Whensoever I take my journey into Spain, I will come to you.

(Romans 15:24)

When things don't seem to work out the way you plan, God is still at work. Paul planned to go to Spain; it was certainly a good idea. But God had a better one, and Paul landed in prison. It was there he wrote his epistles—words that would last far beyond his short lifetime, and touch multitudes far beyond the small group of believers waiting for him in Spain. Listen: "In his heart a man plans his course, but the Lord determines his steps" (Proverbs 16:9 NIV). *Sometimes your disappointments are His appointments.*

Two of my friends recently walked through this very experience. They loved one another dearly and planned to get married. They had even made reservations for a honeymoon in the Bahamas. But God spoke and told them they were not to get married. It hurt! They cried for days, but they knew that God closes a lesser door to open a greater one.

David said, "You ... scheduled each day of my life before I began to breathe" (Psalm 139:16 TLB). Have you asked Him about your schedule? Have you submitted your plans to Him and asked Him to direct your steps?

***

SPAIN MAY LOOK GOOD TO YOU, BUT WHAT DOES GOD WANT FOR YOUR LIFE?

FEBRUARY 24

Learning from Others

All these events happened to them as examples for us....

(1 Corinthians 10:11 NLT)

Have you heard about the man who was really upset because he didn't get a promotion? He told his boss, "I've had twenty-five years experience." His boss replied, "No, John, you've had *one* year's experience—over and over again for the last twenty-five years!"

Repeating the same lessons over and over means you're not learning enough. You need to go *beyond yourself* in learning. Study those who've succeeded where you want to succeed, in order to know what to do and what not to do.

Ben Feldman said, "Only a fool learns from his own experience." Admiral Hyman Rick over said, "Learn from others' mistakes; you'll never live long enough to make them all yourself."

Select a board of directors for your life. For example, when you want to know how to handle repeated temptation, talk to Joseph; or what it costs to put principle over politics, ask Daniel; or about making sacrifices in order to fulfill your destiny, consult Paul, who spent all but seven years of his ministry behind bars; or how to cope with inferiority, talk to Gideon; or how to come back from failure, talk to Peter; or about risk-taking, talk to Esther.

Listen: "All these events happened to them as examples for us" (1 Corinthians 10:11 NLT). The formula for success is H.O.W.—Honesty, Openness, and Willingness.

***

RESPOND HONESTLY, OPENLY, AND WILLINGLY TO WHOMEVER GOD SENDS TO TEACH YOU.

FEBRUARY 25

The "No-Excuse Sunday"

...Let us go to the house of the Lord ... (Psalm 122:1 NIV)

Recently, a church bulletin announced the "No-Excuse Sunday." It read:

To make it possible for everyone to attend church next week we're planning to have:

1. Cots, for those who say Sunday is their only day for sleeping in.
2. Eye drops, for those whose eyes are tired from watching too much TV the night before.
3. Steel helmets, for those who say the roof will fall in if they go to church.
4. Blankets, for those who say the building is too cold, and fans for those who say it's too hot.
5. Hearing aids, for those who say the pastor isn't loud enough, and ear plugs for those who say he shouts too much.
6. Score cards, for those who like to count all the hypocrites.
7. Relatives, for those who say Sunday is their only day to be with the family.
8. Lunch, for those who say they can't attend church and make dinner, too.

9. Trees and grass, for those who say they "see God in nature"—especially   golf courses!
10.   Christmas poinsettias and Easter lilies, for those who wouldn't recognize the church without them.

Now, listen to what David said about going to church: "I love the house where you live, O Lord, the place where your glory dwells" (Psalm 26:8 NIV).

***

DO YOU FEEL THAT WAY, TOO? IF SO—SEE YOU THERE NEXT SUNDAY!

FEBRUARY 26

No Replays

Live one day at a time.

(Matthew 6:34 TLB)

Erma Bombeck wrote: "If I had my life to live over I would have waxed less and listened more. Instead of wishing away nine months of pregnancy and complaining about the shadow over my feet, I'd have cherished every minute of it, and realized that the wonder growing inside me was just a wonderful opportunity to assist God in a miracle. I would have cried and laughed less while watching television, and more while watching life. There would have been more 'I love you,' more I'm sorry,' and more 'I'm listening:' but mostly, given another shot at life, I would seize every minute of it and never give that minute back until there was nothing left of it."

Sadly, life doesn't offer us replays. You can't re-rear your children, or re-pastor your church. Initial impressions can't be re-made, and cutting remarks can't be re-said.

"You mean God won't forgive?" you ask. You know better than that! God will forgive, and most people are amazingly understanding. But our biggest task is usually forgiving ourselves.

***

THE MAIN MESSAGE IS CLEAR. THINK BEFORE YOU SPEAK. PAUSE BEFORE YOU ACT. AND MAKE EVERY MINUTE COUNT.

FEBRUARY 27

A Place for the Hurting

I will ... transform her Valley of Troubles into a Door of Hope.

(Hosea 2:15 TLB)

When your brother or sister falls, what do they need from you? *First, they need a place of anonymity.* A place where it's safe to be honest—where no one points an accusing finger and asks, "How could you have done such a thing?" Peter says, "Love will cover a multitude of sins" (1 Peter 4:8 NKJV). Note, love doesn't spread—it covers.

Next, they need a place of mercy. The God of the Old Testament built cities of refuge, where offenders could run to safety (see Numbers 35:6). In the New Testament Jesus lifted a fallen woman, and restored Peter after his painful chapter of denial. If you can't find mercy in the family of God, where *are* you going to find it?

Finally, they need a place of hope. In Hosea 2:15, God said He would open a Door of Hope in the Valley of Trouble (Achor). *Achor* was where Achan was stoned to death for disobeying God. If you're going through a time of trouble today—even if it's your own fault—remember, God has not abandoned you. Those

He loves experience His correcting hand. But He's not through blessing you. He's going to bring you out stronger than you were when you went in.

***

TODAY, HE'S OPENING A DOOR OF HOPE FOR YOU IN YOUR VALLEY OF TROUBLE.

FEBRUARY 28

Watch What You Say!

This book of the law shall not depart out of thy mouth.

(Joshua 1:8)

Your tongue is one of the greatest gifts God has placed at your command—use it wisely! The Bible says, "Death and life are in the power of the tongue" (Proverbs 18:21). Strong words—yet so often we don't stop to think *before* we speak, or consider the effect our words will have.

Have you ever used words like, *I can't handle this,* or, *This will never change?* I know I have! Your words don't just affect those around you; they affect God. *Faith-talk* is what He responds to. What you *say* about your situation affects what you *believe,* and what you *believe* determines what you'll *receive* from God.

Are you talking about your *expectations,* or are you still rehearsing *past experiences?* Listen: "Out of the same mouth come praise and cursing. My brothers, this should not be" (James 3:10 NIV). It's so easy to slip from speaking faith to speaking fear. Don't do it!

***

MAKE A DECISION TODAY TO GUARD YOUR WORDS CAREFULLY, AND REMEMBER, OTHERS MAY NOT SPEAK WORDS OF FAITH TO YOU TODAY—SO PRACTICE SPEAKING THEM TO YOURSELF!

FEBRUARY 29

Do You Have an Important Decision to Make?

If you don't know what you're doing, pray....

(James 1:5 TM)

Here are some suggestions to help you make better decisions:

(1) *Don't ask God to bless your plans; ask Him to show you His—they're already blessed!* He'll never tell you to do anything that doesn't line up with what He's already told you in His Word (see Isaiah 8:20).

(2) *Make sure your goal is to glorify God.* Sometimes that's hard to do, for the worst pride often masquerades behind feigned humility. The human body's amazing—pat a man on the back and his head begins to swell! (See James 4:6.)

(3) *Use your brain.* God's guidance transcends human reasoning, but it usually doesn't exclude it. God doesn't remove your mind. He renews it—so pray, then put it to work (see Romans 12:2).

(4) *Seasons aren't meant to be ignored.* If it isn't God's timing, wait! In the right season, the plan

will be clear, the people you need will show up, and the funds will be provided (see Ecclesiastes 3:1).

(5) *Never act without the facts, but never limit God to them.* When knowledge won't take you another step, faith will carry you through. It's what connects you to the power of God.

***

NOW LISTEN AGAIN: "IF YOU DON'T KNOW WHAT YOU'RE DOING, PRAY TO THE FATHER. HE LOVES TO HELP" (JAMES 1:6 TM).

MARCH 1

Spirit-Led People

To be carnally minded is death; but to be spiritually minded is life and peace.

(Romans 8:6)

When your mind agrees with your spirit, you're spiritually minded; but when your mind agrees with your flesh, you're carnally minded. That's why you need to read the Word daily. Listen: "A good man out of the good treasure of the heart bringeth forth good things" (Matthew 12:35). First you have to get it into your heart, *then* you can bring it forth. *Anything you can conceive, you can bring forth.* That's why the enemy will do everything he can to keep you out of the Word.

Have you ever changed a baby's diaper? Before you put on the new you have to take off the *old* or you'll have problems. Paul tells us to *"put off your old self, which is being corrupted ... put on the new self, created to be like God"* (Ephesians 4:22, 24 NIV).

He calls this being "renewed in the spirit of your mind" (verse 23). As long as the Prodigal Son had a "hog-pen mentality," he was dead to his father's blessings and his rightful place as his son and heir. But when he remembered, repented, and renewed his mind, things turned around for him. *And it's the same for you.*

***

AS A SPIRIT-LED PERSON, YOU NEED TO RENEW YOUR MIND EVERY DAY, AND TODAY IS ONE OF THOSE DAYS.

MARCH 2

When You No Longer Need God

As long as he sought the Lord, God made him to prosper.

1 Chronicles 26:5)

As a leader, Uzziah was a Lincoln or a Churchill. Listen to his accomplishments: He defeated all the enemies of Israel; created an army of 307,000 elite troops; developed state-of-the-art warfare; built towers and reservoirs; and developed agriculture and cattle farming, so that Israel became the envy of the world. All this happened, *"as long as he sought the Lord."*

But then it all changed. Listen again: "But when he was strong, his heart was lifted up to his destruction" (2 Chronicles 26:16). Learn this lesson well. *It's okay to possess things, so long as things don't possess you.* You don't own anything—you're just the administrator of God's estate, and the executor of His will. So long as you pursue God, His blessings will pursue you.

When the pressure is off we stop seeking God, because we don't *need* Him like we once did. *Things* become more important to us than He is. We get so busy building homes, buying cars, and bringing up families, that before we know it, *He's pushed aside.*

Do you remember when you had such a hunger for Him that you couldn't wait to get to His house? You couldn't wait to read His Word. You talked about Him constantly. But now that fire has become a smoldering ash.

***

TODAY, HE'S CALLING YOU BACK TO YOUR FIRST LOVE, BACK TO THE PLACE YOU ONCE KNEW.

MARCH 3

A God-Altered Perspective

Rejoice in the Lord always...

(Philippians 4:4 NIV)

Paul was in prison when he wrote, "Rejoice in the Lord always." *Around* him was the cruelty of men, but *within* him was the Kingdom of God. How is such joy possible? Paul gives us the key: "We look not at the things which are seen, but at the things which are not seen: for the things which are seen are temporal; but the things which are not seen are eternal" (2 Corinthians 4:18). *Child of God, there are things we see that the world doesn't.*

Paul was saying, "You can lock me up, but you can't keep me in. Outside these bars Caesar rules, but in here Jesus is Lord, and when my assignment is complete, I'm out of here. Go ahead, take your best shot. Beat me, imprison me, behead me, but one second after the axe falls I'll be more alive than I am now." *There's nothing you can do to a man like that. He's beyond your reach.*

Paul was saying, "This is the best it will ever be for you, but you ought to see where I'm going!"

"For we know that if our earthly house of this tabernacle were dissolved, we have a building of God, an house not made with hands, eternal in the heavens" (2 Corinthians 5:1). *That's* a God-altered perspective!

***

WHEN YOU PRAISE HIM, NOT BECAUSE OF WHAT YOU FEEL, BUT BECAUSE OF WHAT YOU KNOW, YOU'LL HAVE JOY THAT TRANSCENDS ANYTHING THAT COMES AGAINST YOU.

MARCH 4

Frail but Not Disqualified

We have not an high priest which cannot be touched with the feeling of our infirmities.

(Hebrews 4:15)

The word *infirmities* is plural, meaning we each have several. Yet many of us struggle to admit to even one. A well-known writer said: "We have carefully hidden our struggles and paraded only our victories, but the whole country is falling asleep at the parade." For God's sake, and a dying world's sake, will somebody *please get real!*

The Greek word for *infirmities* means "malady" or "frailty." All of us have some malady or frailty that incapacitates us to the degree that we need His mercies newly bestowed on us every morning. David succeeded on the battlefield, but failed in the bedroom, yet no man was more used of God. This should encourage you today, for God's not only sympathetic, but He also uses people like you and me, who are affected by the same stimuli and struggles as David.

Paul spelled it out clearly: "We also are men of like passions with you" (Acts 14:15). Only a fool would refuse to lift a diamond out of a drain, and God is no fool. The Church has thrown away thousands of valuable diamonds by denying her wounded soldiers a chance to return to active service.

***

IF GOD IS ABLE TO SYMPATHIZE WITH OUR WEAKNESSES, SHOULDN'T WE BE WILLING TO DO AT LEAST THAT MUCH FOR EACH OTHER?

MARCH 5

We Can't Lose

I want to report to you, friends, that my imprisonment here has had the opposite of its intended effect. Instead of being squelched, the Message has actually prospered.

(Philippians 1:12 TM)

When I read the words, "My imprisonment here has had the opposite of its intended effect," I shouted for joy! And that's not all; listen: "Not only that, but most of the Christians here have become far more sure of themselves in the faith than ever, speaking out fearlessly about God" (Philippians 1:14 TM). The devil thought that by locking Paul up, he could shut him up; but instead, Paul starting writing books that would change the world. Satan thought imprisoning him would intimidate all the other Christians in town; but instead, it ignited them.

And to make matters worse, they changed Paul's guards every few hours, and chained him to another two Roman soldiers. That's what's called a *captive audience.* Every few hours, two new converts would leave, and two new prospects would arrive, until there were "saints in the household of Caesar" (see Philippians 4:22). Finally, they decided that the only thing to do was to kill Paul. Kill what? They could destroy the shell, but they couldn't lay a finger on the treasure. Listen again: "They didn't shut me up; they gave me a pulpit! Alive, I'm Christ's messenger; dead, I'm his bounty. Life versus even more life! I can't lose" (Philippians 1:23 TM).

***

REJOICE, CHILD OF GOD, WE'RE ON THE WINNING SIDE TODAY. YOU CAN'T LOSE!

MARCH 6

Deep-Water Faith!

Nevertheless at thy word I will...

(Luke 5:5)

After they'd fished all night and caught nothing, Jesus said to His disciples, "Launch out into the deep, and let down your nets" (Luke 5:4).

Listen to Peter's response, "...nevertheless at thy word I will let down the net..." (Luke 5:5). That's it! Doubt your doubts, but never doubt God. One word from Him can change everything. Listen: "And when they had this done, they inclosed a great multitude of fishes: and their net brake" (Luke 5:6). There are four lessons here for you today:

(1) *He'll involve you in one thing, to teach you another.* Soon, He was going to involve them in an even bigger miracle—catching multitudes and bringing them into His Kingdom.

(2) *He'll use the familiar to do the incredible.* In their workplace, where nothing special ever happened, He suddenly showed up and changed everything. Look for Him today in the familiar and unexpected places in your life.

(3) *He'll move you from the security of the shore to the risks of the deep.* Why? Because you've

got to risk the great storms if you're going to enjoy great catches. No risks, no rewards!

(4) *When you obey God—nets break, needs are met, minds are blown, and He is glorified.*

***

BUT REMEMBER, THE MIRACLE ONLY BEGINS WHEN YOU SAY, "...NEVERTHELESS AT THY WORD, I WILL..."

MARCH 7

God Can Do So Much With So Little

She hath done what she could.

(Mark 14:8)

Edmund Burke says, "Nobody made a greater mistake than he who did nothing, because he could only do little!" It's one of the best-kept secrets—God can do so much with so little!

Last night in church I met a genuine hero. She's a grandmother who has already raised one family, and all but one of them became great successes. Sadly, that one became a drug addict and abandoned her four children. Into the gap, with a huge heart of love, stepped this grandmother. Alone at sixty-eight years old, she's raising her daughter's children. Every time the church doors are open, she has them there. They're in school making straight As. She's wise enough to know she can't do it by herself, so she has enlisted God's help with the project!

David said that those who are *planted* in the house of God shall *flourish* (Psalm 92:13). She keeps the light burning and the door open, praying for the day when her prodigal will return. But until then, she's molding another generation for God. You'll meet her someday, when Heaven gives out its highest awards. She's like the little woman of whom Jesus said, "She hath done what she could."

***

THE QUESTION IS, HAVE YOU?

MARCH 8

You're Still His

When I was still in my mother's womb he chose and called me.

(Galatians 1:15 TM)

Satan is terrified of those who have been called by God. He'll set traps and initiate attacks to keep you from discovering and fulfilling your destiny. Don't waste your time being terrified of him—he's terrified of *you.* Listen: "The God of peace will soon crush Satan under your feet" (Romans 16:20 NIV). Your struggle is just an indication of *who* you are and *what* your worth is to God. Satan doesn't attack a retreating army; he joins them. You have value in the Kingdom of God. Never forget that!

Satan will do whatever he can today to destroy *your confidence in God* and blind you to how great, how powerful, and how mighty your God is. The enemy wants to sabotage your success because you were created to win, not lose. This morning I read something wonderful, and I believe God wants me to share it with you. Listen:

I pray that your hearts will be flooded with light so that you can see something of the future he has called you to share.... I pray that you will begin to understand how incredibly great his power is to help those who believe him. It is that same mighty power that raised Christ from the dead and seated him in the place of honor at God's right hand in heaven (Ephesians 1:18-20 TLB).

✳✳✳

TODAY, THAT POWER IS YOURS—USE IT!

MARCH 9

"Pharaoh, You Can't Have What Belongs to God"

Let my people go, that they may serve me.

(Exodus 8:1)

The same God who said to Pharaoh, "Let my people go," is saying again, "Pharaoh, you've got something that belongs to Me. You've picked a fight you can't win. I'm going to set this child of Mine free, and there's nothing you can do about it."

For too long Pharaoh has contaminated your mind and caused you to think that you're a zero, a reject, a nothing. That's a lie! God doesn't check your bank account, your nationality, your education, or your talent to see if He can use you. God will use you *in spite of* your broken home, *in spite of* your broken health, and in spite of your broken dreams. *Don't let Pharaoh have your firstborn! Don't let him have your inheritance. Don't let him have your future. Don't let him keep you in Egypt another day.*

Turn to God, and watch what He'll do on your behalf. He'll bring Pharaoh down! He'll open the Red Sea and make a way out for you. *Whom do you think brought you this far?* Just because you couldn't see Him, didn't mean He wasn't watching over you.

***

LISTEN: "DO NOT BE AFRAID. STAND FIRM AND YOU WILL SEE THE DELIVERANCE THE LORD WILL BRING YOU TODAY. THE EGYPTIANS YOU SEE TODAY YOU WILL NEVER SEE AGAIN" (EXODUS 14:13-14 NIV).

MARCH 10

Resting

There remains therefore a rest for the people of God.

(Hebrews 4:9 NKJV)

If the devil can't drive you into carnality, he'll be just as happy to drive you into exhaustion. He tried it with Moses. No man ever had so much trouble with a congregation as Moses had with the congregation of Israel in the wilderness. When he complained to God, God told him, in effect, "I never told you to do it all by yourself. It's *My* work and they're My people, and I'm well able to take care of them."

God's got some players who act like they're the whole team. D.L. Moody once said, "You can either do the work of ten men, or get ten men to do the work." It's called *delegation.*

Our church pews are filled with spectators and "frozen assets." Paul said the responsibility of those who minister is "the perfecting of the saints, for the work of the ministry" (Ephesians 4:12). Are you being trained and equipped to minister to others? Are you discipling and training anyone else? Give these questions some serious thought, because you will be answerable to God.

The Lord told Moses, "My presence shall go with thee, and I will give thee rest" (Exodus 33:14). *There is no burnout in the will of God.* There is, however, in the will of the flesh. In God's will, there is only rest and peace.

***

TODAY, ASK HIM TO HELP YOU ENTER THAT PLACE OF REST.

MARCH 11

Walking With God!

...Walk worthy of the calling with which you were called.

(Ephesians 4:1 NKJV)

You can't just come to God and say, "Here's my idea; please stamp Your approval on it." That's not the way it works! Listen: "He has created us ... so that we can do the good things he planned for us long ago" (Ephesians 2:10 NLT). Your prayer must be, *Lord, show me Your plan.*

You can't compartmentalize your life and say, "In this category I'm doing things my way, but in this other category, I'm being led by God." Every step you take must be synchronized with the beat of the Holy Spirit!

Sometimes what you hear in your spirit will be different from what you hear with your ears. Once you understand that, nothing will be more important to you than keeping pace with Him, for His direction is always right. His timing is always perfect, and His results are always best.

You ask, "But how can I live like that?" (1) By understanding that God works through you as you engage your mind, open your mouth, move your feet, and use your hands to do what He has already put into your heart. (2) By understanding that He never stops calling you to take one more step, do one more thing, and engage in one more act of faith.

***

THAT'S WHAT'S CALLED "WALKING WITH GOD!"

MARCH 12

Are You Keeping Your Covenant?

With thee will I establish my covenant.

(Genesis 6:18)

A covenant is the strongest promise two people can make. Covenant means "to bind together." Sometimes they would exchange swords, signifying that they would always defend each other. Other times, they would pass a sandal between them, pledging to go to any lengths for each other. Again, they would take an annual sacrifice, split it down the middle, and walk between the halves, signifying they were one, and each was incomplete without the other.

God has entered into a covenant to bless you. Listen: "There, in the presence of the Lord your God, you and your families shall eat and shall rejoice in everything you have put your hand to, because the Lord your God has blessed you" (Deuteronomy 12:7 NIV). Read the promises of your covenant: health, safety, prosperity, guidance, victory—*if you obey the rules.* God put those rules into the Ark of the Covenant and when Israel went to war and the Ark went before them, nobody could withstand them. *The covenant was their power source; God himself was their ally in battle. And He is your ally, too.*

The covenant *sword* is God's promise to fight for you. The covenant *sandal* says no matter how far gone you may feel, just call and He'll come. The covenant *sacrifice* means you're an heir to all that He has promised.

***

ARE YOU KEEPING YOUR COVENANT WITH HIM TODAY?

MARCH 13

Staying on Track

He's the one who will keep you on track.

(Proverbs 3:6 TM)

I recently had a real *off day.* A friend asked, "What is God saying to you in all of this? After all, He's not the author of confusion." (Don't you hate it when friends call you to accountability on an *off day?*) I was miserable because I knew the answer, but I didn't like it. Now we can shorten the process, but since I'm stubborn, I took the long route. Finally, my wife said, "You've completely lost your peace, and you need to do something about it."

All those great promises came flooding back: "Thou wilt keep him in perfect peace, whose mind is stayed on thee" (Isaiah 26:3). Or how about this one: "Let not your heart be troubled, neither let it be afraid" (John 14:27). Now if I don't have the peace God promised, it's not His fault.

Finally, I asked Him to forgive me for my lousy attitude and lack of trust in Him. I'd made others my source, and when they didn't *act* the way I wanted them to, I tried to force the issue. Since people can't make *me* do what they want, why would I think I could make *them* do what I want? At last I took all the pieces, threw them at the feet of Jesus, and asked Him to sort them all out. He did! Guess what? I'm back on track again.

***

IS THERE A MESSAGE IN THIS FOR YOU TODAY?

MARCH 14

It Wasn't That He Didn't Know; He Just Didn't Care

The Pharisee ... said to himself, "If this man was the prophet I thought he was, he would have known what kind of woman this is.

(Luke 7:39 TM)

She was a prostitute, and everybody seemed to know it except Jesus. As He ate with some clergymen, she washed His feet with her tears and dried them with her hair. One preacher commented, "If He was a real prophet, He'd know what kind of woman this is." They had been with Jesus, but they didn't know Him at all. They had heard His words, but they didn't know His heart. He knew all about this woman. It wasn't that He didn't *know*—it was that He just didn't *care.* How wonderful!

Your past doesn't matter to Him! Jesus said concerning the Prodigal Son, "When he was yet a great way off, his father saw him, and had compassion, and ran, and fell on his neck, and kissed him ... and said to his servants ... my son was dead, and is alive again; he was lost, and is found. And they began to be merry" (Luke 15:20-24).

We *all* have a past—but the *blood of Jesus* cleanses us from all sin (see 1 John 1:7). Come just as you are. Once you've met Him, you'll never be the same. Listen to what Jesus said concerning this woman: "Her sins, which are many, are forgiven" (Luke 7:47).

***

TODAY HE'S SAYING THOSE SAME WORDS TO YOU.

MARCH 15

Secure Enough to Take Risks

Absolutely nothing can get between us and God's love.

(Romans 8:39 TM)

Once you're secure in God's love, you can afford to take risks, admit failure, seek help, and try again. When you know you are loved based on who you *are,* and not on what you've *done,* you have the ultimate self-esteem born of God's esteem for you.

Once you have that, you can chart your course according to the dream in your heart, and never again be intimidated by the fear of failing. How often did you mess up before you learned to drive? On the field, did you hit a home run the first time you picked up the bat?

Listen, Babe Ruth struck out 1,330 times—almost twice as often as he hit a home run. Yet, he went on to become the greatest home-run hitter in history! R.H. Macy failed seven times before his stores caught on; yet now his name's a household word.

Failing doesn't make you a failure from God's perspective, because in Christ you are always a success. Listen: "Nothing ... in the whole world will be able to separate us from the love of God..." (Romans 8:38 NCV). Think about that—nothing!

Even when you risk and fail, you still succeed. Because (1) your character's strengthened; (2) you grow in wisdom; (3) you inspire others; and (4) you learn to depend on God's strength instead of your own.

**

SO, GO AHEAD—RISK IT! WITH GOD YOU CAN'T LOSE!

MARCH 16

It's Time for the Word to Become Flesh

And the Word was made flesh, and dwelt among us, and we beheld...

(John 1:14)

Jesus didn't just *have* a sermon; He *was* the sermon. He didn't just talk about love; He fed the hungry, ministered to the sick, and lifted the fallen. It wasn't just "a Sunday thing"—they saw "the Word made flesh" seven days a week and in *every* circumstance of His life.

He taught forgiveness by forgiving those who ripped the flesh from His back and nailed Him to the Cross. He called Matthew the tax collector, and told him to bring his pen with him because He wanted him to write a book. How wonderful! The fact that John's nets were empty and his business was failing didn't mean a thing to Jesus, for with Him every loser is a potential winner. They all got the same instructions: "Follow Me."

Talk about spiritual warfare—one-fourth of His ministry was spent confronting the enemy. He prayed before dawn, and often all night. Think of it: *He did—but we don't!* And doesn't it show up in the results?

It's time to get your theology off the drawing board. The Word has got to become flesh in your home, in your job, and in every area of your life.

***

IT'S A "SHOW ME" WORLD OUT THERE, AND THEY DON'T WANT TO SEE YOU; THEY WANT TO SEE JESUS.

MARCH 17

Poured from Vessel Into Vessel

Moab hath been at ease ... he hath ... not been emptied from vessel to vessel.

(Jeremiah 48:11)

The finest wine was perfected by being poured "from vessel to vessel." Each one served a different purpose. The goal was to one day be set on the king's table, and poured out in his service. What a picture of Christian life—*poured from experience into experience.* One of those vessels was called "the vessel of pressure and testing." When the lid was clamped on, the pressure would build. They'd put it in a dark basement and often leave it there for years. As the pressure mounted, it produced the purity and maturity found only in the best wines. Does this sound like where you've been lately?

What you've been *taught* must be *tested* or it has no real value. Before you move from the natural to the supernatural, you'll have to face the wind and the waves. Some lessons can only be learned in the storm. When you tell God you want to grow, don't be surprised if He tells you to get into the boat. That's how you develop real faith and confidence in God. That's how you get to know He's bigger than anything you'll ever face. When He tells you to go over to the other side, nothing can keep you from getting there.

***

TODAY, IF YOU FIND YOURSELF BEING POURED FROM VESSEL TO VESSEL, REJOICE. IT MEANS YOU'RE GETTING READY FOR THE KING'S TABLE!

MARCH 18

Doing What You're Supposed to Do

When ye shall have done all those things which are commanded you, say, We are unprofitable servants: we have done that which was our duty to do.

(Luke 17:10)

Has God ever surfaced in you things you never knew were there? It happened to me recently. I got angry and took my frustration out on the wrong person. It usually happens to me for two reasons: I'm afraid that I'm not going to *get* something I need, or that I'm going to *lose* something I've got. Most of my fears seem to fall into those two categories.

Afterward, I felt rotten. Here I am writing a devotional and telling others they should be loving, patient, and kind, and I act like a spoiled child who doesn't get his own way. So I apologized and felt much better. Then a voice said, "That was big of you—you're really something." No sooner had I heard it, than *another* voice said, *"You're still an unprofitable servant."* Wow—what an ego deflator! No trumpet fanfare, no parades, no words of praise. Listen to these words again: "When you've done everything expected of you, be matter-of-fact and say, 'The work is done. What we were told to do, we did'" (Luke 17:10 TM).

***

THE SONGWRITER PUTS IT INTO PERSPECTIVE WITH THESE WORDS: TAKE UP THY CROSS AND FOLLOW ME, I HEAR MY BLESSED SAVIOR CALL. HOW CAN I MAKE A LESSER SACRIFICE, WHEN JESUS GAVE HIS ALL?

MARCH 19

Don't Come Down

I am doing a great work and I cannot come down.

(Nehemiah 6:3 NAS)

Satan will use anything he can to bring you down! Nehemiah was told to remove the rubbish, rebuild the walls, restore the Temple, and reclaim the people of God—the same assignment that we've been given today! His enemy tried threats, diplomacy, and fifth columns, but Nehemiah stood firm and said, "I am doing a great work, and I cannot come down." And the word for you today is—don't come down!

When they ask you to explain what you're doing, or to defend yourself, *don't come down!* When faint hearts say, "Couldn't we compromise and just get along with them?" *Don't come down!* When human wisdom says, "It's not a good time to move forward; perhaps we should wait," *don't come down!* When doubt and fear say, "The job is too big and God is too small," *don't come down!* Take your sword in one hand and your mortarboard in the other, and whether you have to build or battle, *stay up there* and keep doing the job God has called you to do.

If you even *think* of coming down, you send a signal to the enemy that his strategy is working. You step down to the level of your accuser, and the work God gave you to do is put on hold.

***

STAY UP THERE, AND BEFORE YOU KNOW IT, THE WALL WILL BE BUILT, THE ENEMY WILL BE BEATEN, AND GOD WILL BE GLORIFIED.

MARCH 20

Whatever It Costs – It's Worth It

The sufferings of this present time are not worthy to be compared with the glory which shall be revealed in us.

(Romans 8:18)

This morning I was reading about Paul's calling. It's *different* from much of what I hear today. Listen: "He is a chosen vessel unto me, to bear my name before the Gentiles, and kings, and the children of Israel: For I will shew him how great things he must *suffer* for my name's sake" (Acts 9:15-16). What's this? *Suffer* great things for My name? I thought I was signing up to be prospered, not pulverized. Think again! The blessing of God doesn't *exempt* you from attack; it equips you to handle it. His grace is what carries you through it. Paul spent all but seven years of his ministry in prison.

Where did you get the idea that it's fun being a Christian? You can have joy in jail, and fellowship in suffering, but if you pose any threat to the devil, then get ready for attack, because it's coming. The important part is not what's going on *around* you; it's what is going on *within* you. Listen: "What we suffer now is nothing compared to the glory he will give us later" (Romans 8:18 TLB).

***

REJOICE, YOU'RE PART OF AN ARMY DESTINED TO WIN, AND A KINGDOM THAT'S GOING TO PREVAIL.

MARCH 21

Gracious Words

The words of a wise man's mouth are gracious.

(Ecclesiastes 10:12)

Sometimes gifted and busy people can be harsh or unkind without meaning to be. They live by a schedule, and they get upset when others fail to respect it. But not Jesus. He had the most important job in the world, and yet He stopped for children and spent time with them. Sometimes the only people who matter to us are those who further our goals. *That's not ambition; it's selfishness!*

Jesus had many opportunities to ingratiate himself with the rich and powerful, and He did have friends among them. But mostly He gave himself to common folks. He was so secure in His identity and clear in His purpose that He spent time lifting "losers" like Mary Magdalene.

The law of kindness governed His words, and He taught this law to His disciples. Listen: "Love your enemies, bless them that curse you, do good to them that hate you, and pray for them which despitefully use you" (Matthew 5:44). When I read those words, my heart cries, "Help! I fall so far short of this goal." Jesus didn't berate Peter when he failed—he restored him and made him a leader in the Church. He didn't degrade Thomas for doubting. He strengthened him.

***

TODAY, ASK GOD TO HELP YOU STAY COOL UNDER FIRE, AND BE GRACIOUS TO THOSE YOU MEET.

MARCH 22

The Gentleness of Jesus

A bruised reed shall he not break, and the smoking flax shall he not quench.

(Isaiah 42:3)

I love to talk about Jesus, and I find myself increasingly wanting to be around others who love to talk about Him, too. It's a growing hunger that's becoming an obsession. Today I saw another wonderful thing about Him; Isaiah says, "A bruised reed shall he not break, and the smoking flax shall he not quench." Can you think of anything more worthless than a bruised reed that people have trampled on? Jesus will not walk *by* it, and He will not walk *on* it. He'll stop and gently *strengthen* it in the broken places, and then He'll *straighten* it up so it can grow again.

Can you picture anything more useless than a smoldering wick that once burned brightly? But watch how Jesus works; He carefully pours fresh oil into the empty lamp, and then gently blows on the flax until it ignites again.

I don't know about you, but I've *been* a bruised reed and a smoking flax, and when I couldn't reach up, He reached down and lifted me from hopelessness and despair. He made me strong in the broken places, and fanned the smoldering flax into a flame of love. And He's done it *for you,* too, hasn't He?

***

TAKE A FEW MOMENTS TODAY AND TELL HIM HOW MUCH YOU LOVE HIM.

MARCH 23

Rebuilding Trust

Love ... always trusts, always hopes, always perseveres.

(1 Corinthians 13:6-7 NIV)

Has your trust been violated? Have you become distrustful, questioning things you never did before? Sometimes you can't receive the love you need because your wounded spirit says, "Nobody will ever do that to me again." The real damage lies not in what you've been through, but in what you're left with—terrible doubt. When the woman at the well met Jesus, she didn't know He was different from the men she had known before. He had to remove her defenses or she'd have missed the greatest experience of her life.

Now Jesus is "the same yesterday, and to day, and for ever" (Hebrews 13:8). You can't go back, but He can. He can heal your wounded areas and break the chains that bind you to memory. Listen: "The former [things] shall not be remembered, nor come into mind" (Isaiah 65:17). You don't have to wait until you get to heaven to experience this. He can do that for you *now.* But you'll never experience what He's promised until you learn to trust again. Trust

God. Trust the people He sends to bless you. Sure, you'll be disappointed; don't look for perfection from imperfect people. You'll get lots of practice forgiving—that's Christian life.

***

ASK HIM TODAY TO HELP YOU TAKE DOWN THE WALL OF FEAR SO YOU CAN TRUST AGAIN, AND START LIVING.

MARCH 24

The "I Only" Syndrome

And I, even I only, am left; and they seek my life, to take it away.

(1 Kings 19:10)

Elijah was convinced he was the only man of God left in the world. Imagine it—the only ministry still preaching righteousness and standing up to Jezebel and her corrupt religious system. God soon disillusioned him: "I have left me seven thousand in Israel, all the knees which have not bowed unto Baal" (1 Kings 19:18). What a humbling revelation. You may be a great quarterback, but you're not the whole team. God has others!

Sometimes leaders fall into the trap of turf-guarding. From there it's only a short step to believing that "our church is the only place where God is moving—so if you're mature and love the truth, you'll walk and worship with us." Elijah really believed he was the only standard-bearer of truth in the land, and when that happens, you become critical of others. Usually you say, "They're not very deep, or they're not very spiritual, or what have they ever done for God anyway?" When someone else has had an experience different from ours, we diminish and dismiss it.

Check your heart, child of God. Jesus said, "By this shall all men know that ye are my disciples, if ye have love one to another" (John 13:35).

***

TODAY, ASK GOD FOR THE GRACE TO RECOGNIZE HIS WORK IN OTHERS. THEN REACH OUT TO THEM IN HIS LOVE.

MARCH 25

Your Time Has Come

None of my words will be delayed any longer.

(Ezekiel 12:28 NIV)

The Living Bible says, "All delay has ended! I will do it now!" Rejoice, child of God, your delivery date has come. The waiting is over. God is about to answer your prayer.

When Peter was imprisoned, the Church began praying around the clock. It worked. The angel of the Lord came and delivered Peter to the very door where they were praying. But when they heard Peter was at the door, they said, "It couldn't be." When it was confirmed, they said, "It must be an angel." Finally, when they saw him, Scripture says, "They were astonished" (Acts 12:16). They were praying, but not believing. They were locked into a posture of asking, but not expecting. Maybe that's where you are, expecting little or nothing. Today God is saying to you, *The answer is knocking at your door, go and open it.*

Don't wait until the walls fall—shout *now.* When praise fills your mouth, expectation will fill your heart, and God will move on your behalf. When God gives you a word, act on it! Before their prison doors opened, Paul and Silas filled the place with praise, for that produces a climate in which faith can grow. So start praising Him now for what He is about to do.

***

HIS WORD TO YOU TODAY IS, "ALL DELAY HAS ENDED. I WILL DO IT NOW!"

MARCH 26

How to Have a Relationship with God

I can of mine own self do nothing: as I hear, I judge.

(John 5:30)

Jesus spent three and a half years showing us how to build a relationship with God. He didn't respond to *need.* He only responded to the *Father.* Listen to these words: "I can't do a solitary thing on my own: I listen, then I decide" (John 5:30 TM). The *King James Version* says, "As I hear, I judge." What a way to live. When you hear from God, people can no longer control you or set your agenda. Unmet needs can no longer discourage you, for you're listening to one voice only—His.

Jesus spent whole nights in prayer, and often rose before dawn to pray. What was He doing? Making *deposits* early in the morning, so that He could make *withdrawals* all day long.

Listen again: "For the Father loves the Son, and shows Him all things that He Himself does" (John 5:20 NKJV). You don't reveal yourself to just anyone—only to those with whom you're intimate. Power flows from intimacy. Wisdom flows from intimacy. Authority flows from knowing you've been with God.

The Bible tells us that Jesus called the disciples to be *with* Him, and then He sent them *out from* Him. Don't try to go out for Him until you've first spent time with Him.

***

DON'T TRY TO BUILD A MINISTRY UNTIL YOU'VE FIRST BUILT A RELATIONSHIP, AND IF THAT MEANS REARRANGING YOUR PRIORITIES, THEN DO IT.

MARCH 27

A New Measuring Rod

Among you, those who are the greatest should take the lowest rank, and the leader should be like a servant.

(Luke 22:26 NLT)

In this devotional we often write about goal setting, perseverance, motivation, and destiny. And we should—for without a goal, a strategy, and a committed heart, you'll never fulfill your life's purpose.

But in your quest for success and recognition, Jesus gives you a new measuring rod. Listen: "Normally the master sits at the table and is served.... But not here! For I am your servant" (Luke 22:27 NLT).

In Jesus' day, foot-washing was a task reserved not just for servants, but for the lowest ranking among them. Every group has its pecking order, and household workers back then were no exception. The servant at the bottom was expected to be on his knees with the towel and basin.

What a sight. The one *here* with the towel and basin is Jesus! The hands that formed the stars now wash away street filth. The fingers that formed the mountains now dry the rough feet of common fishermen. Hours before His death, Jesus's singular concern is to make sure the disciples know that in His Kingdom the way up is down, and the way to the top is not through intelligence or manipulation, but through humility and service. Living that way is not natural—it's supernatural!

***

YOU CAN ONLY DO IT AS YOU SURRENDER DAILY TO THE INDWELLING POWER OF HIS SPIRIT.

MARCH 28

Call It Grace!

I am the Lord ... the merciful and gracious God.

(Exodus 34:6 NLT)

God loves you just as you are, but He loves you too much to let you stay that way! Do you think God's love for you would be stronger, if your faith was stronger? If so, you're confusing God's love with human love. Human love increases with performance and decreases with mistakes. But not God's love. He loves you just as you are.

Having trouble accepting that? Listen to how God introduces himself: "I am the Lord, the merciful and gracious God. I am slow to anger and rich in unfailing love and faithfulness" (Exodus 34:6 NLT). In spite of failures, David could say, "I will sing of the mercies of the Lord for ever: with my mouth will I make known thy faithfulness to all generations" (Psalm 89:1). Need more to convince you? Paul writes, "God showed his great love for us by sending Christ to die for us while we were still sinners" (Romans 5:8 NLT).

Get rid of your do-it-yourself righteousness! Salvation's not, "Do! Do! Do!" It's, "Done! Done! Done!" It's a finished work; therefore, you can stand before Christ in His name and not your own.

Perhaps you're thinking, *This sounds too easy.* Wrong! There was nothing easy about it! The cross was heavy, the blood was real, and the price was staggering. It would have bankrupted you or me, so He paid it for us.

***

CALL IT SIMPLE—CALL IT A GIFT—CALL IT WHAT IT IS: GRACE!

MARCH 29

More on Walking With God

...Walk worthy of the calling with which you were called.

(Ephesians 4:1 NKJV)

The moment you say yes to God, and move in obedience to His voice, He gives you the ability to perform His will. He doesn't give it to you first, then call you next; no. He calls you; then, as you step out and obey Him, He imparts it to you.

God is never content with the status quo. Never! Every day in countless ways He'll call you, mold you, and develop you into a greater and greater likeness of His Son.

You see, you're not out for a stroll—you're going somewhere! God has a destiny in mind for you! Every day you'll be given new experiences and put into situations that'll mature you to the point where you have ... the same attitude ... the same perspective ... and the same discernment as Him.

When you understand that, walking with God will take on a whole new meaning. You'll realize that your walk with Him is the only walk that will ever satisfy you, or fulfill your purpose for being on this Earth.

***

YOU'LL ALSO EXPERIENCE THE GREATEST JOY YOU'VE EVER KNOWN—AND BRING CREDIT TO HIS NAME EVERY DAY!

MARCH 30

The Ministry of Worrying

Be anxious for nothing.

(Philippians 4:6 NKJV)

Some of us were trained to worry by parents who weren't there when we needed them. Others were trained by religious systems that had no power, so they said, "God doesn't do that anymore." And some were told that once God saved us, the rest was up to us. So we work hard and worry a lot.

The hardest people to deal with are those who feel called to *the ministry of worrying.* Bishop Malcolm Smith says, "I once had an old aunt who showed up every Christmas, and always seemed to know when we were in trouble. Her stock phrase was, 'Well, I can't really help, but I'll worry for you.'" Worry has become such a way of life for some of us, that we worry if we're not worried!

Today, I came across a wonderful translation of Philippians 4:6 in *The Message.* It may be just what you need:

Instead of worrying, pray. Let petitions and praises shape your worries into prayers, letting God know your concerns. Before you know it, a sense of God's wholeness, everything coming together for good, will come and settle you down. It's wonderful what happens when Christ displaces worry at the center of your life.

***

PAUL DOESN'T SAY, "DON'T LOOK AT THE PROBLEM." HE SAYS, "LET CHRIST DISPLACE WORRY AT THE CENTER OF YOUR LIFE." IT'S THE ONLY WAY TO LIVE.

MARCH 31

More Isn't Always Better

If riches increase, set not your heart upon them.

(Psalm 62:10)

God longs to bless you in every area of your life. But when you have more, you get more responsibility, more pressure, more insurance, more wear and tear, and more bogged down by the very thing that was supposed to be such a blessing. Can I ask you something? When you had *less,* did you have more time to read the Word and more time to pray? The danger comes when the *things* we have consume so much of our time that we've little or nothing left for *Him.* And ministers fight this. It's a lot easier to get involved with the work of the Lord than it is to get involved with the Lord of the work.

Did you think a new home or a new car would satisfy you? Shouldn't any joy that costs that much last a little longer? The Bible says, "Let us lay aside every weight" (Hebrews 12:1). Lighten up for the race. What drains you and diverts you from being all that you were meant to be? Paul says, "I am bringing all my energies to bear on this one thing ... to reach the end of the race and receive the prize" (Philippians 3:13-14 TLB).

***

TODAY, ASK YOURSELF, WHERE AM I PUTTING MY ENERGIES?

APRIL 1

Do You Feel Used?

The Lord is my helper; I will not be afraid what can man do to me?

(Hebrews 13:6 NIV)

When your trust has been betrayed, you feel angry and want to strike back. Something inside you cries, *It's not fair!* You want to even the score.

Don't do it! Turn to Jesus instead! He, too, was betrayed, so He understands. Through this you can learn how to forgive and become more gracious. Don't sink to the level of the person who hurt you. Take the high road!

When David's friends turned against him, he first prayed, "Tell me what to do, O Lord." Then he continued, "I am expecting the Lord to rescue me ... once again I will see his goodness to me" (Psalm 27:11-13 TLB). Cry out to God for help, and then be confident that He'll answer you!

Go ahead—ask Him to help you forgive those who've turned against you. Don't let bitterness rob you of the wisdom you can gain through this, or the blessings that await you on the other side of it.

When you think you'll never be able to trust again, that is when you must place your trust in God and let Him heal your heart and mind. Pray: "Father, I am hurt, but I won't let it infect my spirit or destroy my faith in You.

***

"I NEED TO FORGIVE THOSE WHO HAVE BETRAYED ME. I DO SO TODAY IN YOUR NAME. AMEN."

APRIL 2

Persistence

Staying with it—that's what God requires. Stay with it to the end. You won't be sorry.

(Matthew 24:13 TM)

Abraham Lincoln said, "Success is going from failure to failure without losing your enthusiasm." Elbert Hubbaid wrote, "There is no defeat, except in no longer trying; no really insurmountable barrier, save our own inherent weakness of purpose."

Charles Lindbergh said, "Success is not measured by what a man accomplishes, but by the *opposition* he encountered and the courage he maintained in his struggle against it."

The University of Chicago conducted a five-year survey of twenty top performers in various fields, including musicians, athletes, sculptors, mathematicians, physicians, actors, artists, scholars, and chief executives. They also interviewed the families and teachers of these celebrated high-achievers to find out how they did it.

What they discovered was that drive and determination—not talent—led to their success! Imagine that! Just plain old stick-toit-iveness!

Anybody who ever did *anything* worthwhile persevered. The Master Teacher himself gives us the formula for success in these words:

***

"STAYING WITH IT—THAT'S WHAT GOD REQUIRES. STAY WITH IT TO THE END. YOU WON'T BE SORRY" (MATTHEW 24:13 TM).

APRIL 3

When You're Waiting

Wait on the Lord, and keep his way, and he shall exalt thee.

(Psalm 37:34)

Waiting is not wasted time! When David was called by God to be Israel's next king, he was in a cave hiding in fear for his life, and wondering, *Where is God in all this?* So how do you behave in a cave? What do you do in a waiting period?

First, David encouraged himself in the Lord. (See 1 Samuel 30:6.) He reminded himself of God's faithfulness, and so should you. God told Moses to put Aaron's rod and some manna into the Ark of the Covenant as constant reminders of His great faithfulness. Abraham built seven altars during his life as memorials to God's goodness. *Start remembering!*

Next, David thought of Joseph's experience. Listen: "Until God's time finally came—how God tested his patience!" (Psalm 105:19 TLB). David learned from Joseph; whom are you learning from?

When Potiphar threw Joseph into prison, he didn't lie there thinking, *This is the break I've been waiting for.* No, waiting can be rough. That's why you have to fill your cave *with praise* and make your waiting room a worship room! It will help you hold on a little longer. Stay shut in with God, and when the time is right He'll come and get you.

***

GOD DID IT FOR DAVID AND JOSEPH, AND HE WILL WORK IT OUT FOR YOU, TOO—IF YOU'LL ONLY WAIT.

APRIL 4

Paganini's Violin

Great gifts mean great responsibilities.

(Luke 12:48 TM)

Paganini, one of the greatest violinists of all time, performed his first concert at age eleven. He revolutionized violin technique in Europe forever. When he died in 1840, he willed his violin to his birthplace, Genoa, on one condition—that no other artist ever play it again. The city fathers agreed, and put it in a beautiful case, where thousands came to view it.

But wooden instruments have a certain peculiarity. So long as *they're played,* they show no wear. But left unused they decay, which is what happened to Paganini's violin. It became worm-eaten and useless. Other violins of the same vintage, handed down through generations from one gifted musician to another, continue to bless the world. *But today, Paganini's instrument remains a crumbling relic of what it might have been.* What a lesson!

Paul told his spiritual son, Timothy, "Do not neglect the spiritual gift you received" (1 Timothy 4:14 NLT). Success is an on-going thing. It involves growth and development. It involves achieving one thing, and using that as a stepping-stone to accomplishing the next. There's no stopping place.

What you don't nurture decays. But by consistently working on your gift, you'll produce something that will not only give you joy, but will also serve and bless others.

***

THAT'S WHAT GIVES LIFE REAL PURPOSE!

APRIL 5

Just One!

Be an example ... in the way you live.

(1 Timothy 4:12 NLT)

We all need heroes—people we admire for their achievements and character. People who aren't afraid to be different, and who dare to stand "a cut above." *Real* human beings with flaws and failures, yet ones who inspire and bring out the best in us, by modeling excellence when no one's looking—or, for that matter, when half the world is looking! It seems to me that we're running short of folks like that.

Here's a question for you. Would you be surprised to know that for some people, *you* are that person? That's right! It may be where you work, even though nobody's mentioned it. It may be where you live, even though no neighbor has had the nerve to say to you, "You're the one we all watch." It may be at school, where you've decided to stand out, rather than just blend in with the crowd.

One thing is for sure, if you knew how many people really felt that way, you'd be a *lot* more careful, wouldn't you? You see, it takes real commitment to make a difference. Mediocre people impact nobody—at least not long-term.

***

BUT ONE COMMITTED PERSON—JUST ONE—CAN
CHANGE SO MUCH! TODAY, ASK GOD TO MAKE YOU
THAT PERSON.

APRIL 6

Four Seasons

Come before winter.

(2 Timothy 4:21)

Spring speaks *of youth,* summer *of manhood,* autumn *of old age,* and winter *of death* and the judgment beyond. The word to you today is, "Come before winter." Mark Twain said, "Some folks get bothered about the Scriptures they don't understand, but it's the ones I *do* understand that bother *me."* Here's one that would bother me if I didn't know Jesus: "It is appointed unto men once to die, but after this the judgment" (Hebrews 9:27).

A legend from Baghdad tells of a wealthy merchant, who sent his servant to the market. The servant returned empty-handed and frightened. He said he had just met Death, and she had made a "threatening gesture" toward him.

He borrowed the fastest horse from his master's stable and left Baghdad to flee to Samaria, believing Death would never find him there. That afternoon the master himself met Death in the marketplace and asked, "Why did you frighten my servant with a threatening gesture?" Death answered, "Sir, you're mistaken; that was merely an expression of surprise.

I did not expect to see your servant in Baghdad, *for I have an appointment with him this evening in Samaria!*"

***

ALL OF US HAVE AN APPOINTMENT IN SAMARIA. WILL YOU BE READY WHEN IT ARRIVES?

APRIL 7

Guard Your Thoughts

Anyone who looks at a woman lustfully has already committed adultery with her in his heart.

(Matthew 5:28 NIV)

Are you tempted to entertain certain thoughts in the privacy of your mind? After all, who would know? Why be concerned? Because *you will ultimately become whatever you meditate on.* The Bible says, "As [a man] thinketh in his heart, so is he" (Proverbs 23:7). When Satan wants to tear down your character, he doesn't start with an act; he always starts with a *thought.*

He'll plant seeds in the form of thoughts. These thoughts aren't yours just because they come to mind. They *become* yours when you allow them to move in and rearrange the furniture.

A thought left to ramble can attach itself to the pain of the past, and feed on it until it grows like a virus. The stronger it gets, the weaker you become, until all your strength has been drained. Don't let that happen. Listen: "You'll do best by filling your minds and meditating on things true, noble, reputable, authentic, compelling, gracious—the best, not the worst" (Philippians 4:8 TM).

***

NOW THAT YOU KNOW, START PUTTING IT INTO PRACTICE.

APRIL 8

There's No Need to Hide

Everything is uncovered and laid bare before the eyes of him to whom we must give account.

(Hebrews 4:13 NIV)

God knows your every thought! You can't lie to Him; He knows you inside out. Just be honest and say, "Father, this is what's tempting me; please help me! Cleanse me and give me strength. Thank You for loving me in spite of all You know about me. Forgive me for judging others. If it were not for Your mercy, I would be guilty of the very things for which I have condemned them. Help me to be more like Jesus."

The Book of Hebrews doesn't stop by telling us God *sees* and *knows* everything about us. Listen: "For we have not an high priest which cannot be touched with the feeling of our infirmities" (Hebrews 4:15). Great news! You have a high priest, and He has provided forgiveness for *all* your sins.

Today, if you're frustrated by your failures, and discouraged over your defeats, listen: He can be touched with the feeling of your infirmities. He's been to your point of despair. He's faced the tempter in every area—*and defeated him.* All He asks is an invitation to cleanse your heart and mind.

***

YOU DON'T HAVE TO HIDE ANYMORE—HE'S WAITING TO FORGIVE AND RESTORE YOU. ALL YOU HAVE TO DO IS ASK HIM.

APRIL 9

He Won't Give Upon You

So shall my word be that goeth forth out of my mouth: it shall not return unto me void, but it shall accomplish that which I please.

(Isaiah 55:11)

The reason I keep urging you to get into God's Word is that the more you hear His thoughts, the more you start thinking like Him! Peter became so dependent upon the words of Jesus, that when others walked away, he said, "Lord, to whom shall we go? Thou hast the words of eternal life" (John 6:68). Job said that he considered God's words more necessary than food. (See Job 23:12.) It's through the Word that God speaks to you, comforts you, counsels you, and deals with your problems.

God's Word will accomplish what He sends it to do. He won't stop in the middle of the job, and He won't give up on you. He'll keep hammering until the foundation is secure and the building is strong. And the wonderful thing is that no one will ever know that you were in such terrible shape! He'll cover you with His precious blood even while He works on you. Think of it: you're covered while you're being changed into

His image. In a world void of commitment, isn't it comforting to know that God won't give up on you?

***

IF ANYBODY OUGHT TO PRAISE THE LORD, IT'S YOU!

APRIL 10

The King and I

I will surely shew thee kindness for Jonathan thy father's sake.

(2 Samuel 9:7)

Mephibosheth, Jonathan's son, was lame because he was dropped when he was a baby. Years later. King David, who had a covenant with his father, redeemed him and gave him a place at the king's table. What a story—lifted from the fall, saved because of another, and made a child of the king! Sounds like your testimony and mine, doesn't it?

But there was a problem in his *thinking.* Although he'd been redeemed, he still saw himself as *worthless.* Listen: "And he bowed himself, and said, What is thy servant, that thou shouldest look upon such a dead dog as I am?" (2 Samuel 9:8). He thought of himself as a dead dog, so he lay on the floor like one. Not only were his feet lame—his thinking was also.

The word of the Lord to you today is: "You've been on the floor long enough. It's time for a resurrection, and it must start in your thinking. Just because you've been treated like a dog, doesn't make you one. Get up off the floor and take your seat at the King's table—He has made you worthy. You have a right to be there. Not because of *your goodness,* but because of *His grace!"*

***

LET GOD HEAL YOUR THINKING SO THAT YOU CAN ENJOY WHAT HE IS DOING IN YOUR LIFE RIGHT NOW!

APRIL 11

Devoted

I will love thee, O Lord, my strength.

(Psalm 18:1)

It's easy to get distracted and grow cold. That's a battle you'll fight constantly. Listen: "For the sinful nature desires what is contrary to the Spirit, and the Spirit what is contrary to the sinful nature. They are in conflict with each other" (Galatians 5:17 NIV). Every day you'll have to make a decision. If you don't, your flesh will decide for you, and you'll finish up asking, "How did I ever get here?" And the answer is, "Because you never decided not to!"

When two people are devoted to each other, they don't mind sacrificing for their dream. Their relationship may come under attack, but it only draws them closer. Temptation may try to lure them away, but they find strength in each other's arms. To them, giving is not a *discipline;* it's a *delight.* David cried, "Lord, how I love you! For you have done such tremendous things for me" (Psalm 18:1 TLB).

***

YOU SEE, WHEN YOU REALLY LOVE HIM, IT'S EASIER TO OBEY HIM, SERVE HIM, AND FOLLOW HIM.

APRIL 12

Grounded and Steady

Stay grounded and steady ... constantly tuned in to the Message.

(Colossians 1:23 TM)

We live in an entertainment-based society, and we've brought it into the Church. Great emphasis is placed on *feeling good.* One pastor told me, "People have had a hard week, and when they come to God's house they should have a good time." In a sense that's true. David said, "In thy presence is fullness of joy" (Psalm 16:11). But when there's a cancer, do you tell the patient, or just keep him feeling good until his condition is hopeless?

Jeremiah was told "to root out, and to pull down ... to build, and to plant" (Jeremiah 1:10). Now, building and planting are more exciting than rooting out and pulling down, and definitely draw bigger crowds. But what if the patient dies?

Let's read carefully what Paul told Timothy: "You're going to find that there will be times when people will have no stomach for solid teaching, but will fill up on spiritual junk food—catchy opinions that tickle their fancy. They'll turn their backs on truth and chase mirages. But *you*—keep your eye on what you're doing" (2 Timothy 4:2-5 TM).

***

AS WE GET CLOSER TO THE COMING OF CHRIST, THE ONLY THING THAT WILL SUSTAIN YOU IS KNOWING HIS WORD, AND YOUR RELATIONSHIP WITH HIM.

APRIL 13

John and Judas

And Jesus said unto him, "Friend."

(Matthew 26:50)

God's purposes in your life are tied to relationships—and not always enjoyable ones. But God can turn rejection into direction. Sometimes He opens doors; other times He closes them. Personally, I'm grateful for some of the doors He has closed, for had I been allowed to walk through them, I would have been destroyed. But that doesn't mean people can just walk in and destroy God's plan for your life. Their access to your future is limited by the shield of His divine purpose and protection. What a comfort! God can still hang Haman on the gallows he built for you. (See Esther 7:10.) Paul said the purposes of God for him permitted, "false brethren" (2 Corinthians 11:26). The pain *they* caused him made the shipwrecks look easy!

As you look back, you realize *persecution* taught you *perseverance,* and *rejection* taught you *forgiveness.* They produced Christian character. *It's much easier to forgive the actions of men when you understand the purposes of God.* The challenge is to sit at the table with John and Judas, knowing each one's agenda, and love them equally. We all want a friend like John, who'll love us, or Peter, who'll fight for us. Peter's misguided love would have stopped Jesus from going to the Cross—through Judas He fulfilled His destiny.

***

THAT'S WHY JESUS KISSED JUDAS AND CALLED HIM "FRIEND."

APRIL 14

To Thine Own Self Be True

Blessed is the man who perseveres under trial, because when he has stood the test, he will receive the crown of life.

(James 1:12 NIV)

When you violate your own values, you stop enjoying your own company. When you talk one way and live another, you become somebody you can't respect, and it's hard to be alone with a person like that. Everybody deals with temptation, and if you don't learn how to handle it, it will run over you like a steamroller. For example, cheating the tax man is one of the more "acceptable" transgressions in the Kingdom. But how do you feel afterward? If you save on your taxes but lose your integrity, what have you gained? Does money mean that much to you?

And what about Joseph? Potiphar's wife was beautiful, she was lonely, and she was available. She didn't try to entice Joseph just once; she did it for months. But Joseph didn't consult his flesh—he consulted his spirit. He didn't ask, "Can I get away with it?" He asked, "Can I live with it afterward?" The house you're building today is the one you're going to live in tomorrow. Every time you say no to sin and yes to God, you add one more brick to the wall of character.

***

REMEMBER, AFTER YOU PASS THE TEST, YOU'LL RECEIVE THE CROWN OF LIFE!

APRIL 15

Hindsight

This I recall to my mind, therefore have I hope.

(Lamentations 3:21)

When Jacob was facing the crisis of his life, God visited him, but he didn't realize it until later. Listen: "Surely the Lord is in this place; and I knew it not" (Genesis 28:16). *Sometimes you can't see God's hand until you look back.*

When Jeremiah wrote Lamentations, he was going through tough times. Listen: "All peace and all prosperity have long since gone ... I have forgotten what enjoyment is" (Lamentations 3:17 TLB). I'm glad that men of God not only experienced real life, but recorded it so we wouldn't feel terminally unique. They not only shared the problem, but they also shared the solution. Listen again: "This I recall to my mind, therefore have I hope." Go ahead, start recalling. Do you remember when Jesus stood on the bow of your ship and spoke peace to the storm that terrified you? When you think of what He's brought you *through,* and what He's kept you from, it's only by His grace that you've made it!

Here's the word for you today: "It is of the Lord's mercies that we are not consumed, because his compassions fail not. They are new every morning: great is thy faithfulness" (Lamentations 3:22-23). This morning you woke in His arms, surrounded by His love. *Nothing* can get to you without first coming through Him.

***

TODAY, HE'LL FORGIVE YOU, LIFT YOU, AND STRENGTHEN YOU, SO THAT YOU'LL LOOK BACK AND SAY, "GREAT IS THY FAITHFULNESS."

APRIL 16

Fly United

Bind yourselves together with peace.

(Ephesians 4:3 NLT)

There's a legend about a covey of quails that lived in a forest. They were happy together, apart from having to avoid their enemy, the quail-catcher. But he was clever; he'd imitate their calls, and then when they all got together, he'd throw his net over them and carry them off to market.

One day, however, the birds devised a plan to outwit him. The next time he threw his net over them, they put their heads together, flapped their wings in unity, lifted the net, and flew off with it. However, this only worked well until they began to fight over who was carrying most of the weight, and who deserved most of the credit. (Sound familiar?) Once that happened, the quail-catcher, seizing his opportunity, threw the net over them again and carried them all off.

You see, they were so busy complaining and competing with each other, that they failed to help one another and stay on guard against the enemy. What a lesson!

They evidently had this problem in Paul's time, too. Listen: "Be patient with each other, making allowance for each other's faults because of your love. Always keep yourselves united ... bind yourselves together with peace" (Ephesians 4:2-3 NLT).

Until you learn how to give graciously to others, you'll remain unfulfilled. And until you learn to receive graciously, you'll remain incomplete.

***

ASK GOD TODAY TO HELP YOU TO CARE—REALLY CARE—ABOUT OTHERS.

APRIL 17

Exercising Discernment

But strong meat belongeth to them ... who by reason of use have their senses exercised to discern both good and evil.

(Hebrews 5:14)

When God wants to bless you, He'll send a person. When Satan wants to bother you, he'll also send somebody. That's why you need *discernment.* The world calls it "a gut feeling" or "intuition," but the Bible calls it the discerning of spirits. Not just evil spirits—all sorts of spirits. When someone comes into your life, he brings his spirit. Have you ever been around someone with a controlling spirit? Or a resentful spirit? Even the business world tries to screen out those with the *right* abilities but the wrong attitudes by using "Personality Profile Testing."

Now, discernment is something you have to *exercise.* You need to give it a daily workout. The reason children need protection is because they lack discernment. Predators and pedophiles feed on ignorance. So does the devil. If you are to have mature discernment, you must move from milk to meat—the strong meat of the Word.

Like a knife sharpened on a well-oiled stone, your sense of discernment will be sharpened as you *live in the Word* and *stay filled with His Spirit.*

***

WHEN BOTH ARE ACTIVE, YOU'LL DISCERN WHAT IS AT WORK IN OTHERS AND HAVE THE WISDOM TO DEAL WITH IT.

APRIL 18

The Ingredients of an Anointed Life

Take ... pure myrrh ... it shall be an holy anointing oil.

(Exodus 30:23, 25)

One of the ingredients in anointing oil was *myrrh,* which speaks of *change.* It was used to anoint the living and embalm the dead—before the birth of the new we experience the death of the old. Before Elisha received a double portion, he had to break his plough. That wasn't easy, for it put food on his table and gave him his identity as a farmer. But if you want to become a prophet, you have to break your plough. Moses was the meekest man on Earth. (See Numbers 12:3.) How did he become that way? Forty years in the wilderness will do it every time!

What makes change so difficult are the opinions of others. Most denominations never make it beyond the point of their greatest revelation. They celebrate it, institutionalize it, and stop it. To backslide you don't have to go back, you only have to stay in the same place while God moves on. Solomon says, "The path of the just is as the shining light, that shineth more and more unto the perfect day" (Proverbs 4:18). *You'll never become what you're called to be by remaining what you are.*

✳✳✳

GOD HAS WORDS YOU'VE NEVER HEARD, PLACES YOU'VE NEVER BEEN, AND JOYS YOU'VE NEVER EXPERIENCED. OPEN YOUR HEART AND LET HIM LEAD YOU TODAY.

APRIL 19

Inner Cleansing

Take ... cassia ... it shall be an holy anointing oil.

(Exodus 30:23-25)

Another ingredient in anointing oil was cassia, and it was used as a laxative for *inner cleansing.* The problem is not just that we sin, but that we try to hide it, defend it, and rationalize it. A man told me, "Maybe I do sin, but I'm no worse than anyone else." I said, "You're measuring by the wrong standard."

When my son was little, he hated the evening ritual of having a bath. One night he said, "Pop, give me a break!" I said, "What do you have in mind?" He smiled and said, *"Couldn't you just dust me off a little?"* Most of us do the same thing. Instead of repenting, we go to church for a light religious dusting. But it doesn't work because sin is a heart condition.

Most of us know about David's sin, but have you ever read his prayer of repentance? Listen: "Against thee, thee only, have I sinned, and done this evil in thy sight.... Purge me with hyssop, and I shall be clean: wash me, and I shall be whiter than snow" (Psalm 51:4, 7). God heard David, forgave him, and totally restored him. His greatest psalms were written *after* his failure, and his greatest days were lived after this prayer.

***

YOURS CAN BE, TOO. BUT TO BE ANOINTED, YOU MUST HAVE A CLEAN HEART.

APRIL 20

A Mother's Influence

Her children arise up, and call her blessed.

(Proverbs 31:28)

Helen Young writes:

There will come a time when there'll be no more slamming of doors, no more toys to pick up on the stairs, no more childhood quarrels, and no more fingerprints on the wallpaper. Then, may I look back with joy and not regret.

May I have the wisdom to see that today is my day with my children; that there are no unimportant moments in their lives;

That no career is more precious, no work more rewarding, and no task more urgent.

May I not defer it, nor neglect it, but accept it gladly—and understand that my time is short and my time is now, for my children won't wait.

There would be no Samuel without a Hannah; no John Mark without a Mary; and no Timothy without a Eunice. These men became great because of the mothers they had!

What was the secret of that winning combination? Mother with child—just that simple. So, please, Mom

... stay with it! Don't ever forget the permanence of your imprint.

At times your children may seem ungrateful and act irresponsibly. They may ignore your reminders and forget your advice.

***

BUT BELIEVE THIS: THEY CANNOT ERASE YOUR INFLUENCE!

APRIL 21

When Mice Roar

His huge outstretched arms protect you—under them you're perfectly safe.

(Psalm 91:4 TM)

Max Lucado tells the following story. "Two-year-old Sarah sits on my lap. We're watching a comedy on television about a guy who has a mouse in his room. He is asleep. He opens one eye and finds himself peering into the face of the mouse. I laugh, but Sarah panics. She turns away from the screen and buries her face in my shoulder. Her little body grows rigid. She thinks the mouse is going to get her. 'It's okay, Sarah,' I assure her. Still, she's afraid. But with time I convince her, and she goes from white-knuckled fear, to peaceful chuckles. Why? Because her father spoke, and she believed him. Would to God that we could do the same!

"Got any giant mice on your screen? Got any fears that won't go away? I wish the fears were just television images. But they aren't. They lurk in hospital rooms and funeral homes. They stare at us from divorce papers and eviction notices. They glare through the eyes of a cruel parent, or an abusive mate. There are times when mice roar. Times when you need the strong arms of God to run to and hide in."

Listen: "His huge outstretched arms protect you—under them you're perfectly safe" (Psalm 91:4 TM).

***

TODAY YOU HAVE NOTHING TO FEAR!

APRIL 22

It's Time to Move On

How long wilt thou mourn for Saul ... fill thine horn with oil, and go ... for I have provided.

(1 Samuel 16:1)

Samuel was still mourning the loss of King Saul, when God visited him and told him it was time to move on. There's another step beyond death, and that's *burial.* It separates the living from the dead, and the past from the future. Some of us get through it faster than others. Some *never do.* They talk only of the past, because they stopped living years ago.

Anytime you discuss the past as if it were the present, it's because you've let the past *steal* the present from you. Don't do it! Rise up and take it back. Listen again to God's Word to Samuel: "Go ... for I have provided." Did you hear that, child of God? He's provided everything you need to start again.

Here's your choice: You can keep lamenting what nobody can change, or you can live in the present and plan for the future. God says, "I have provided." There are friends who want to be part of your life the moment you decide to live again. Don't go back to the past—you've already been there!

***

TAKE ALL YOUR TIME, LOVE, AND ENERGY, AND GIVE THEM TO YOUR FUTURE. IT'S TIME TO MOVE ON!

APRIL 23

When Moses Dies

As I was with Moses, so I will be with thee.

(Joshua 1:5)

Stop thinking God will use everybody but you, or bless others more than you. Moses spoke for God, stood up to Pharaoh, and worked miracles—but he died. And there are some things you'll never know until your Moses dies. When Joshua wanted to know if God would be with him, too, God said, "I will." What faithfulness!

People will enter and leave your life. Circumstances change overnight. Life hits you like a tornado. You struggle to get back up, and wonder if you can go on. But through your tears you'll hear God say, "As I was with Moses, so I will be with you."

Listen to Jesus: "The stone which the builders rejected, the same is become the head of the comer: this is the Lord's doing, and it is marvellous in our eyes" (Matthew 21:42). Imagine—the rejection of men can be "the Lord's doing." He'll take what is painful and make it "marvellous in our eyes." Are you grieving over something, as though you had no God to direct it, and no grace to correct it? See it from *His* perspective! When you do, you may well see that the worst possible thing that you thought could have happened to you, was the Lord's doing, and it will suddenly look marvelous in your eyes.

***

REJOICE, CHILD OF GOD, AND BE STRONG, FOR HE IS WITH YOU.

APRIL 24

Are You Ready?

Behold, I will do a new thing; now it shall spring forth.

(Isaiah 43:19)

If God says He's going to bless you—ignore your circumstances, and believe the God who cannot lie. You're too important to Him to be destroyed by a situation designed to build character and give you direction. God's grace will enable you to make it through. God proved that He can bring you out of the fire without even the smell of smoke, and out of the lions' den without so much as a bite mark. If you want to know what God can do, look at what He's already done for you—and start praising Him.

And that's not all. Listen: "Behold I will do a new thing; now it shall spring forth." After feeling like you've waited forever, God will suddenly move, and if you're not ready, you'll miss Him.

When the Church was born, we read: "Suddenly there came a sound from heaven as of a rushing mighty wind, and it filled all the house where they were sitting" (Acts 2:2). When God decided to bring Paul and Silas out of prison, we read: "And suddenly there was a great earthquake ... and immediately all the doors were opened" (Acts 16:26). Are you ready for God to move *suddenly?* Are you ready for doors to open?

***

THE WORD TO YOU TODAY IS, "I WILL DO A NEW THING; NOW IT SHALL SPRING FORTH."

APRIL 25

Christian Life Isn't Natural; It's Spiritual

But we have this treasure in earthen vessels, that the excellency of the power may be of God, and not of us.

(2 Corinthians 4:7)

As a young Christian, the love of God I saw demonstrated was based on *performance,* like a merit system. If I did well, He loved me—if I failed. He didn't. What a roller coaster! To make matters worse, I constantly heard testimonies from people who seemed to live in unending bliss. They never had a Monday morning—at least, never one I heard about! I thought they woke up swinging from the rafters, never had a down day, terrorized the devil, and heard from heaven regularly. Meanwhile, I soldiered on. Sometimes I felt ashamed, but mostly I felt insecure. I felt like something was missing, and even though I was a babe in Christ, I always felt like I should be further along. Sound familiar?

Then I read, "I don't mean to say I am perfect. I haven't learned all I should even yet, but I keep working toward that day when I will finally be all that

Christ saved me for and wants me to be" (Philippians 3:12 TLB). The mighty Apostle Paul said that! Today, I understand that the Christian life isn't *natural,* it's *spiritual.* (See Matthew 5:44.)

***

IT'S ENOUGH TO DRIVE YOU INTO THE ARMS OF JESUS—AND THAT'S THE WAY HE PLANNED IT!

APRIL 26

The New Birth Produces a New Battle

Now there was long war between the house of Saul and the house of David: but David waxed stronger and stronger, and the house of Saul waxed weaker and weaker.

(2 Samuel 3:1)

Saul represents the flesh, and David the spirit; and the war between them lasted a long time. It takes faith and patience to produce in any of us the nature of Christ. Today, in *The Message,* I read a remarkable statement by Paul: *I decide to do good but I don't really do it; I decide not to do bad, but then I do it anyway. My decisions, such as they are, don't result in actions. Now if that sounds familiar, listen to what he says next: I've tried everything and nothing helps. I'm at the end of my rope. Is there no one who can do anything for me? ... The answer, thank God, is that Jesus Christ can and does.* (See Romans 7:17-25.) To feed David and starve Saul, you've got to move closer to Jesus.

Paul says, "My little children, of whom I travail in birth again until Christ be formed in you" (Galatians

4:19). Only God knows the process it will take for the Christ who saved you to be formed in you. That's when you really begin to resemble your Father.

***

THIS ONLY HAPPENS AS THE HOUSE OF SAUL GROWS WEAKER AND THE HOUSE OF DAVID GROWS STRONGER IN OUR LIVES.

APRIL 27

Character, Class, and Christianity

He will sift out everything without solid foundations, so that only unshakable things will be left.

(Hebrews 12:27 TLB)

The Lord often uses trials to re-align us, and storms to attack everything in us that can be shaken. Everybody God uses goes through experiences that cause them to let go of the temporal and take hold of the eternal. Some wake up in hospital rooms with beeping monitors to discover the things they thought were important actually mean nothing at all. Others discover it when the person they thought was everything, walks away and leaves them. Job went through it. One day he had everything, and the next day—nothing. His health was in shambles, his children dead, and his marriage a joke. At times like that you discover what's meant by "things which cannot be shaken," things that are worth living for. Things like character, class, and Christianity.

Character is not what you *know;* it's what you *are.* *Class* doesn't show in what you *have;* it shows in the way you *act* and even more in the way you *react*. *Christianity* is not a culture; it's a way of life. It's seeking to be Christ-like—not just to observe rules and impress people, but to please Him. That's why Paul calls it "the high calling of God in Christ Jesus" (Philippians 3:14).

***

REMEMBER, WHEN THE SUN RISES TOMORROW, YOU'LL HAVE ONE DAY LESS. GIVE YOUR LIFE TO THINGS THAT CANNOT BE SHAKEN.

APRIL 28

Have You Been Specific?

Let your requests be made known unto God.

(Philippians 4:6)

Too often we talk to everybody about our problem, except the One who can do something about it. God says, "Let your requests be made known unto [Me]." Have you done that today? Have you talked to God about the *specific* things you're so concerned over? If you'll be specific with Him. He'll be specific with you. Jesus said, "Whatever you ask for in prayer, believe that you have received it, and it will be yours" (Mark 11:24 NIV). How do you think you would act if you knew for sure that your prayer had already been answered? Wouldn't you praise the Lord? Wouldn't you speak confidently?

Perhaps you're having difficulty believing. Then the Word for you today is, "If two of you on earth agree about anything you ask for, it will be done for you" (Matthew 18:19 NIV). Join your faith with the faith of others—multiply your impact before the throne. Unite and get results! When someone asks you to pray for them, take it seriously. Don't just promise to pray—do it! The Bible is about *us,* not *you!*

We are told to pray for one another, encourage one another, and bear one another's burdens.

**

TODAY, "LET YOUR REQUESTS BE MADE KNOWN."
THE DOOR IS OPEN—HE'S INVITING YOU TO COME.

APRIL 29

Don't Go Until He Sends You

I waited patiently for the Lord; and he inclined unto me.

(Psalm 40:1)

Don't jump the starter gun, or you'll be disqualified from the race. Don't come out until God has finished working on you, or you won't be ready for the job.

There's never been a day like this. Listen: "Woe to the Earth and the sea, because the devil has gone down to you! He is filled with fury, because he knows that his time is short" (Revelation 12:12 NIV). Forces have been released that no previous generation ever faced, and if we're not strong and well-equipped, we won't be able to cope with them, much less conquer them.

How long did it take to prepare Ananias to lead Saul of Tarsus to Christ? And after he did, we never hear of him again. He was born for a purpose, and when it was fulfilled, he disappeared. That's hard on the ego. We want to be *permanent.* We want to be *featured.* But John the Baptist said, "He must increase, but I must decrease" (John 3:30).

In the wilderness, Moses learned reverence and dependence, and he built a relationship with God that would sustain him for the rest of his life. Child of God, stop looking for a door out of your wilderness.

✳✳✳

IF YOU DON'T STAY WHERE HE HAS PLACED YOU TODAY, YOU WON'T MAKE A DIFFERENCE WHERE HE SENDS YOU TOMORROW.

APRIL 30

Set Free!

Go, sell the oil, and pay thy debt, and live thou and thy children of the rest.

(2 Kings 4:7)

In Old Testament days, if you couldn't pay your bills, your creditor took your children and made them work off the debt. In 2 Kings 4, the widow of a prophet was in that position. But she turned to a man of God—and that's always a wise move, because if you can hear from a *messenger of God,* you can hear from *God.* (See John 13:20.)

The prophet asked her, in effect, "What have you got?" (See 2 Kings 4:2.) God always uses what you've got to create what you need, and all she had was a little pot of oil. But no matter how little you have, when you put it into His hands, it multiplies. Remember this principle: *When what you have isn't enough to be a harvest, make it a seed!* Don't eat it. Don't keep it. Sow it and start a harvest. The woman was instructed to borrow all the empty vessels she could, and "pour out."

That's the key—*pour out!* Find something outside yourself, something bigger than you, and pour your time, your life, and your resources into it. The oil from her little pot kept pouring until her debt was paid and her children were redeemed. And the character of God *never* changes; today He wants to lift your burden, cancel your debts, and set you free to really live.

***

TAKE A FEW MOMENTS AND TALK TO HIM ABOUT IT. HE'LL TELL YOU WHAT TO DO.

MAY 1

How Badly Do You Want It?

Let us throw off everything that hinders.

(Hebrews 12:1 NIV)

You'll start getting well when getting well is what matters most to you. Let your desperation drive you beyond concern about the opinions of others. As long as you're more conscious of *people* than you are of *God,* you'll never get what you need.

When Hannah, Samuel's mother, prayed in the Temple, there was so much locked inside her that when she began to pour her heart out, Eli thought she was *drunk.* (See 1 Samuel 1:13.) God is raising up people who will confound us—radical Christians. Like those on the Day of Pentecost, they're hungry for God. They'll raise the roof to get to Jesus. They'll interrupt carefully laid plans, and cry like blind Bartimaeus, "Jesus, thou Son of David, have mercy on me" (Mark 10:47). When you're blind, all that matters is receiving your sight.

When it looks like there's no way out for you—start shouting! Faith is born in the storm and conceived in the incubator of impossibility. Don't panic. Don't quit. Don't stop short of the prize. The greater the conflict, the greater the conquest. There's something good inside you, and God wants to bring it out.

***

SO, HOW BADLY DO YOU WANT IT?

MAY 2

Intercession or Accusation?

Then you will call, and the Lord will answer ... "If you remove the yoke from your midst, the pointing of the finger and speaking wickedness...."

(Isaiah 58:9 NAS)

Has your healing failed to come? Do troubles follow you more than blessings? Are your prayers seldom answered? The reason could be a yoke in your life called, "The pointing of the finger and speaking wickedness." God promised through Isaiah that things will change radically when you remove this yoke!

There are two ministries that go on continually before the throne of God. One is *intercession.* The other is *accusation.* Jesus lives to intercede for His people, and if you abide in Him, you will intercede for them, too. (See Hebrews 7:25.) On the other side, Satan is "the accuser of our brethren" (Revelation 12:10). When you give him access to your life, you'll become increasingly critical of others.

You've got to make a choice about which of these ministries will be yours. You may ask how Satan can continually accuse the saints before God, if he's been thrown out of heaven. The answer is, *he uses the saints to do it for him.* Any time you see one believer accusing another, he's at work. Satan knows the authority God has given to any two who will agree in prayer. (See Matthew 18:19.)

***

SO, WALK IN LOVE TODAY, AND BECOME A DIRECT THREAT TO HIS DOMAIN.

MAY 3

Laying It All Aside to Serve

He riseth from supper, and laid aside his garments; and took a towel ... and began to wash the disciples' feet.

(John 13:4-5)

They would never forget this night. Jesus alone had the right to be called *Master,* but He laid it aside to serve. Paul said, "Let this mind be in you, which was also in Christ Jesus: ... Who ... took upon him the form of a servant" (Philippians 2:5-7).

The secret of great ministry lies in what we lay aside to respond to God's call. Laying aside the comforts of home to go where His name hasn't been heard. Laying aside the things we most enjoy, to experience those that few will ever know.

There are evangelists, pastors, and workers who never sold a tape or wrote a book, never drew a crowd, nor gained national fame, but they paid the price. Like Noah, whose membership never exceeded eight souls, they ministered faithfully. They wanted to do more, and they thought they would go further. But they *laid it all aside to serve the few.* They said, "If I'm not called to help *everybody,* then please, God, let me help *somebody.*" Child of God, ask yourself today, *Am I willing to lay it all aside to follow Him?*

***

IT'S ONE OF THE MOST IMPORTANT QUESTIONS YOU'LL EVER ANSWER.

MAY 4

Can You Receive From Others?

Whoever accepts anyone I send accepts me.

(John 13:20 NIV)

You'd be surprised at how many people live beyond help, because they have an image to uphold. It's a dangerous place to be. When trials come, not only must you be open to the Lord, but also to whomever He sends. Listen: "And he was there in the wilderness forty days, tempted of Satan; ... and the angels ministered unto him" (Mark 1:13). *Even Jesus needed ministry.*

He created the angels, yet He permitted them to minister to Him. The greater was willing to receive help from the lesser. What a lesson for you! When your pain levels get high enough, you won't care whom God uses. If you were in a burning house you wouldn't care who the firemen were. Their education, denomination, and ethnic background would mean nothing to you, because of the urgency of your need.

Perhaps your problem is that you need *someone,* but you don't trust *anyone. Start trusting God!* Whom do you think brought you this far? Listen: "'Though the mountains be shaken and the hills be removed, yet my unfailing love for you will not be shaken nor my covenant of peace be removed,' says the Lord, who has compassion on you" (Isaiah 54:10 NIV). When God extends His love and compassion to you, don't be too proud to accept it.

***

WHEN YOU ACCEPT IT, YOU ACCEPT HIM!

MAY 5

Position Yourself to Receive

If you hold anything against anyone, forgive him.

(Mark 11:25 NIV)

Sometimes forgiving is the hardest thing you'll ever do. Jesus said, in effect, "Don't just *dismiss* it—throw the case out of court!" Make a decision never to discuss it again. When you consider how often God has forgiven you, how could you think of doing less? Don't wait for the other person to ask, and don't criticize them if they never do—that's between God and them. Forgiveness is for *your* benefit! You're removing the roadblocks between you and His blessing.

In Mark 11:23, Jesus told His disciples to tell the mountain to move and it will move. Perhaps you're thinking, *I spoke to my mountain and it grew.* But notice that Jesus also said, "Whatever you ask for in prayer, believe that you have received it, and it will be yours" (Mark 11:24 NIV). Perhaps you're saying, "I prayed, I claimed, I believed, and *nothing* has happened."

Then maybe you need to focus on this verse, "If you hold anything against anyone, forgive him, so that your Father in heaven may forgive you your sins"

(Mark 11:25 NIV). Go ahead, open your heart, close the door on the past, stand in His presence, and say, "Lord, I've done what You asked. I've forgiven *any* and *all,* as You've forgiven me, and I'm ready now for everything You have for me today."

***

THESE WORDS COULD BE THE KEY TO YOUR DELIVERANCE AND THE DOOR TO YOUR FUTURE.

MAY 6

The "Nobodies" of the Bible

The Lord God hath opened mine ear.

(Isaiah 50:5)

God can speak to you today through anybody. The question is, can you hear Him? Naaman, the commander-in-chief of the Syrian army, was dying of leprosy. Did he want to be healed? Yes! *But he wanted it his way.* First, since he was a man of rank and prestige, he wanted Elisha to come personally and speak to him. But instead Elisha sent his servant out to say, "Go, wash yourself seven times in the Jordan" (see 2 Kings 5:10). But Naaman, who didn't like the Jordan because it was dirty, asked, "Are there not cleaner rivers?" (See 2 Kings 5:12.) But God wouldn't accommodate his pride—and He won't accommodate yours either.

Naaman received his healing only after he humbled himself and became *willing to listen*—first to a slave in his kitchen, and then to some regular soldiers in his army who said, "If the prophet had told you to do some great thing, wouldn't you have done it?" (2 Kings 5:13 TLB). Our problem is, if God doesn't speak to us in a certain familiar way, we won't receive it. But He can use anybody to speak to you—a kitchen maid, a waitress, a nameless soldier, or somebody you know.

***

TODAY, BE SENSITIVE, BE HUMBLE, AND BE WILLING TO HEAR.

MAY 7

Acting or Reacting

He that is soon angry dealeth foolishly.

(Proverbs 14:17)

The little girl was in a bad mood, so she took her frustration out on her younger brother. At first she just teased him, then she punched him, pulled his hair, and finally kicked him in the shins. He could take it all until the kicking began. That hurt! So he went crying to his mother, who said to her daughter, "Mary, the devil made you pull your brother's hair and kick his shins."

She thought it over for a moment, and then answered, "Maybe the devil did make me pull his hair, *but kicking him was my own idea.*"

Blaming the devil for everything can be a cop-out. All the evil in the world doesn't necessarily come from him. A lot of it comes from the hearts of people. Jesus said, "Out of the heart proceed evil thoughts, murders, adulteries, fornications, thefts, false witness, blasphemies" (Matthew 15:19). What we do with our anger and frustrations is subject to our will.

You can *choose* how you respond to stress, and to the behavior of others. You either *act* or you *react.* When you react, you give control to other people and other things. But *when you act according to the Word,* you can change that person or circumstance, and end up feeling better about yourself.

***

TODAY, YOU'RE GOING TO GET ANOTHER CHANCE TO DO IT GOD'S WAY!

MAY 8

Find Your Place

And they stood every man in his place round about the camp: and all the host ran, and cried, and fled.

(Judges 7:21)

It's one of the greatest military victories in the Bible. Three hundred men willing to *stand in their places,* and as a result, the enemy was routed. All Gideon needed was a consecrated few, and God did the rest. *Have you found your place yet?* Are you totally identified with the cause of Christ? Is your light shining?

Perhaps things are not going well in your local church, and you wonder what to do. The answer lies in a small group of believing Christians who will join with you to fast, pray, bring in the lost, and refuse to yield an inch to the enemy. The New Testament Church started with 120, and before it was over they were accused of turning "the world upside down" (Acts 17:6).

Revival can begin with two or three people seeking the face of God, and refusing to settle for anything less. If you haven't found *your* place yet, get into God's presence and ask Him about it. He'll reveal it to you, and when He does, you will find greater joy there than anywhere else you've ever been.

***

UNTIL YOU FIND YOUR PLACE, YOUR SUCCESSES WILL BE HOLLOW, AND YOU'LL FEEL LIKE A MISFIT.

MAY 9

Victory

Use every piece of God's armor to resist the enemy whenever he attacks, and when it is all over, you will still be standing up.

(Ephesians 6:13 TLB)

During World War II, Winston Churchill's words inspired the British people to believe in victory. Listen:

You ask, what is our policy? It is to wage war by sea, land, and air, with all our might and all the strength that God can give us ... You ask, what is our aim? I can answer in one word: Victory! ... at all costs. Victory! ... in spite of all terror, Victory! ... however long and hard the road may be; for without victory there is no survival.

We shall go on to the end, we shall fight in France, we shall fight on the seas and oceans, we shall fight with growing confidence and growing strength in the air, we shall defend our island, whatever the cost may be; we shall fight on the beaches, we shall fight on the landing grounds; we shall fight in the fields and in the streets, we shall fight in the hills; but we shall never, never, never surrender.

Child of God, never give up. You're on the winning side. No matter how bad things may look today, His

Word to you is, "The Lord himself goes before you and will be with you; he will never leave you nor forsake you. Do not be afraid; do not be discouraged" (Deuteronomy 31:8 NIV).

***

THE WORD TO YOU TODAY IS, "VICTORY!"

MAY 10

Spread the "I Love You" Virus

A new commandment I give to you, that you love one another.

(John 13:34 NAS)

A deadly virus rocked the computer world a while ago. Millions logged on one morning to read their e-mail, only to find their computers infected by a virus masquerading as the message, "I love you." Whomever sent it was clever; they understood the tug of those words. After all, who could resist opening an e-mail with that title?

Jesus told His disciples "By this all men will know that you are My disciples, if you have love [not doctrinal agreement] for one another" (John 13:35 NAS). We never lose our need to feel loved and appreciated. Never! Even when we act tough and put on a front. So, don't act like the crusty old Irishman who said to his wife, "I told you I loved you when I married you fifty years ago—and if it ever changes, I'll let you know."

Lower your guard. Open your heart. Take the time today to tell at least *one* person that you love them—and really mean it. You'll be amazed at how good it'll make you *both* feel.

The famed psychiatrist Carl Menninger said, "Love cures people; both the ones who *give* it, and the ones who *receive* it."

***

TODAY, ASK GOD TO HELP YOU DEMONSTRATE LOVE.

MAY 11

Do It Now

Redeeming the time, because the days are evil.

(Ephesians 5:16)

How many times have you said, "I'll do it tomorrow"? Sometimes you put something off because you don't think you know enough, or can't do it well enough. The fact is, there is no magic age at which excellence emerges and quality suddenly surfaces.

Thomas Jefferson was thirty-three when he drafted the Declaration of Independence. Charles Dickens was twenty-four when he began his *Pickwick Papers,* and twenty-five when he wrote *Oliver Twist.* Isaac Newton was twenty-four when he formulated the Law of Gravity.

A second danger is to think that creativity and invention belong only to the young. Not so! Emmanuel Kant wrote his finest philosophical works at age seventy-four. Verdi, at eighty, produced *Falstaff.* Goethe was eighty when he completed Faust. Tennyson was eighty when he wrote *Crossing the Bar,* and Michelangelo completed his greatest work at eighty-seven. Moses was eighty when he led God's people out of Egypt, and 120 when he got to Caanan.

Seize the day! Redeem the *now* moments of your life—because the time and age you're waiting for may never arrive!

***

THE MOMENT, ONCE PASSED, WILL NEVER RETURN. SO DO IT NOW!

MAY 12

True Greatness

Whatsoever ye would that men should do to you, do ye even so to them.

(Matthew 7:12)

One afternoon in 1953, reporters and city officials gathered at a Chicago railroad station to welcome the Nobel Peace Prize winner. A giant of a man with bushy hair and a large mustache stepped from the train. Cameras flashed as city officials approached him with hands outstretched, and began telling him how honored they were to meet him.

The man politely thanked them, and then, looking over their heads, asked to be excused for a moment. He quickly walked through the crowd until he reached the side of an elderly woman who was struggling with two suitcases. He picked up the bags, and with a smile escorted her to a bus. After helping her aboard, he wished her a safe journey. Returning to the greeting party, he apologized, "Sorry to have kept you waiting."

That man was Dr. Albert Schweitzer, the famous missionary doctor who spent his life helping the poor in Africa. In response to Schweitzer's action, one member of the reception committee said to a reporter next to him, *"That's the first time I ever saw a sermon walking."* Today, look for an opportunity to be kind—to *go out of your way* to bless someone, even if it costs you to do it.

***

REMEMBER, "WHATSOEVER GOOD THING ANY MAN DOETH, THE SAME SHALL HE RECEIVE OF THE LORD" (EPHESIANS 6:8).

MAY 13

When You're Following Him, You Can Face Anything

He goes on ahead of them, and his sheep follow him because they know his voice.

(John 10:4 NIV)

When you face something bigger and stronger than you, remember that it's not bigger than your God! He shut the mouths of the lions for Daniel, and He quenched the fire for the three Hebrew children. He opened the prison door for Peter, who was about to be executed the next day. Why? Because Peter's assignment wasn't yet completed, *and nothing could happen to him until it was.*

Don't be afraid today. David said, "Commit thy way unto the Lord; trust also in him; and he shall bring it to pass" (Psalm 37:5). You can either commit it, or sweat it.

You can look at the mountain, or look at the Mountain Mover. If you've tried running away, or manipulating the situation, or giving in to doubt and despair, stop and give it to Him. Peter said, "Casting all your care upon him; for he careth for you" (1 Peter 5:7). He may not do it in your time frame, and He may not do it the way *you* think it should be done, but He'll do it *right.* Give it to Him! Surrender is simply turning it over one more time than you take it back.

***

DO IT, AND YOU'LL DISCOVER THAT WHEN YOU'RE FOLLOWING HIM, YOU CAN FACE ANYTHING.

MAY 14

Falsely Accused?

Blessed are you when people insult you, persecute you and falsely say all kinds of evil against you....

(Matthew 5:11 NIV)

Have you been judged unfairly? Are you struggling with resentment? Do you feel like striking back? Read this prayer, and make it yours today:

Lord, I'm tired of being misrepresented; of dodging verbal bullets and ducking insults. You know I'm not guilty of the things they say I've done. Clearly they're out to get me, to make me the brunt of their jokes. How could they be so cruel?

And then I think of what You endured while You walked on this Earth. They made jokes about You, too. You were despised, and rejected, and crucified. They even dared You to prove Yourself while You were hanging on a cross taking Your dying breath—for them, and for me! That's when You said, "Father, forgive them. They don't know what they are doing.

Lord, forgive me for my pity party; help me to deal with this—Your way. Give me compassion in the face of criticism, and grace in the face of contempt.

Above all, help me to turn it over to You, knowing that You are my Defender and my Provider.

Send the Spirit of Truth into every aspect of this situation. Make me strong in You. Keep me focused on the path You've set before me. Make my heart big enough to forgive, as You've forgiven me.

***

"THANK YOU, FATHER, THAT WHAT OTHERS MEANT FOR EVIL, YOU WILL USE FOR MY GOOD. AMEN."

MAY 15

Contentment Isn't Getting What You Want; It's Enjoying What You've Got

I have learned to be content.

(Philippians 4:11 NIV)

A farmer had spent his life on the same farm. It was a good one with fertile soil; but with the passing of years he began to think, *Maybe there's something better for me.* So he went out to find a better plot of land to farm.

Every day he found a new reason to disparage his old farm, until finally he decided to sell. He listed it with a real estate broker, who promptly prepared an advertisement emphasizing all its advantages: ideal location, modern equipment, healthy stock, acres of fertile ground, high yields on crops, well-kept barns and pens, nice two-story house on a hill above the pasture.

When the agent called to read her ad to the farmer for his approval prior to placing it in the local paper, the farmer heard her out. And when she had finished, he said, "Hold everything! I've changed my mind. I'm not going to sell. *I've been looking for a place just like that all my life!"*

When you start seeing the good in your situation, you're likely to find it far outweighs the bad. Paul says, "Dwell on the fine, good things in others. Think about all you can praise God for and be glad about" (Philippians 4:8 TLB).

***

TODAY, WHEN YOU LOOK FOR THE GOOD IN YOUR CIRCUMSTANCES, YOU'LL FIND IT!

MAY 16

Satan's Schemes

In order that Satan might not outwit us. For we are not unaware of his schemes.

(2 Corinthians 2:11 NIV)

God has a plan for your life, and when you walk in it, you'll have peace, joy, and real fulfillment. Satan also has a plan for your life, and he counts heavily on one thing—*your ignorance!* If he can keep you in the dark, then he can wreak havoc with your life.

His scheme is to keep you *spiritually dull,* so that you can't discern the needs in other people's lives. He wants to keep you *spiritually weak,* so that you can't respond. He wants to keep you living in *condemnation,* so that you feel unfit and unworthy to minister to others—so that those who might have heard through you will be lost. In other words, Satan's goal is not just you, but those he can *reach through you.*

Once you know this, you've destroyed his advantage, and taken your first step toward victory. Take the weapon out of his hand today. Jesus said, "I give unto you power ... over all the power of the enemy" (Luke 10:19). Today, that power is found in His Word, in the place of prayer, and in fellowship with His people.

***

AS YOU WALK IN OBEDIENCE, YOU'LL DISCOVER YOU HAVE THE POWER TO DEFEAT SATAN ON EVERY FRONT AND DO THE JOB GOD HAS CALLED YOU TO DO.

MAY 17

Trust

Trust God from the bottom of your heart; don't try to figure out everything on your own. Listen for God's voice in everything you do, everywhere you go; he's the one who will keep you on track.

(Proverbs 3:5-6 TM)

Faith has many facets, but I think the most brilliant is trust! Trust is something you already have; you just have to decide where to place it. You're going to trust somebody; the question is—who will it be?

For you to put your trust in the right place, you must be able to look back and see who delivered you in the past, and who takes care of you daily.

Trust has two major characteristics. (1) *It's not easily* upset, because it has found a place of rest and confidence in Christ (Matthew 11:28). (2) *It's not easily confused,* because it doesn't need to figure everything out. In other words, it doesn't indulge in human reasoning. Instead, it allows God to be in charge!

Where are you placing your trust today? Your job? Your bank account? Your natural talents? Your track record? Your friends? Yourself?

All these things are temporal and subject to change. (See 2 Corinthians 4:18.) *The only One who doesn't change is God! He alone is the Rock that cannot be moved.*

***

PLACING YOUR TRUST IN HIM MAY REQUIRE GREATER FAITH—BUT IT PAYS GREATER DIVIDENDS!

MAY 18

Rise Above Your Fear

With him on my side I'm fearless, afraid of no one and nothing.

(Psalm 27:1 TM)

Ray Blankenship looked out of his window one morning to see a little girl being swept along in a rain-flooded drainage ditch beside his home. He knew that further downstream the ditch disappeared underneath the road, and then emptied into a main culvert. Nobody could survive that!

He raced along the side of the ditch trying to get ahead of the girl. Finally, he hurled himself into the water and when he surfaced, he was able to grab the child's arm. The two tumbled end over end, and then within three feet of the culvert, Ray's free hand felt something protruding from the bank. He clung to it desperately, while the force of the water kept trying to tear him and the child away.

Amazingly by the time fire department arrived, Ray had pulled the child to safety. Both were treated for shock, but in that heroic moment Ray Blankenship was truly a hero. You see, *he couldn't swim!*

Today, let your courage respond to the needs that you see, not the fear that you feel. God is just waiting for you to do what you *can,* then He'll do what you *can't.*

***

WHEN YOU MAKE THE EFFORT, GOD WILL DO THE REST—BUT NOTHING WILL HAPPEN UNTIL YOU MAKE THAT FIRST MOVE!

MAY 19

To Be Like Jesus

And we ... are being transformed into his likeness.

(2 Corinthians 3:18 NIV)

Teaching is very important, but people are not changed by doctrine. Some of the most critical, self-righteous, self-serving people I've ever met, held positions in the Church. Some were even Bible school graduates, and taught the Word. But try to do business with them, and you'll always end up with the short end of the stick! Don't cross them, for they have tempers like tornados! When some of them are far away from home, it's amazing where you'll find them.

Don't get me wrong, sound teaching is critically important and we must have it. *But a few minutes in the manifest presence of the Lord, can accomplish more than weeks or years of theology.* Remember Saul on the Damascus Road? (See Acts 9.)

Teaching that's anointed by His Spirit will lead those who hear it into God's presence, where truth is transmitted from the head to the heart. *The Living Bible* says, "As the Spirit of the Lord works within us, we become more and more like him" (2 Corinthians 3:18 TLB).

***

MAKE THE GOAL OF YOUR LIFE TODAY TO BE LIKE JESUS.

MAY 20

Ambassadors

We are ambassadors for Christ.

(2 Corinthians 5:20)

An ambassador holds a position of great honor and responsibility. They have to know the mind of your king and represent *his* interests only. Someone who gives his own opinions would never qualify.

Often kings would recall ambassadors after only two or three years. They were afraid that if they stayed in another country too long, they would become more concerned with that country's interests than those of their own king.

We, too, must guard our hearts from becoming more attuned to the interests of this present age than to those of Christ. Paul writes, "Demas hath forsaken me, having loved this present world" (2 Timothy 4:10). It can happen easily; Demas was seduced by *things* and lured away by the appeal of the world.

The Lord doesn't change His ambassadors every few years; you have a lifetime commission. Therefore, you must be careful to keep your mind and heart set on God's interests alone. Paul said, "If I were still trying to please men, I would not be a servant of Christ" (Galatians 1:10 NIV). As long as you fear men and seek their praises, you can never properly represent your King and His Kingdom.

***

TODAY, ASK GOD TO TRULY MAKE YOU HIS AMBASSADOR. WHAT A CALLING!

MAY 21

Are You a Secret Disciple?

Joseph of Arimathea, being a disciple of Jesus, but secretly for fear of the Jews....

(John 19:38)

Years ago a famous atheist gave a talk to 2,000 students in a North American university. For an hour she ridiculed religion, defied God, and attacked the Bible. When she finished, a Christian girl at the back of the auditorium stood up and began to sing, "Stand up. Stand up for Jesus, ye soldiers of the Cross, lift high His royal banner, it must not suffer loss."

For a moment there was stunned silence. Then in another section of the auditorium, a young man stood to his feet and joined in, singing, "From victory unto victory, His army shall He lead." Others jumped to their feet and joined in, until all over the auditorium hundreds of students were singing, "From victory unto victory, His army shall He lead, 'til every foe is vanquished, and Christ is Lord indeed."

Enraged, the atheist stormed from the podium, swearing she would never be back. What she had tried to build for the devil in an hourlong speech was torn down in a few moments by the commitment and the courage of a young Christian who refused to be a secret disciple. Are you a "closet Christian," like Joseph of Arimathea?

***

TODAY, GOD IS GOING TO GIVE YOU AN OPPORTUNITY TO SPEAK UP FOR JESUS. DON'T MISS IT!

MAY 22

Don't Stop Praying

God forbid that I should sin against the Lord in ceasing to pray for you.

(1 Samuel 12:23)

Prayer is one of the highest expressions of love. It's "standing in the gap" (see Ezekiel 22:30) on behalf of another. It's both a privilege and a great responsibility. James says, "Pray one for another, that ye may be healed" (James 5:16). When times are discouraging and things seem to be getting worse, *keep praying.* Paul says, "I make mention of you always in my prayers" (Romans 1:9).

A dear Christian friend of mine who died in his nineties could recall the names of scores of people others seemed to have difficulty remembering. When asked how he could do this, he said, *"Because I pray for them by name every day."* You can't forget somebody you're praying for.

God works through your prayers. Listen: "Call unto me, and I will answer thee, and shew thee great and mighty things, which thou knowest not" (Jeremiah 33:3). Your prayers become the bridge over which the answers pass, and the wire through which God's power flows into the situation. *When you stop praying, a door closes. God comes by invitation.* Even though Israel was in rebellion, Samuel knew that it would be a sin to stop praying for them. God says, "You who call on the Lord, give yourselves no rest, and give him no rest" (Isaiah 62:6-7 NIV).

***

KEEP PRAYING, CHILD OF GOD, FOR PRAYER CHANGES THINGS.

MAY 23

The Tongue

He who guards his lips guards his life.

(Proverbs 13:3 NIV)

"The boneless tongue, so small and weak, can crush and kill," declares the Greek.

"The tongue destroys a greater hoard," the Turk asserts, "Than does the sword."

A Persian proverb wisely saith, "A lengthy tongue—an early death"; or sometimes takes this form instead, "Don't let your tongue cut off your head."

"The tongue can speak a word whose speed," the Chinese say, "outstrips the steed", while Arab sages this impart, "The tongue's great storehouse is the heart."

From Hebrew wit this maxim sprung, "Though feet should slip, ne'er let the tongue."

The sacred writer crowns the whole, *"Who keeps his tongue doth keep his soul."*

James says, "If anyone can control his tongue, it proves that he has perfect control over himself in every other way" (James 3:2 TLB). If this is the standard by which we are measured, how well are *you* doing? It's so hard to keep quiet, especially when you have strong opinions, or when you're constantly provoked.

Listen: "They called him [Jesus] everything in the book, and he said nothing back. He suffered in silence, content to let God set things right" (1 Peter 2:23 TM). As I read these words, my heart cries, *Lord, help me! I fall so far short of this standard.*

***

MAYBE THAT'S A PRAYER YOU ALSO SHOULD PRAY TODAY.

MAY 24

When Things Fall Apart

The Lord ... rescued me. He is for me! How can I be afraid? ... The Lord is on my side.

(Psalm 118:5-7 TLB)

Things can change fast. One minute it's smooth sailing; the next you're in the biggest storm of your life. Is that where you are today? Take heart; nothing surprises your Heavenly Father. Everything that gets to you must first pass through Him, and He knows every detail. Today, here's a prayer to stand on:

Lord, just yesterday everything was so different. I can't believe how suddenly things can change—and how completely. Just moments ago my life was happy and secure. Now I feel as though I've stepped on a land mine. My world is shattered. I have nothing left but You.

I can't express everything I need from You, and I'm not even sure how to pray about this. I have to rest in the promise that You know my every need and that You will provide.

Please send Your Holy Spirit to bring truth, to bring wisdom, to bring deliverance, and to bring an understanding of what to do next.

As I said, I have nothing left but You. But You are all I need. You are my rock, my one stable place, and my only sure foundation. Thank You for being there.

***

I LEAVE IT ALL IN YOUR CAPABLE HANDS TODAY, CONFIDENT THAT YOU WILL WORK IT OUT FOR MY GOOD. AMEN.

MAY 25

How Big Is Your "Mistake Quota"?

...Give yourselves fully to the work of the Lord [which God has given you to do] because ... your labor in the Lord is not in vain. (1 Corinthians 15:58 NIV)

We're much too quick to judge things as "failures" when they're merely "learning experiences." Knowing what *doesn't* work moves you one step closer to knowing what *does.* Thomas Edison said, "Many of life's failures happened because people didn't realize how close they were to success when they gave up."

The key to victory is having the commitment to move through your failures, learning as you go, and taking hold of the success that lies just beyond them. And it's there—waiting for you!

Chuck Braun of Idea Connection Systems allows each of his trainees a "Mistake Quota." It works like this. They can each make up to thirty mistakes during a training session without worrying. If they use up all thirty, then Chuck gives them *another* thirty!

As a result, they overcome the fear of failure, and begin to see mistakes as a creative part of the essential learning process—and they can then go on to excel!

Did you grow up in an environment where failure was unacceptable? Was it rewarded with embarrassment, shame, and condemnation? If so, your perception of failure must be changed before you can begin to move forward (see Psalm 37:24).

***

TODAY GIVE YOURSELF A BIGGER "MISTAKE QUOTA"—GOD HAS!

MAY 26

Be a Friend to Those in Need

Be kind to each other.

(Ephesians 4:32 TLB)

In the book, *Feeding the Soul,* Carolyn Adams Miller writes: "My greatest lessons in the value of kindness, gentleness, and love have been as a result of having had those same qualities *withheld* from me when I needed them most. Although some people were supportive, others drew feelings of superiority from treating me like a beggar, and not even extending common courtesies, like returning a phone call, or being polite.

"A friend who commiserated with me wasn't surprised. He reminded me that many people won't visit sick friends in hospital, for fear of contracting the same illness; and that injured sports players who are forced to sit on the bench during the game, are often shunned by their healthier teammates." How sad!

Don't wait until you are the victim of somebody else's cruelty before you learn to be a friend to those in need. Extend yourself to that one who needs love and support today. Jesus said, "Do to others [at all times] as you would have them do to you" (Luke 6:31 NIV).

Listen to these two Scriptures: (1) "Love [the kind God gives] is very patient and kind, never jealous or envious" (1 Corinthians 13:4 TLB). (2) "Practice tenderhearted mercy and kindness to others" (Colossians 3:12 TLB).

***

NOTE THE WORD PRACTICE—YOU HAVE TO WORK AT BEING KIND. OTHERWISE IT'LL BE THE LAST THING THAT COMES TO MIND!

MAY 27

Get Up and Fight

Fight the good fight of faith ... whereunto thou art also called.

(1 Timothy 6:12)

Some of us are strong in faith but weak in fight. Without fight, Caleb would never have gotten his inheritance. Listen: "Now therefore give me this mountain ... if so be the Lord will be with me, then I shall be able to drive them out" (Joshua 14:12).

To subdue Goliath, David had to fight. What a scene! "Then said David to the Philistine ... And all this assembly shall know that the Lord saveth not with sword and spear: for the battle is the Lord's" (1 Samuel 17:45-47). Did you hear that? "All shall know that the battle is the Lord's!" The world wants to know if the God we talk about is bigger than the Goliath they're looking at. Their weapons don't work, and they're wondering if ours do.

Jesus challenged religious systems that enslaved people with rules that nobody could live up to, including those who made a living by preaching them. He had something to say, and He had the courage to say it. How about you? It's a lot easier to admire Jesus than it is to follow Him. The moment you really decide to follow Him, you're in for the fight of your life—in the workplace, the community, the home, and anywhere else you happen to be.

***

REMEMBER, BIG BATTLES PRODUCE BIG VICTORIES, AND THAT'S WHAT GOD HAS IN STORE FOR YOU TODAY.

MAY 28

Make Prayer a Lifestyle

Aaron shall burn ... sweet incense every morning.... And ... at twilight ... a perpetual incense before the Lord.

(Exodus 30:7-8 NKJV)

Aaron was to burn incense first thing each morning and last thing each night, so that there would be "perpetual incense before the Lord." If you begin and end your days with prayer, you'll stay in a perpetual attitude of prayer. The Lord doesn't want you to talk to Him once in a while. He wants you to *abide* in Him. (See John 15:7.)

How would your lifestyle change if the Lord appeared in person and went everywhere with you today? Are there places you wouldn't go, and things you wouldn't say or do? Would your attitude undergo a radical change? The truth is, if the eyes of our hearts were opened, we would see Him in all we do, and the reality of His presence would be greater than what we see with our physical eyes. Ask the Holy Spirit to make Jesus real to you, so that you can *see* Him and *sense* Him in everything you do.

When Paul said, "Pray without ceasing" (1 Thessalonians 5:17), he was talking about being conscious of God *at all times,* and staying in constant communication with Him.

***

MAKE PRAYER YOUR LIFESTYLE TODAY.

MAY 29

Make a Clean Break

Make a clean break with all cutting, backbiting, profane talk.

(Ephesians 4:31 TM)

Criticism is one of the ultimate manifestations of pride, because it assumes superiority! God's reaction to it should be the only warning we need: "God resisteth the proud, but giveth grace unto the humble" (James 4:6).

The Bible says God is at work in each of us. (See Philippians 2:13.) So when you criticize your brother, you're actually saying that "God's workmanship" does not meet with your approval, and that He could have done it better. What arrogance! The truth is, we all struggle and fall far short, so on what basis do you point out the faults of another? When you criticize somebody's children, who gets upset? *The parents!* It's the same with God. When we judge His people, we're really judging Him. When we judge His leaders, we're saying that God doesn't know what He's doing by permitting such leadership. Look out! That puts you on very dangerous ground.

Grumbling and complaining kept the first generation of Israelites out of the Promised Land. They spent their entire lives wandering in dry places. Could this be why you've been going through such a dry spell lately? They went around the same mountain (problem) over and over again. Think about it! Paul says, "Make a clean break with all cutting, backbiting, profane talk."

**

DON'T YOU THINK IT'S TIME TO TAKE THESE THINGS SERIOUSLY?

MAY 30

Gracious Words

Let your speech be always with grace...

(Colossians 4:6)

Legend has it that the sun and the wind got into an argument one day over who was the stronger. When a traveler came down the road, they decided to settle it by seeing who could force him to take off his coat. As the sun hid behind a cloud, the wind blasted the man, but that just made him wrap his coat around him more tightly. Then the sun came out with its gentle, caressing warmth, and shone on the traveler—forcing him *to take his coat off.* Think about that!

Angry words only make others withdraw, shrivel, and shut down. But gracious words help them to ... open up ... discover what's *good* about themselves ... and motivate them to reach higher.

Paul writes, "Watch the way you talk.... Say only what helps, each word a gift" (Ephesians 4:29 TM). Solomon says, "...there is healing in the words of the wise" (Proverbs 12:18 TM).

People tend to reproduce the seeds we plant in them. If you keep telling them that they're incapable or worthless, they'll probably fail. But if you keep praising them, and pointing to what's good in them, they'll make every effort to justify your confidence. Listen again: "Let your speech be always with grace..."(Colossians 4:6).

***

TODAY, TRY TO MAKE YOUR WORDS GRACIOUS.

MAY 31

Act on What You Hear

Don't fool yourself into thinking that you are a listener when you are anything but, letting the Word go in one ear and out the other. Act on what you hear.

(James 1:23-25 TM)

Charles Spurgeon said that for every ten men who would *die* for the Bible, he could find only one who would *read* it. I doubt if much has changed! You'll find *ten* men and women who will fight for prayer in public schools, for every one who actually prays with his or her own children at home. You'll find *ten* men and women who complain about sex and violence on television, for every *one* who refuses to watch it. This must change! Our power to be salt and light in the world doesn't depend on what we *applaud;* it depends on what we *apply!*

You can go to church, enjoy great preaching, and yet leave and do nothing about it. On the road to Emmaus, the disciples' eyes were opened when they recognized that it was the Lord who was breaking the bread. It's the same with us. When we see Jesus as the one breaking the bread regardless of the earthly vessel, then our eyes will begin to open.

God help us to get our doctrine off the drawing board and into daily practice, that men and women may be drawn to Jesus.

***

IT'S TIME TO START ACTING ON WHAT YOU HEAR.

JUNE 1

Who Are You Living For?

Those who live should no longer live for themselves but for him who died for them and was raised again.

(2 Corinthians 5:15 NIV)

The fire on the altar of incense was lit from the fire on the altar of sacrifice. It takes sacrifice to pray. We must give up our selflife. The Lord is not after a few minutes of our day—He wants our every *thought* taken captive and brought into obedience to Him.

The Apostle Paul is one of the great examples. He died to *self daily.* He did all things for the sake of the Gospel. He sacrificed his own *will, safety,* and *comfort* to serve the Lord and His people. Paul's great effectiveness in ministry can be directly tied to the degree to which he laid down his life for the purposes of God. Are you willing to do that today?

There is power in sacrifice. The Cross was the ultimate sacrifice, and it is the ultimate power. The degree to which you will take up your cross daily will be the degree to which you experience the power of God in your daily life. The priesthood is about intercession, and *intercession is not prayer for yourself, but for others.*

Listen:

Others, Lord, yes others,
Let this my motto be;
Help me to live for others,
That I may live for thee.

***

WHOM ARE YOU LIVING FOR?

JUNE 2

Learning to Pray

After this manner therefore pray ye: Our Father...

(Matthew 6:9)

When you say "Our Father," you're acknowledging you belong to God's family, and that includes all the rights and privileges that go with it. Have you learned what they are yet? One of the first words most babies say is "daddy." Knowing your father helps you understand your own identity as a son or daughter. I need to know who my Father is and how He feels about me. If you had an abusive father, or one who wasn't there when you needed him, it will take you some time to believe and act on the fact that God's your loving Heavenly Father. It will be difficult to learn that you can come to Him any time day or night, and He'll be there for you.

Prayer is just talking with the One you call "Father." So, why don't we spend more time talking to Him? One reason is that while His love draws me, His holiness intimidates me. When Isaiah saw the Lord, he cried, "Woe is me! For I am undone" (Isaiah 6:5). Have you ever felt that way? I have. Thank God David saw His compassion and said, "Like as a father pitieth his children, so the Lord pitieth them that fear him"

(Psalm 103:13). All of us long to be understood. It's exhausting to be around people who audit your every move and demand that you qualify every statement. But "our Father" isn't like that. We don't have to labor to create what's already there. He knows what your *speech* and your *silence* suggest, and sometimes you can say it all in just two words—*"Heavenly Father."*

***

WHY DON'T YOU TAKE A FEW MOMENTS TODAY AND DO JUST THAT?

JUNE 3

Take Control of Your Life

We ought to obey God rather than men.

(Acts 5:29)

No matter how timid you are, don't allow anybody to dominate or direct your life. Get back into the driver's seat and take the wheel, for only *you* know where God has told you to go!

Too often our actions are dictated not by a sense of purpose, but by a need to please. We care so much about what certain people think, that with every step we take, we're looking over our shoulder to see whether they're smiling or frowning.

Hear this clearly: Your first responsibility is to please God, not people. In the end, you're accountable to Him alone (see Romans 14:12).

Listen: "You shall have no other gods before me" (Exodus 20:3 NIV). But you say, "I don't worship idols." You *do* when you dedicate your life to impressing people instead of obeying God.

"But who am I to assert myself?" you ask. Who are you *not* to? As a child of God, your first responsibility is to please your Father and your second is to live your life to its fullest!

***

TODAY, IT'S TIME TO TAKE CONTROL OF YOUR LIFE AND GET BACK IN THE DRIVER'S SEAT!

JUNE 4

His Touch and His Word

[He] touched me and gave me strength.... When he spoke to me, I was strengthened.

(Daniel 10:18-19 NIV)

What you need today is a *touch* and a *word* from God, especially if you're battling sin, sickness, or depression.

Daniel sought God with all his heart for an answer, but for three weeks he got nowhere. If that's where you are today, don't give up. *Things are happening that you don't fully understand yet.* There's a battle going on, and when it's over you're going to come out a winner.

Listen to what the Angel of the Lord told Daniel: "From the first day you set your heart before God, your words were heard. But for twenty-one days an evil spirit blocked my way. Then Michael, one of the top officers of the heavenly army, came to help me so that I was able to break through" (Daniel 10:12-13, paraphrase).

When God assigns, Satan attacks. Expect it! It may come from a source you least expect, even a family member. Remember Joseph and his brothers? But God has an answer for you today—His *touch* and

His *Word*—and they can both be found *in His presence.* So take some time today to get together with Him.

***

ASK HIM TO TOUCH YOU AND SPEAK TO YOUR HEART.

JUNE 5

The Rejection Test

He came unto his own, and his own received him not.

(John 1:11)

How many of us would spend our last night with someone if we knew they were going to betray us the next day? Jesus did. He was faithful even when others were not. There is no greater opportunity for you to grow in Christian love than when you are rejected and abused. Jesus asked the Father to forgive those who crucified Him. Amazing!

How you handle rejection reveals whether you have truly died to self and to the world. It's impossible for a dead man to feel rejection. On the other hand, being rejected without being offended is one of the greatest demonstrations of spiritual maturity—it's being Christ-like.

In the Old Testament, a priest was not allowed to minister if he had scabs. (See Leviticus 21:20.) A scab is an unhealed wound. And when you have unhealed spiritual wounds, you're touchy, you can't function the way God wants you to, and it will show up in the things you say. You need to be healed, because only when you pass the "rejection test" can you reach out in love and make others whole.

***

ASK GOD TO HELP YOU PASS THE TEST!

JUNE 6

Like a Tree

He shall be like a tree planted by the rivers of water ... whatsoever he doeth shall prosper.

(Psalm 1:3)

The Bible likens the prosperous man to a tree because:

1) *It's stable.* That's because it draws continually from underground streams. If you want to succeed, learn how to draw daily on the indwelling power of God's Spirit. Not all of the answers are in heaven; some of them are within you waiting for expression.

2) *It's productive.* Note the words, "Whatsoever he *doeth* shall prosper" (Psalm 1:3). You've got to *do* something to be blessed! You say, "But I'm praying about it." That's good; prayer releases the favor of God—but work releases the force of man! When one is in harmony with the other, you're unstoppable. Don't just pray for a better relationship with your husband or wife—give them more attention. Don't ask for better credit, or more money—set a budget and start living within your means.

3) *It's connected.* Without additional sources to draw from, a tree may survive, but it'll never reach its full potential for fruitfulness. And neither will you. You can't beg or borrow *somebody else's fruit,* but there's a lot to be said for using a little of their *pollen* to stimulate what God's already placed within you. Joshua drew from Moses. Timothy drew from Paul.

***

FROM WHOM ARE YOU DRAWING TODAY?

JUNE 7

Do You Care?

Refuge failed me; no man cared for my soul.

(Psalm 142:4)

Nobody knew who he was, and nobody seemed to care. They found him lying in a heap with his throat slashed. A doctor used black thread to suture the gash, and then the man was dumped into a paddy wagon and dropped off at Bellevue Hospital, where he languished until he died.

A friend seeking him went to the local morgue, and there, among dozens of nameless corpses, he found him. His only possessions were a ragged coat that smelled of liquor, with thirty-eight cents in one pocket and a scrap of paper in the other, on which was written, "Dear friends and gentle hearts." It almost sounded like the words of a song somebody was going to write.

Which would have been correct—for in another time, this man had written songs that made the whole world sing. Songs like "I Dream of Jeannie with the Light Brown Hair," "My Old Kentucky Home," "Oh! Susannah," and 200 more, with deep roots in our culture. The man's name was Stephen Collins Foster. You may have heard of him.

So many people around you today are hurting. Some are hard to spot because they wear the mask of success. Others are clearly down-and-out.

But how do you change the world around you? You do it one life at a time! But you've got to have enough love to restore and rekindle the flame life has snuffed out.

***

TODAY, TOUCH ONE PERSON—JUST ONE—WITH GOD'S LOVE!

JUNE 8

Taking Possession!

How long will you wait before you begin to take possession?

(Joshua 18:3 NIV)

God promised the children of Israel the land, and Joshua led them right to it. Yet seven of the tribes of Israel had done *nothing* to possess it. Is that where you're at today? Just because you know your destiny, and understand what God's promised you, doesn't mean you'll ever fulfill it!

The Old Testament Saul might have been one of Israel's greatest kings, but instead David took his place. Saul died tragically on Mount Gilboa, with the words captioning his life, "I have played the fool, and have erred exceedingly" (1 Samuel 26:21). But what a difference we find in the New Testament Saul: "I have fought a good fight, I have finished my course" (2 Timothy 4:7). *Your destiny is determined by your decisions; so seek God and consult His Word before you make them.*

Perhaps you're saying, "But I'm too busy." Doing what? God doesn't only reward your *efforts*, He rewards your *obedience!* Build your life on what's *important*, not what's *urgent.* Prayer may not seem important at the moment, but in the final analysis, nothing is more important. Getting into God's Word may not seem urgent, but in the light of your destiny, can you think of anything more important? Set your priorities according to your destiny, and you'll suddenly begin to see what really matters in your life today.

***

HOW LONG WILL YOU WAIT BEFORE YOU TAKE POSSESSION OF THE LAND THE LORD HAS GIVEN YOU?

JUNE 9

Thinking God's Way

Be renewed in the spirit of your mind.

(Ephesians 4:23)

How you process information and arrive at conclusions must always be subject to the will of God. Listen: "...be made new in the attitude of your minds..." (Ephesians 4:23-24 NIV).

When you first start thinking God's way, it'll feel strange to you. It may even feel like a "put-on." But it's not!

It works like this: You have to (a) *practice* being nice until you automatically become nice; (b) *practice* going to church on Sunday until going anywhere else seems strange to you; (c) *practice* giving to God until it becomes as natural to you as shopping at the mall; (d) *practice* speaking the truth until even the smallest lie tastes bad in your mouth; (e) *practice* speaking kindness until every cynical, negative word is purged from your vocabulary. It's all a matter of practice!

But you ask, "Isn't that hypocritical—feeling one way and speaking another?" *No, it's re-training yourself to walk God's way, and restraining yourself from walking any other way!* You are literally declaring, "Lord, it's no longer a matter of anything goes...

***

"FROM NOW ON, IT'S WHAT YOU SAY, AND WHAT YOU DIRECT ME TO DO."

JUNE 10

Just Be Yourself!

A man must be content to receive the gift which is given him from heaven.

(John 3:27 AMP)

Have you ever considered how much "they" control your life? How often have you said, "Well, you know what *they* say?" You see, *"they"* set the standard, and we wear it ... drive it ... or do it! And while that may be fine in some areas, it's *not* when it comes to your life's direction. Jesus said, "If the son ... [makes you free men] ... you are ... unquestionably free" (John 8:36 AMP). That means: (1) free from the pressure of others' expectations; (2) free to be who God has called you to be; and (3) free to look to Him for answers, instead of running to other people.

Listen: "A man must be content to receive the gift which is given him from heaven" (John 3:27 AMP). Because of my background I struggled with insecurity. I was competitive. I kept comparing myself to others. I was jealous of their possessions, abilities, and accomplishments. I tried to keep up with certain people—or to be just like them! As a result, I was constantly frustrated because I was operating *outside* of what God had called *me* to be. *In other words, I wasn't being myself!*

When I finally realized that I could only be who God had ordained me to be, I began to say, *"I am who I am. I can't be anything other than who God has called me to be. So I'm going to concentrate on being the best 'me' that I can be."*

*** *

YOU NEED TO SAY THAT, TOO!

JUNE 11

Wolf-Proofed!

Be on guard ... savage wolves will come in among you, not sparing the flock.

(Acts 20:28-29 NAS)

You never reach a place spiritually where opposition and attacks disappear. Never! The wolves will constantly circle, and their "target of choice" will always be: (1) the sheep that strays too far from the protection of the fold; (2) the sheep that can't discern the Shepherd's voice, or won't follow His instructions; (3) the sheep that think they only need to be fed on Sunday mornings and (4) the sheep that think wolves are not so dangerous and get too close to them.

Who are these wolves? Listen: "From among your own selves men will arise, speaking perverse things, to draw away the disciples after them. Therefore be on the alert..." (Acts 20:30-31 NAS). Did you hear that? "From among your own selves..."

"How can I protect myself?" you ask. Listen again: "And now, brethren, I commend you to God, and to the word of his grace, which is able to build you up..." (Acts 20:32). There it is—God's Word is your greatest line of defense! That's what will keep you protected and allow you to prevail over the wolves when they come against you.

***

THAT'S WHAT'S KNOWN AS BEING "WOLF-PROOFED"!

JUNE 12

Coming Out and Going In!

Do not give the devil a foothold.

(Ephesians 4:27 NIV)

Before God's people escaped out of Egypt, Pharaoh made them three offers. To each Moses said, "No," or they'd never have made it out.

First, Pharaoh said, "Go, but leave your *children* here." Then he said, "Go, but leave your *business* here." Finally, he said, "Go, but *don't go too far.*" Listen to how Moses replied, "There shall not an hoof be left behind..."(Exodus 10:26). And that's what you've got to do, too—look the enemy in the eye and say, "No! I'm taking my family, I'm taking my business, and I'm going *all* the way with God!" That's what it takes to get out of Egypt!

But what about getting into the Promised Land? That only happens one city at a time ... one habit at a time ... one attitude at a time ... one step of faith at a time.

It happens when you break the enemy's hold on your finances and put God first. It happens when you take the remote control out of his hand, and protect your family from a culture that corrupts. It happens when you refuse to contradict what God has said about you in His Word.

***

RISE UP IN FAITH TODAY AND ANNOUNCE, "I'M COMING OUT, AND I'M GOING IN!"

JUNE 13

How to Leave

For ye shall go out with joy, and be led forth with peace.

(Isaiah 55:12)

It's always easier to leave a difficult situation than to stay and grow in grace.

But when it's truly time to leave, how should you do it? You can leave *offended,* and try to negatively influence as many others as possible. When you see yourself as a victim, you'll blame those whom you think hurt you, and you'll try to justify your resentment. However, when you do, you lose!

Listen to these words: "For ye shall go out with joy, and *be led forth with peace."* That's how you should leave—*because God led you to do it peacefully.*

Churches aren't like cafeterias; you can't pick and choose what you like! Paul says, "But now God has set the members ... in the body just as He pleased" (1 Corinthians 12:18 NKJV). You are not the one who chooses where you go to church—God does!

Satan will always try to offend you and get you out of the place where God wants to bless you and make you spiritually fruitful. David says, "Those that be planted in the house of the Lord shall flourish in the courts of our God" (Psalm 92:13).

***

IF GOD PLANTS YOU, HE'S THE ONLY ONE WHO SHOULD UPROOT YOU!

JUNE 14

Who Gave You the Right to Sit This One Out?

Moses said to the Gadites and Reubenites, "Shall your countrymen go to war while you sit here?"

(Numbers 32:6 NIV)

The world respects an ex-president. The world salutes an excaptain or general. But the world despises an ex-Christian There is no retirement in the service of the King of kings! At seventy, Paul said he was ready to go to Rome. For Paul, Rome meant death, but death for him held no terrors. Listen: "Since future victory is sure, be strong and steady, always abounding in the Lord's work, for you know that nothing you do for the Lord is ever wasted" (1 Corinthians 15:58 TLB).

Did you hear that? This is the only *"sure thing"* you can invest your life in. Everything else, regardless of how highly you may value it, is scheduled for demolition. Child of God, *live*—until the very day and hour you die!

If your "get-up-and-go" has "got-up-and-gone"— *get up and go after it!* Get involved in something that will outlive you—something that will make a difference.

The God who asked His people of old,, "Shall your countrymen go to war while you sit here?" is asking you the same question today.

***

HOW ARE YOU GOING TO RESPOND?

JUNE 15

Don't Take the Bait

It is impossible that no offenses should come.

(Luke 17:1 NKJV)

Jesus said that it is impossible to live in this world and not be offended. So why then are we so shocked when it happens to us? The Greek word for *offense,* literally means "a trap with bait in it," and when we take offense, we have taken the devil's bait, and we finish up in a trap. We become self-absorbed and resentful. We lose our joy and can't function properly.

So what can you do? Jesus told the end-age believers to "anoint thine eyes with eye salve, that thou mayest see" (Revelation 3:18). See what? See your own attitude in all of this! *You'll only repent—when you see your own condition of heart and stop blaming other people.*

The wonderful thing is, when the Spirit of God shows you your sin, you will feel *conviction,* not *condemnation.* When He does, don't carry that offense another step.

***

FORGIVE THE OFFENDING PARTY, AS GOD HAS
FORGIVEN YOU—THEN MOVE ON.

JUNE 16

What Time Is It?

All of us must quickly carry out the task assigned us ... for there is little time left before the night falls and all work comes to an end.

(John 9:4 TLB)

When you're a child, time is endless. As you grow older, it begins to fly. In later years, it's a gift to be used wisely.

When He was thirty-three, the Master said, "I have finished the work which thou gavest me to do" (John 17:4). At seventy, Paul said, "I have fought a good fight, I have finished my course" (2 Timothy 4:7). Let me ask you a question: *Have you found the will of God for your life yet?* There isn't a more important question. If you want to know what His will is, ask Him. As you wait in His presence, I promise He'll reveal it to you (see James 1:5).

The next question is: *Are you doing the will of God?* When your life ends, will you be able to say, "I have finished the work which thou gavest me to do"? Is your life making a difference? Will there be souls in heaven because you witnessed, prayed, and gave so that they could hear the Gospel? Please think about this, for it's eternally important.

***

ONE OF AMERICA'S FIRST MISSIONARY MARTYRS IN THE AMAZON SAID, "HE IS NOT A FOOL WHO GIVES WHAT HE CANNOT KEEP, TO GAIN WHAT HE CANNOT LOSE."

JUNE 17

Robbing God

Will a man rob God? Surely not! And yet you have robbed me. "What do you mean? When did we ever rob you?" You have robbed me of the tithes and offerings due to me.

(Malachi 3:8 TLB)

"If He already owns everything, how could I be robbing Him?" you ask.

First, you're robbing Him of the joy of blessing you. God says He wants to open the windows of heaven and "pour out a blessing so great you won't have room enough to take it in!" (Malachi 3:10 TLB). As a father, I am thrilled when my children are blessed—don't rob God of that joy!

Next, you're robbing Him of the honor of having first place in your life. Often the reason we don't tithe is that we have nothing left over. How dishonoring to God! He doesn't want your *leftovers.* He wants *your first fruit.* Listen: "Honor the Lord by giving him the first part of all your income" (Proverbs 3:9 TLB).

Finally, you're robbing His house of resources (see Malachi 3:10). In the Old Testament, believers gave over 25 percent of their income to the work of God, and widows, orphans, and those in need were cared for.

**

SHOULD WE DO LESS UNDER GRACE THAN THEY DID UNDER THE LAW?

JUNE 18

No Reserve, No Retreat, No Regrets

Well done, thou good and faithful servant.

(Matthew 25:21)

Bill Borden, of the famous Borden Milk family in America, turned his back on fame and fortune and went to China as a missionary. His friends in America thought he'd taken leave of his senses by walking away from a life of comfort and riches. He'd been missing for days when they found his body in a tent. Under his thumb was a note that read, *"No reserve! No retreat! No regrets!"*

Think of it, child of God: "No reserve"—holding nothing back. "No retreat"—never looking back or turning back from what God called you to do. "No regrets"—"a workman that needeth not to be ashamed" (2 Timothy 2:15).

Today, the spotlight is on *commitment.* When you look at yourself, what you see may not be a very nice picture, but be honest with yourself—painfully honest. Ask God to help you rebuild your altar, and then place your life on it.

***

REMEMBER, THERE'S ONLY ONE WAY TO DO IT: NO RESERVE. NO RETREAT. NO REGRETS!

JUNE 19

An Open Mind

But the wisdom that comes from heaven is ... peace-loving and courteous. It allows discussion and is willing to yield to others.

(James 3:17 TLB)

The wisdom God gives is not contentious or argumentative. It will make you humble enough to listen to the counsel of others. God will share His wisdom through them as well. The real test of knowing whether the wisdom we receive is from God or man is that *God's wisdom brings peace!*

Over the years I've found that people who are determined to have their own way, and who are not open to correction or change, often say "The Lord told me..." When I hear that, I know then the door is closed and all they really want is my approval. When I can give it, I do. When I can't, I offer them my prayers and my love, and urge them to keep an open mind.

Read this verse again, and then ask God for the gift of an open mind. When you need an answer. He will place it within your spirit.

***

WHEN HE DOES, YOU'LL KNOW IT'S HIS WISDOM
WORKING THROUGH YOU.

JUNE 20

He Frames Your Life in Pictures – One Day at a Time

This is the day the Lord has made. We will rejoice and be glad in it.

(Psalm 118:24 TLB)

So often if we don't like our present scene, we try to escape into the next picture. But each picture the Lord paints makes us a little *more* like Him, and a little *less* like we used to be. This is not a Polaroid shot, or "one day" service—it's lesson after lesson learned on the canvas of life. Day by day the picture changes, and we move from weakness to strength, and from spiritual babyhood into full stature. In the picture there are mountains and valleys, storms and sunsets. It's all part of growing up. God wants you to see that the real joy in life is not in arriving; it's in *the journey itself.*

Be where you are today! *Live in the present, for that's where God is.* That's where victory is. That's where growth is. That's where joy is. Check the words that come out of your mouth. If the window you are looking through is framed by doubt and negativity, then this word is for you. You have the power to change your focus and your speech. Rejoice and be glad. In what? In this day that the Lord has made and given to you.

$$* * *$$

TODAY IS THE ONLY ONE YOU'VE GOT—MAKE IT COUNT!

JUNE 21

Either It Works or It Doesn't!

Give away and become richer! ... Hold on too tightly and lose everything. Yes, the liberal man shall be rich! By watering others, he waters himself.

(Proverbs 11:24–25 TLB)

It's not the seed you keep that multiplies; it's the seed you sow. That seed will never leave your life; it moves from your present into your future. It goes ahead of you to rearrange tomorrow in your favor.

The world doesn't understand this principle, and some of God's children don't either. And because they don't, they're living on the wrong side of God's blessings.

Giving is proof that you have conquered *greed.* It's also proof that you have conquered *fear.* When you give, your gift tells God that He is first in your life. It says you're totally confident that He is going to meet your needs and bless you. If you're not sowing, *you're robbing yourself of the harvest.* Read it again: "It is possible to give away and become richer! It is also possible to hold on too tightly and lose everything." *Make giving your style of living.* Be alert today, for God will give you opportunities to water others—and as you do, watch it begin to pour back into your own life. Either it works or it doesn't.

***

DON'T YOU THINK IT'S TIME YOU FOUND OUT FOR YOURSELF?

JUNE 22

Today – He's with You

Blessed be the Lord, Who bears our burdens and carries us day by day.

(Psalm 68:19 AMP)

When the pressure is on, one of our greatest temptations is to try and escape into tomorrow. We dream about the day when we will be "out of this mess." The problem is, today is the tomorrow you dreamed about yesterday. And each time you do it, you lose another day and another opportunity to grow. You lose a chance to learn a lesson—even if it's painful—that could enrich your life and prepare you to make tomorrow better. Listen to the promise again: "Blessed be the Lord, Who bears our burdens and carries us day by day."

Remember: *Yard by yard, life is hard—but inch by inch, life's a cinch.* Use today to "inch" closer to Jesus than you were yesterday, to add another layer to your strength, and to make a new discovery of who you really are in Christ.

Worry is *faith in the wrong thing.* Are you worried about your health? Your finances? Your kids? Your future? Are you projecting into the future? Don't do it! God won't give you tomorrow's answers today. He won't give you tomorrow's supply today. He wants you to enjoy *this day.*

***

AND WHEN YOU GET TO TOMORROW, HE'LL BE THERE, TOO!

JUNE 23

In Harmony with God

According as he hath chosen us in him...

(Ephesians 1:4)

The word *holy* simply means *"exclusively yours,"* and that kind of lifestyle is unnatural to us. One of the keys to living that way is in understanding the word *according.* It's a musical term that means *"to be in harmony with."*

But in order to be in harmony, you've got to understand four things: (1) the melody must always take the lead; (2) the harmony must have an ear to hear and a willingness to follow; (3) it takes time and practice to get it right; and (4) an instrument can be thrown off-key by lack of use or poor maintenance.

Your job today is to recognize God's purpose for your life, and choose *only* those things that harmonize with it!

That means yielding to Him each day, and saying, "Lord, turn me upside down and empty out anything that's not in accordance with Your will. Then turn me right side up and fill me with Your Spirit, so that I may walk in Your ways."

One of life's greatest experiences is to be wanted and chosen by another person. It's the supreme antidote to loneliness, depression, and low self-esteem. But as wonderful as that is, it pales in comparison to being wanted and chosen by God.

* * *

IMAGINE: GOD CHOSE YOU TO LIVE IN HARMONY WITH HIM! WHAT A PRIVILEGE!

JUNE 24

A Passion for Unity!

With longsuffering, forbearing one another in love; endeavoring to keep the unity of the Spirit...

(Ephesians 4:2-3)

If unity was a wall, each of us would be a brick, no two of us would occupy the same slot, and all of us would be held together by the mortar of "longsuffering."

Without a passion for unity, we'll never have it, for there's a cost attached. The cost involves: (a) yielding to one another and preferring one another (see Romans 12:10); (b) persevering regardless of the difficulties (see Galatians 6:9); and (c) protecting that unity, because ultimately it's the source of our blessing (see Ephesians 4:13).

Listen: "Behold, how good and how pleasant it is for brethren to dwell together in unity! It is like the precious ointment upon the head, that ran down upon the beard, even Aaron's beard: that went down to the skirts of his garments ... for there the Lord commanded the blessing" (Psalm 133:1-3).

Did you hear that? Unity must start at the head and flow down, undiluted by personal agendas, contentious spirits, and fleshly desires. It must be the same at the bottom as it is at the top—pure and undefiled.

∗∗

WHEN THAT HAPPENS, GOD WILL COMMAND HIS BLESSING TO BE UPON ALL THAT WE DO!

JUNE 25

My Steps and My Stops

The steps of a good man are ordered by the Lord.

(Psalm 37:23)

Clinton Utterbach, who wrote "Blessed Be the Name of the Lord" and several other great songs, said, "My *steps* and my *stops* are ordered of the Lord!" He explained it this way: "In music, a rest is as much an action as a note; it's an important part of the whole score." Think about it! David said, "He maketh me to lie down" (Psalm 23:2). Why? To restore my soul, to strengthen and refresh me by green pastures and still waters. In other words, to keep me from burning out and falling apart. When He orders you to *stop,* it's because He knows what lies ahead, and He wants you to be prepared for the journey. Don't be anxious; a *delay* is not a *denial.* Isaiah said, "They that wait upon the Lord shall renew their strength" (Isaiah 40:31).

If the door is closed, don't try to force it open. If He's giving you a red light, don't keep driving, for when you move beyond obedience you move beyond protection. He knows what's on the other side of that closed door, no matter how appealing it may seem to you. David said, "He guides the humble in what is right and teaches them his way" (Psalm 25:9 NIV). And if you need more, listen: "For this God is our God for ever and ever; he will be our guide even to the end" (Psalm 48:14 NIV). Jesus said that the Holy Spirit would guide us (see John 16:13). The bottom line is—it's a "trust issue"!

***

WILL YOU TRUST HIM TODAY TO LEAD YOUR STEPS AND YOUR STOPS?

JUNE 26

What Do You Really Stand For?

If you do not stand firm in your faith, you will not stand at all.

(Isaiah 7:9 NIV)

A man went to Sodom one day hoping to save it from God's judgment. He tried to talk to one individual after another, but nobody would talk to him. Next, he tried carrying a picket sign that had "REPENT" written in large letters, but nobody paid attention. Finally, he went from street to street, shouting, "Men and women, repent! What you are doing is wrong. It will destroy you!"

The people laughed at him, but still he continued shouting. One day someone stopped him and said, "Stranger, can't you see that your shouting is useless?" The man replied, "Yes, I see that." He asked, "Then why do you continue?" The man replied, "When I arrived in this city I was convinced that I could change them. Now I know I cannot. But I continue shouting *because I don't want it to change me!*"

Speak out for those things you believe in. If you remain silent others may interpret your silence as agreement. Evil can only prevail if good people do nothing. Jesus said, "Let your light so shine before men, that they may see your good works, and glorify your Father which is in heaven" (Matthew 5:16).

***

TODAY, LOVINGLY BUT FIRMLY, TAKE YOUR STAND.

JUNE 27

Are You in the Fire Today?

Think it not strange concerning the fiery trial which is to try you.

(1 Peter 4:12)

If you could talk to the three Hebrew children about the fiery furnace, perhaps they'd describe their experience this way:

"The fire was all over us. Our robes were ablaze, but amazingly, our skin was unaffected. We had no idea what was going on. Then something moved among the ashes; *we were not alone!*

"Suddenly, out of the smoke came a shining, gleaming figure ... We never got His name ... He never said it ... He never said anything. *But just knowing He was there brought us comfort in the fire. His presence gave us protection in the midst of the crisis.*

"Now, we don't mean that the fire went out. No, it still burned; but the brightness of the flames was eclipsed by the brilliance of His presence.

"We never saw Him again; *He only showed up when we needed Him most.* But one thing is certain; looking back we're glad they dragged us from the presence of the wicked one, into the presence of the

Righteous One! For in His presence we learned that, 'No weapon that is formed against [us] shall prosper'" (Isaiah 54:17).

Are you walking through fire today? If so, you're not alone—He's there with you! Take courage!

***

WHEN HE BRINGS YOU OUT, YOU'LL KNOW HIM BETTER, TRUST HIM MORE, AND YOU'LL HAVE SOMETHING REALLY WORTHWHILE TO SHARE.

JUNE 28

Do You Have Trouble With Your Temper?

He that hath no rule over his own spirit is like a city ... without walls. (Proverbs 25:28)

When a person loses his temper, we say he "flew off the handle." This refers to the head of a hammer coming loose from its handle as the carpenter uses it. When this happens, three things always follow:

First, the hammer becomes useless. When you lose your temper, you lose your effectiveness. You lose respect, you lose control, and anything you say is usually unproductive.

Second, the hammer head will hurt anything in its path. Our children can carry the scars of our anger with them until the day they die. We may not realize we inflicted scars, and we may never have intended to. But angry words cause wounds and become the pattern of abuse that our children pick up and use with their children. Anger has a long reach.

Third, repairing the damage can take time. The person who loses his temper may recover quickly, but the victim of that anger rarely does. Solomon says, "He that is slow to anger is better than the mighty;

and he that ruleth his spirit than he that taketh a city" (Proverbs 16:32).

***

ASK GOD TO HELP YOU KEEP YOUR TEMPER TODAY—NO ONE ELSE NEEDS IT!

JUNE 29

God, I Need to Find You!

You will ... find me when you seek me with all your heart.

(Jeremiah 29:13 NIV)

More and more I find myself searching for the assurance of His presence, rather than the answer to my problem. After all, what's a problem if He's there? He doesn't have to do anything but just *be there,* and all is well!

If you're searching for God today, He may be closer than you think. Job said, "Behold, I go forward, but he is not there; and backward, but I cannot perceive him: On the left hand, where he doth work" (Job 23:8-9). Listen: *Job just told you where to find God!*

If you were looking for someone and you knew where he or she worked, you wouldn't have far to look. Job said, "He works on the left hand..."

We always look on the right hand, because it symbolizes the place of power. But the left hand is where His strength is made perfect in our weakness (see 2 Corinthians 12:9), and His grace can be seen working in the ashes of our disappointment and failure.

Perhaps you think God's only at work when blessings come. No! It's when the blessings are *delayed* that He's working on your faith and character. His blessing is the reward that comes *after* you learn obedience through your experience (see Hebrews 5:8).

***

I WOULDN'T TAKE ANYTHING IN EXCHANGE FOR WHAT I'VE LEARNED DURING HARD TIMES, FOR IT WAS THEN THAT GOD HAD MY COMPLETE ATTENTION. HOW ABOUT YOU?

JUNE 30

He's the Lighthouse

I am the Lord, I change not. (Malachi 3:6)

One night the captain of a battleship spotted a strange light rapidly closing in on them. He ordered his signalman to flash a message to the unidentified vessel: "Alter your course ten degrees to the south." Back came the reply, "Alter *your* course ten degrees to the north." More determined, he snapped a second order. "Alter *your* course ten degrees—I am the CAPTAIN!" The response came back, "Alter *your* course ten degrees—I am Seaman Third Class Smith!" By this time the light was growing brighter and larger. Infuriated, the captain personally signaled, "Alter *your* course. *I am a battleship!"* The reply came back quickly, "Alter *your* course; *I am a lighthouse!"*

Over six hundred times in the Bible, Jesus is called "Lord"—that means He's the boss. New Testament believers greeted one another by saying, "Jesus is Lord!" It meant His word is final. He can call for any change He wants or demand any price He chooses. His Word demands it, and His love deserves it!

***

EVEN IF YOU THINK YOU'RE A BATTLESHIP,
REMEMBER, HE'S THE LIGHTHOUSE!

JULY 1

Don't Do It!

Grieve not the Holy Spirit. (Ephesians 4:30)

The Holy Spirit can be grieved easily! When you decide to do your own thing, He backs off and says, *I can't be a party to that.* When that happens, you've cut yourself off from His help and His function in your life. Now that doesn't mean He leaves you, for you are "...sealed [by the Holy Spirit] unto the day of redemption" (Ephesians 4:30). What it means is you're disconnected from His favor, His strength, and His guidance. Can you afford to live without those?

There are certain things the Holy Spirit will and won't do. For example, He won't help you to cheat and escape the consequences of getting caught. But He will lead you to repentance, help you to make restitution to those you've wronged, and begin to walk in honesty. He won't help you to seduce somebody, cover it up, and escape the pain that comes from it. But He will help you to resist temptation, terminate the relationship, seek His forgiveness, and walk in purity.

The Holy Spirit delights in helping you by: (1) giving you the wisdom you need to make better decisions; (2) motivating you to act righteously and courageously; (3) enabling you to stand up to evil and do what's right.

***

TODAY, TREASURE YOUR RELATIONSHIP WITH THE HOLY SPIRIT, AND PURPOSE IN YOUR HEART NEVER TO GRIEVE HIM!

Do You Really Want to Get Well?

Do you want to get well? (John 5:6 NIV)

That's what Jesus asked this man. For thirty-eight years his condition had brought him the sympathy of others. It also gave him an excuse to say, "I'm not responsible." Wrong! *All* of us are responsible for two things—our attitudes and our decisions!

We've all been hurt, but if you're still using it twenty years later, you're not a victim of *circumstance,* you're a victim *by choice.* You see, a victim's somebody who thinks negative attention is better than none at all.

Jesus said, "If ye do not forgive, neither will your Father which is in heaven forgive you" (Mark 11:26). Those words presuppose that somebody has hurt you. They also hold you responsible for your reaction. Jesus said, "If you don't forgive, you won't receive forgiveness." Others may have taken from you in the past, but if you remain bitter they'll take even *more* from you in the future.

Maybe you're thinking, *If they'd only come back and ask for my forgiveness.* ..Is that what you're waiting for? Don't waste your time! The key to happiness is in *your* hands, not *theirs;* that key is forgiveness!

Are you waiting for someone to say, "I forgive you," before you can forgive yourself and move on? What if he or she never does? Here's what you need to do: (1) apologize; (2) make amends if you can; (3) forgive yourself; and (4) move on (see Philippians 3:13).

***

IF YOU REALLY WANT TO GET WELL, THESE ARE THE STEPS!

JULY 3

Learning From Your Elders

The four and twenty elders ... cast their crowns before the throne, saying, Thou art worthy..."

(Revelation 4:10-11)

There are two extremes you need to beware of. The first is *wanting to spend time with God—but failing to touch others with His love.* Isaiah saw God's glory in the Temple as few men ever had, and it caused him to exclaim, "Woe is me!" (Isaiah 6:5). Getting close to God tends to have that effect on you. Next, he heard the words, "Whom shall I send?" and he responded, "Here am I; Send me." (Isaiah 6:8). You see, he'd moved from storing up to pouring out, from receiving to giving. Have you made that transition yet? Remember, you're blessed to be a blessing to others (see Genesis 12:3).

The second extreme is *working for God—but never spending any time with Him!* Listen: "The four and twenty elders ... cast their crowns before the throne, saying, Thou art worthy..." In God's presence, crowns lose their luster, the accolades of men are unimportant, and our greatest accomplishments seem like dusty stones gathered by bored children. When the elders found that place, they were willing to relinquish all their accomplishments (their crowns), for one moment of intimacy with God.

Imagine turning away from the things that others crave and celebrate, because of an emptiness at the core of your being that only His presence can fill.

***

HAVE YOU MADE THAT DISCOVERY YET?

JULY 4

Listen to His Voice!

He that hath an ear, let him hear what the Spirit saith.

(Revelation 2:7)

Learn to recognize the voice of the Holy Spirit. Your future depends on it! God may speak to you through others, but He wants you to learn how to recognize His voice for yourself. That's why Paul says, "The man without the Spirit does not accept the things that come from the Spirit ... because they are spiritually discerned" (1 Corinthians 2:14 NIV).

Unless you learn how to recognize His voice, you'll be like the pilot whose instruments failed, so he announced to the passengers, "Ladies and gentlemen, I don't know where we're going, but you'll be happy to know we're making great time!"

Remember these five guiding principles: (1) *Listen to His voice before you listen to the voice of doubters.* Without faith you have no future! (2) *Listen to His voice before you listen to the ideas and suggestions of others.* Ideas are not commands. (3) *Listen to His voice and your attitude will change miraculously.* When you've heard from Him, you can face anything. (4) *Listen to His voice before you make any commitment of your time, resources, and strength.* They're too precious to waste. (5) *Listen to His voice before you make any significant change in your life.* Otherwise, you may regret it.

Recognizing His voice is what will enable you to ... know your assignment ... discern pitfalls ... and release your faith for the next season of achievement.

***

TODAY PRAY, "LORD, TEACH ME TO DISCERN YOUR VOICE. IN ALL THINGS LET ME BE LED BY YOUR PRECIOUS HOLY SPIRIT. AMEN."

JULY 5

Lessons From Lepers

Jesus ... said, Were there not ten cleansed? but where are the nine?

(Luke 17:17)

If you take a moment today to read how Jesus healed these ten lepers, you'll learn three very important lessons.

1. *They seized the moment!* Listen: "They lifted up their voices, and said ... Have mercy on us" (Luke 17:13). Desperate people do desperate things. Who cares about appearances when you're dying? Jesus was passing! The most frightening thing that can happen to any of us is for Jesus to pass us by. That's why they seized the moment, and cried out to Him. You see, nobody can hear you like Jesus (see Psalm 118:5).

2. *They had to "walk it out."* Their healing was not immediate—it was a process. Listen: "As they went, they were cleansed" (Luke 17:14). Often that's how it works. It's not simply one step, but a relentless plowing through obstacles and insecurities until you get to your miracle. But you appreciate it more when you have to "walk it out" day by day, depending on God.

3. *Only one returned to give thanks.* That's why Jesus asked, "Where are the nine?" (Luke 17:17). Were they too busy? Too self-absorbed? Or just plain forgetful? He said to the one who came back, "Thy faith hath made thee whole" (Luke 17:19). You see, healing can be found in many places, but you can only become whole when you spend time daily with Jesus!

***

HAVE YOU BEEN DOING ANY OF THAT LATELY?

JULY 6

Old Belief Systems

Don't become so well-adjusted to your culture that you fit into it without even thinking.

(Romans 12:2 TM)

Our culture consistently markets misinformation and half truths. Our parents, who grew up in this same culture, handed us the same old grid with which to interpret life—and we came up with some very wrong conclusions.

Here are a few examples: (1) *There's a special person out there who can make me happy!* Listen, only God can fix you! Hurting people only hurt others. (2) *When I have a particular position, or a certain amount of money, I'll be okay.* That's the "as-soon-as" lie, and it breeds frustration and discontent. (3) *I can't help it; it's just the way I am.* That's the "I'm-not-responsible" lie, and it's a shortcut to heartache.

When it comes to excuses, here are a few more real winners: (1) *I'm not the only one!* If everybody does it, does that mean God won't take it seriously? (2) *I don't see any harm in it.* Just who gave .you authority to play God? (3) *I'll just try it once.* If you do, does that mean there'll be no consequences?

What are the lies behind your excuses? Examine them—for they're keeping you in spiritual bondage! They must be unearthed and removed! The Bible calls this "renewing your mind" (see Romans 12:2). Jesus said when you know the truth, your old belief systems will be exposed, and you'll be free. (See John 8:32.)

***

IMAGINE BEING FREE TO BECOME ALL GOD HAS CALLED YOU TO BE!

JULY 7

Tenderheartedness

...Be ye kind ... tenderhearted...

(Ephesians 4:32)

Picture a mother caressing her child and singing softly to him. It makes no difference to absolutely no bearing on the love and tenderness she feels, for this is her child! God feels that way about you, and it's His desire that you learn to feel that way toward others.

But you say, "I don't feel very tenderhearted toward them!" Then ask God to change how you feel! The Bible doesn't say *feel* tenderhearted; it says *be* tenderhearted! It works like this: when you don't know what to say to the person grieving in the funeral home, just sit quietly beside them—that's being tenderhearted. When you don't know what to say to the friend lying in a hospital bed, just utter a prayer for them—that's being tenderhearted.

Sometimes tenderheartedness simply means picking up that person who needs a ride to church; or holding that crying baby while his mother deals with an upset toddler; or secretly leaving groceries on a back porch, because that family is going through a hard time financially.

Listen: "Be ready with a meal or a bed when it's needed. Why, some have extended hospitality to angels without ever knowing it!" (See Hebrews 13:2 TM.)

***

THAT'S BEING TENDERHEARTED!

JULY 8

Are You Hurting?

He healeth the broken in heart, and bindeth up their wounds.

(Psalm 147:3)

If you're not hurting, before this day is over you'll meet someone who is. Behind the smile you'll find a broken heart or a wounded spirit—and you have the answer: "He healeth the broken in heart." Often it's because someone took a wrong direction, or never consulted God in the first place. After Peter denied his Lord, he went out and wept bitterly. He remembered how wonderful it had been to walk with Jesus. He remembered the Master's words, "You will deny Me three times" (Matthew 26:75 NAS). He was so sure that it could never happen to him—but it did. Sound familiar?

Maybe you find yourself today in circumstances you never dreamed you would be in. Divorced? Unemployed? Sick? Depressed? No will to live? Never discuss your problem with someone who is incapable of solving it—take it to Jesus. He's a heart specialist. He has walked every path and felt every pain. Everything you need is available through Him today, but you've got to reach for Him. "Cast thy burden upon the Lord, and he shall sustain thee" (Psalm 55:22). That doesn't mean He'll take you out, but it does mean He'll bring you *through.*

✳✳✳

WHY DON'T YOU GO TO HIM TODAY? HE'S THE HEALER OF BROKEN HEARTS.

JULY 9

Learning to Live Together

All of you together are Christ's body, and each one of you is a separate and necessary part of it.

(1 Corinthians 12:27 NLT)

Take away one link and the chain breaks. Take away one player and the game's lost. Even a tiny screw missing from your carburetor can bring the entire car to a screeching halt. What's the point? Simply this—we need each other! The poet John Donne wrote, "No man is an island." So let's stop *acting* like one!

To make life work you've got to learn how to: (1) lean on others, yet know how to lend them your support; (2) be generous enough to give, yet humble enough to receive; (3) be honest enough to confess, yet always willing to forgive. Are you getting the idea?

Love and acceptance are not optional—neither are tolerance, understanding, and patience. *You know—all the qualities you need from others when your "humanity" crowds out your "divinity"!*

Listen carefully, "...Take delight in honoring each other ... Be patient in trouble, and prayerful always.

When God's children are in need, you be the one to help them out" (Romans 12:10-13 TLB).

You ask, "Why should I do that?" Because each of us is worth it, even when we don't act like it, *feel* like it, or *deserve* it. Furthermore, since none of us is an independent, self-sufficient, super-capable, all-powerful hotshot, let's quit acting like one!

***

LIFE CAN BE LONELY ENOUGH WITHOUT PLAYING THAT GAME!

JULY 10

Ya Gotta Have Heart!

Be strong and courageous ... for the Lord ... goes with you

(Deuteronomy 31:6 NAS)

In San Diego's famous Sea World, you can actually see ducks on roller skates. But when you get close, you'll notice—their heart's just aren't in it! You may smile, but many of us are like that!

If you want your life to count, find a cause greater than yourself, and put everything you've got into it (see John 12:24). Remember Nehemiah? He risked his all to rebuild Jerusalem. In spite of constant threats and hostility, he finished in record time. Why? Because "the people had a heart and mind [the courage] to work" (Nehemiah 4:6 AMP).

In an 1828 copy of *Webster's Dictionary,* the word *courage* is defined as "that quality which enables us to face difficulty and danger ... without fear or depression."

Then Daniel Webster, a committed Christian, added the words of Moses as he handed over the leadership to Joshua. Listen: "Be strong and courageous, do not be afraid ... for the Lord your God is the one who goes with you. He will not fail you or forsake you"

(Deuteronomy 31:6 NAS). Even at 120 years old, Moses was still telling the people, "Ya gotta have heart!" Why? *Because anything worth having is worth fighting for!*

It takes "heart" to deal with a child's willful defiance ... or face your own fears ... or pick up the pieces and start over again. It's easy to *talk* about what's wrong, but it takes "heart" to *do* something about it. That kind of courage only comes from God.

***

HAVE YOU TALKED TO HIM TODAY?

JULY 11

How Do You Treat Hurting People?

We must help the weak. (Acts 20:35 NIV)

Don't get side-tracked by people's pain or problems. After all, it's probably just the result of their sin. Get them converted and the problem will solve itself. Anyway, feeding the poor is something "liberals" do! Who thinks like that? I used to—*but not anymore!*

We can be conservative and still be compassionate. Jesus wouldn't give an inch when it came to the truth, but around hurting people, "He was moved with compassion" (Matthew 9:36).

Sadly, a lot of us are only moved with indignation, but then, that's easier, isn't it? That way we don't have to ... get our hands dirty ... take risks ... feel what it's like to hurt ... or deal with the thorny side of an issue that has no easy answers. Look out! *People don't care how much you know, until they first know how much you care!*

Listen to this conversation between God and some very religious people in the Old Testament. They said, "Why don't you see our sacrifices? Why don't you hear our prayers?" (Isaiah 58:3 TLB). *God's answer should make all of us do some real soul searching.* Listen:

"Feed the hungry! Help those in trouble! Then ... the Lord will guide you continually, and satisfy you with all good things, and keep you healthy too" (Isaiah 58:10-11 TLB). What a promise!

Jesus said that we'll be judged and rewarded according to how we treat hurting people. (See Matthew 25:34-40; Colossians 3:12-14; and James 4:11.)

***

SO, ASK YOURSELF TODAY, "HOW DO I TREAT THEM?"

JULY 12

The Power of Habit

He kneeled upon his knees three times a day, and prayed.

(Daniel 6:10)

People don't decide their futures. They decide their habits, and their habits decide their futures. Recently I decided to rise earlier and spend the first hours of my day in prayer and the Word. To do it I had to give up late night television. Experience has taught me that if I don't get into God's presence and stay there, nothing else goes right. It was a decision of my spirit—my flesh has been opposed to it from day one. Some days are easier than others, *but the rewards are worth it!*

The people who made a difference were "creatures of habit." Even in the face of death, Daniel "kneeled upon his knees three times a day, and prayed." Paul said, "I ... cease not to give thanks for you, making mention of you in my prayers" (Ephesians 1:15-16).

In the life of every great man or woman of God, you will discover a foundation of holy habits from which the power and the presence of God flows.

***

TAKE SOME TIME TODAY AND THINK ABOUT YOUR HABITS—ESPECIALLY THE ONES YOU NEED TO ESTABLISH.

JULY 13

Getting Back Up

As the disciples stood round about him, he rose up, and came into the city.

(Acts 14:20)

When a crowd stoned Paul and left him for dead, the other disciples stood around waiting to see if he would get back up. *And if you're waiting for others to come and lift you, it probably won't happen.* The first move is up to you—when you make it, God will send others to help.

Paul said, "We were troubled on every side; without were fightings, within were fears. Nevertheless God, that comforteth those that are cast down, comforted us by the coming of Titus" (2 Corinthians 7:5-6). We need more believers like Titus, with the ministry of encouragement. We give in so quickly. We blame circumstances or we blame others. Adam started it all: "The woman whom thou gavest to be with me, she gave me of the tree, and I did eat" (Genesis 3:12). When God asked Eve about it, *she blamed the devil!*

Until you accept responsibility for yourself, you won't get anywhere with God. Until you accept correction without resentment, your life will remain on hold.

Get up! Your problems aren't unique—you're not the first person to fail. You would be amazed at how many of us are fighting the same battles, and showing some of the same scars. *Your problem isn't that you fell; it's that you haven't gotten back up!*

***

BE LIKE THE MAN WHO SAID, "I'M NEVER DOWN. I'M ALWAYS GETTING BACK UP!"

JULY 14

The Grateful Heart

Giving thanks always for all things unto God.

(Ephesians 5:20)

A monk in a monastery took a vow of silence. Every seven years he was permitted to speak. When asked if he had anything to say after his first seven years, he replied, "Yes. The bed is too hard." Another seven years went by, and he was asked again if he'd like to say something. He said, "Yes. The food is terrible." Finally, another seven years passed, and he was asked once again if he had anything to say. He plied, "Yes. I quit." Whereupon the head of the monastery said to him, *"I'm glad, because you've done nothing but complain since you got here!"* The point is—what will you be remembered for—the good you always found, or the bad you never failed to point out?

Jesus once healed ten lepers, but only one came back to thank Him: "And Jesus answering said, 'Were there not ten cleansed? But where are the nine?'" (Luke 17:17). Can you hear the disappointment in His voice? He noticed their lack of gratitude, and He still does. Then He turned to the one who came back and said, "Thy faith hath made thee whole" (Luke

17:19). What a statement! The others were *healed,* but the one who had a grateful heart was made *whole.*

***

TODAY—CULTIVATE AN ATTITUDE OF GRATITUDE!

JULY 15

Tested by Success

Promotion and power come ... from God.

(Psalm 75:6-7 TLB)

Success exposes you to four things:

1. *Jealousy from those around you.* In the story of the Prodigal Son, his elder brother was angry, because the attention he once had was now focused on somebody else, and he couldn't stand it. When God blesses you, resistance and resentment will surface in those who feel left out.

2. *Insecurity in those around you who are fearful.* When you move to a new level of blessing, it usually involves change, and that's threatening to those who only know how to do things a certain way.

3. *The attacks of the enemy.* He doesn't mess with low impact Christians. He always targets those who are of special value to God. So you had better put on your armor and get ready for battle today.

4. *A test of every relationship in your life.* Those who feel dwarfed or displaced by your success will often say, "He's just not the same anymore."

Some will seek to control you out of the fear of losing you.
You'll be tested—so get ready.

***

REMEMBER, WALK IN LOVE TOWARD EVERYONE, FOR THE ONE WHO PROMOTED YOU CAN DEMOTE YOU JUST AS EASILY!

JULY 16

Keep Looking Through the Storm Until You See Him

Be of good cheer; it is I; be not afraid.

(Matthew 14:27)

Jesus sent His disciples into the storm knowing that they would be different when they came out. They had seen Him heal the leper, and even raise the dead, but they didn't know He had authority over the wind and the waves.

There are things you can only learn by getting into the boat and going through the storm. *He revealed himself to them in the worst experience of their lives.* He defied impossible conditions to reach them. He proved there is no circumstance you're facing today in which He will not be with you.

Peter said, "Lord, if it be thou, bid me come unto thee on the water" (Matthew 14:28). When Jesus said, "Come," Peter did not step out on the *water;* he stepped out on the *Word.*

He believed that if Jesus told him to do the impossible, *the power to obey would be inherent in His Word!* So why did Jesus rebuke him? *Because he stopped short of what might have been. He accepted less than he could have had.* Sound familiar?

***

HIS WORD TO YOU TODAY IS, "BE OF GOOD CHEER; IT IS I; BE NOT AFRAID."

JULY 17

Time Out!

Come ye yourselves apart ... and rest a while.

(Mark 6:31)

If the light on your inner dashboard's flashing red, you're probably carrying too much, too far, too fast. If you don't pull over, you'll be sorry, and so will those who love you. But, if you've the courage to pull over and make some changes, you'll be well rewarded. Be forewarned, however, about three problems you'll encounter:

First, you'll experience "false guilt." By saying no to people to whom you've always said yes, you'll feel a twinge of guilt. Ignore it—it's false guilt based on wrong thinking and screwed-up values. Retime your conscience to God's Word and the priorities of His Kingdom.

Second, you'll experience hostility and misunder-standing. Certain people won't understand your slower pace—especially those who are still in the sinking boat you just stepped out of. Stick to your guns. In time, those who matter most will see the wisdom of what you're doing. Hey, they may even follow you!

Third, you'll gain some personal and painful in-sights. By not filling every spare moment with activity, you'll begin to get in touch with the real you—and you may not like some of what you see. But if you stick with it, you'll turn the corner and be well on the road to a healthier, happier, freer, and more fulfilling life.

***

YOUR GOAL IS TO FULFILL YOUR DESTINY, AND IN THE PROCESS, TO STAY IN BALANCE, IN GOOD HEALTH, AND IN GOD'S WILL!

JULY 18

Be Specific

Let your requests be made known unto God.

(Philippians 4:6)

Have you talked to God yet about the specific things that are troubling you? Only when you've made specific requests, can you identify specific answers when they come, and praise God for them. Listen: "...Whatever you ask for in prayer, believe that you have received it, and it will be yours" (Mark 11:24 NIV). Sometimes we pray in generalities to keep from being disappointed or to "rationalize" our lack of results. Ever do that?

Your concept of God will determine how you approach Him every time. How do you see Him? As caring or condemning? Isolated or involved? Willing or reluctant? Here are a few helpful insights to make your prayers more effective:

(1) *Remove any hindrance.* Listen: "...If our hearts do not condemn us, we have confidence before God and receive from him anything we ask" (1 John 3:21-22 NIV). (2) *Stand on His Word.* Listen: "If ye abide in me, and my words abide in you, ye shall ask what ye will, and it shall be done unto you" (John 15:7). (3) *Refuse to speak doubt.* Listen: "...He that cometh

to God must believe that he is ... a rewarder of them that diligently seek him" (Hebrews 11:6).

***

TODAY, GET INTO HIS PRESENCE AND "LET YOUR REQUESTS BE MADE KNOWN."

JULY 19

A Hunger for God

My soul thirsts for God.

(Psalm 42:2 NIV)

What comes to mind when you think of the word *godliness?* Rules? Regulations? Religious people who point fingers and say, "Thou shalt not"? Little wonder people avoid us! Is godliness even possible in this age of fast-lane drivers and Internet shoppers? Or do we need to return to the days of *Little House on the Prairie* to live godly lives?

No! Godliness is not a culture—it's an attitude of heart. It's got little to do with how a person looks (although some of us get hung up on that), or what they drive, or where they live. It has nothing to do with personal preference, or the "standards" that some of us like to impose on others. Listen: "Man looketh on the outward appearance, but the Lord looketh on the heart" (1 Samuel 16:7). Godliness is an "inside job."

I'm convinced that the person who is truly godly is one ... whose heart is sensitive toward God ... who takes God and His Word seriously ... and who hungers and thirsts for more of Him. David cried, "My soul thirsts for God" (Psalm 42:2 NIV). That's it!

You can be rich or poor, young or old, urban or rural, follower or leader, black or white, married or single, Democrat or Republican—*none* of that matters!

***

WHAT MATTERS IS YOUR INNER CRAVING TO KNOW GOD, TO LISTEN TO HIM, AND TO WALK WITH HIM.

JULY 20

Staying Clean

How can a young man stay way pure...?

(Psalm 119:9 TLB)

In Psalm 119 God gives us rules for living clean in a dirty world. Here they are:

1) *Seek the Lord on a regular basis.* Listen: "I seek you with all my heart; do not let me stray from your commands" (verse 10 NIV). Include God in all your decisions, your plans, your struggles, and even your fun times.

2) *Hide His precepts in your heart.* Listen: "I have hidden your word in my heart that I might not sin against you" (verse 11 NIV). Commit the Scriptures to memory. Once they're on deposit, you can withdraw them any time you need to.

3) *Talk to others about God.* Listen: "I recount all the laws that come from your mouth" (verse 13 NIV). Something wonderful happens when you begin to talk about the things of God; you grow stronger in the process.

4) *Rejoice in Him.* Listen: "I rejoice in following your statutes" (verse 14 NIV). Smile—others are watching. Let your delight show!

5) *Meditate on His Word throughout the day.* Listen: "I meditate on your precepts and consider your ways" (verse 15 NIV). Weave it into your driving time, your workouts, your quiet time in the morning, and before you go to sleep each night.

***

THAT'S HOW TO STAY CLEAN IN A DIRTY WORLD!

JULY 21

Don't Just Sit There!

Be strong and of good courage, and do it...

(1 Chronicles 28:20)

Larry Walters got tired of sitting around doing nothing. So on July 2, 1982, he rigged forty-two helium-filled weather balloons to a lawn chair, and lifted off. Armed with a pellet gun to shoot down a few balloons should he fly too high, he was shocked when he quickly reached 16,000 feet—and he wasn't the only one! Pilots reported seeing "some guy in a lawn chair floating through the sky." Forty-five minutes later, when he landed in Long Beach, he was asked why he did it. He replied, *"It was something I had to do. I just couldn't sit there any longer."*

When the Prodigal Son finally got sick and tired of being sick and tired, he said, "I will arise and go to my father..." (Luke 15:18). He refused to sit in his hog pen another day! When Israel came to the River Jordan, God told the priests carrying the Ark to step into the water and it would dry up. But nothing happened until they took that first step!

There could be a song in you that's never been sung, a sermon that's never been preached, a gift that's just waiting to be released! The moment you stop holding back, the doors will open, the right people will come, and the resources will be provided.

***

BUT YOU'VE GOT TO TAKE THAT FIRST STEP!

JULY 22

Two Kinds of Honor

How can ye believe, which receive honour one of another, and seek not the honour that cometh from God only?

(John 5:44)

Honor comes from two sources—Christ or the crowd. If you see the crowd as your source, then pleasing them becomes everything. John the Baptist publicly rebuked the sins of a king, and it cost him his life. The three Hebrew children refused to bow to another god—they wouldn't even *nod* in his direction. Paul rebuked Peter for his racial prejudice, and God put it in the Bible for all of us to learn from it.

These men didn't know crowd psychology or marketing strategies. *They knew God,* and that's why they prevailed. Daniel said, "The people that do know their God shall be strong, and do exploits" (Daniel 11:32).

What we need is not more talent and pulpit finesse; *we need men and women who hear from God,* and who aren't afraid to declare what He says. They may not be popular with the crowd, but God will honor them. And when it is all said and done, can you think of anything more important?

***

MAKE HONORING HIM YOUR LIFE'S GOAL.

JULY 23

Keep Your Eyes on Jesus

No doubt about it. God is good ... But I nearly missed it ... I was looking the other way.

(Psalm 73:1-3 TM)

David almost went "over the edge" looking at other people. The ones who really bothered him were those who broke all the rules, yet seemed to prosper. It's one of the oldest weapons in the devil's arsenal—getting you to look at others. The trouble begins when you try to figure it out. God will settle the score. The first time Jesus came to save; the next time He'll come to *reign*—and settle all accounts.

When you're tempted to ask, "What's going on here?" just remember, the last chapter hasn't been written. John said, "And I saw the dead, small and great, stand before God; and the books were opened" (Revelation 20:12). There will be an audit.

But if you're not careful, you can develop a negative attitude and ruin your own future. You don't have to understand everything, and thank God you don't have to explain it. David said, "When I thought to know this, it was too painful for me; until I went into the sanctuary of God; then understood I their end" (Psalm 73:16-17). Just ask God to give you patience under provocation, and love in the face of injustice. Above all, never let your attitudes and actions be determined by other people.

***

KEEP YOUR EYES ON JESUS—HE'S YOUR SOURCE, YOUR SECURITY, AND YOUR PEACE!

JULY 24

A Prayer for Every Day

Order my steps in thy word.

(Psalm 119:133)

David knew from painful experience where his flesh would take him, and he didn't want to go there anymore. So he cries, "Order my steps in thy word: and let not any iniquity have dominion over me" (Psalm 119:133). *Iniquity* means "to bend in the direction of" or "incline toward." He's asking God to deliver him from a nature that is bent toward sin, and always inclined to go the wrong way. Sure sounds familiar to me. How about you?

In the Christian life, the only way to win is to surrender. *You* can't live it, but *He* can. Listen to Paul: "I live; yet not I, but Christ liveth in me" (Galatians 2:20). Slide out from behind the wheel today and let Him take over. You know what happens when *you* drive!

Maybe you're asking, "But what's my part in all of this?" First, *to live in the place of constant surrender to Him;* and second, *to fill your heart with His Word.* Listen: "Thy word have I hid in mine heart, that I might not sin against thee" (Psalm 119:11). Also, remember to stay filled with the Spirit, for the Christian life is not the product of fleshly effort; it's the fruit of the Spirit (see Galatians 5:22-23).

***

TODAY AND EVERY DAY PRAY, "ORDER MY STEPS IN THY WORD."

JULY 25

Before and After

But ye shall receive power, after that the Holy Ghost is come upon you. (Acts 1:8)

The best argument in favor of a Spirit-filled life is those who live it. No illustration is more powerful than the life of Peter. *Before* the Day of Pentecost, he denied Jesus in weakness. *After* it he faced the crowd with boldness and proclaimed that Jesus is Lord. That day, 3,000 were born into God's family.

Before Pentecost Jesus gave Peter one of the harshest rebukes in the Word of God, "Get thee behind me, Satan ... for thou savourest not the things that be of God, but those that be of men" (Matthew 16:23). Peter was opinionated, critical, and often spoke without thinking.

But what a difference we find in Peter *after* Pentecost. Now he is *filled, broken,* and *channeled.* Listen to him: "You should be like one big happy family ... loving one another with tender hearts and humble minds. Don't repay evil for evil. Don't snap back at those who say unkind things about you. Instead, pray for God's help for them, for we are to be kind to others, and God will bless us for it" (1 Peter 3:8-9 TLB).

Is this the same guy? No! He's the new Spirit-filled model, and he's an example of what God wants you and me to be.

***

SO, GET INTO GOD'S PRESENCE TODAY AND ASK HIM TO FILL YOU AGAIN WITH HIS SPIRIT.

JULY 26

Mother, Stand by the Cross!

Now there stood by the cross of Jesus his mother.

(John 19:25)

Where were His disciples? Listen: "Then all the disciples forsook him, and fled" (Matthew 26:56). Couldn't you have understood if His mother had turned her back and walked away, too? Or collapsed under the pain of watching them crucify Him? But the record reads for all time, "Now there stood by the cross of Jesus his mother." I'm convinced that *few things can get the attention of God faster than the prayers of a godly mother.* More than once, in the worst moments of our lives it has been a mother's prayers that sustained us and kept us alive. Many of the blessings we've enjoyed have simply been *transferred credits* from their lives and walk with God.

Many times in the Bible it was a woman's voice that settled the issues and changed history. Remember Deborah, Huldah, and Ruth? Solomon says, "Charm is deceptive, and beauty is fleeting; but a woman who fears the Lord is to be praised" (Proverbs 31:30 NIV). If, as we are told, men are what their mothers make them, then what we need today is an *army of commit-*

ted Christian mothers who will stand by the Cross and refuse to allow one more generation to go to hell.

***

MOTHER, ARE YOU LIVING FOR JESUS TODAY?

JULY 27

Get to Know Him!

The Lord is good, a strong hold in the day of trouble; and he knoweth them that trust in him.

(Nahum 1:7)

What you believe about God will determine everything else in your life. If you believe He is *good,* then you'll have the confidence to go to Him in the day of trouble. If you're not *convinced* of this, you'll turn to everybody and everything else—and only when you've exhausted all other possibilities will you turn to Him. Listen: "When trouble comes, he is the place to go! And he knows everyone who trusts in him!" (Nahum 1:7 TLB). He also knows those who *don't!*

Now, there are two parts to this. First, *what you know* and believe about God; and second, *what God knows* and believes about you. Many of us wait until the day of trouble to discover the faith we *thought* we had isn't there. You can't even approach God without faith, and you certainly can't please Him without it. (See Hebrews 11:6.)

Child of God, are you so wrapped up in business and other things that you've neglected your spiritual life? If you are, then start doing something about it today. Get into God's Word. Get acquainted with just how good He is, and how great His promises are.

***

GET TO KNOW HIM NOW, SO THAT WHEN TROUBLE COMES HE'LL KNOW YOU!

JULY 28

Keep It Simple

What would please the Lord? ... Do what is right ... love mercy ... walk humbly with your God.

(Micah 6:7-8, paraphrase)

Listen to these words: "With what shall I come to the Lord ... burnt offerings ... thousands of rams ... rivers of oil? Shall I present my firstborn ... for the sin of my soul?" (Micah 6:6-7 NAS). Do you sometimes feel like you can *never* live up to certain religious standards, or please God? Does religion look to you like a long, drawn-out series of deeply painful acts, designed to appease a deity who delights in watching you squirm?

Thank God for Micah, who tells us to "keep it simple." Listen: "What would please the Lord?" He gives us three answers:

1) *To do right!* That means even when nobody else is. Why? Because you want to maintain your confidence before God. (See 1 John 3:21-22.) Nothing is more important than that!

2) *To love mercy!* Do you remember the words to the old song: "These boots were made for walkin', and that's just what they'll do. One of these days these boots are gonna walk all over you"? Good

tune—terrible theology! Jesus went through life *lifting* people, not *walking on* them, and His Word to you today is, "Go, and do thou likewise" (Luke 10:37).

3) *To walk humbly with your God.* When God promotes you, your greatest challenge will always be to make sure *He* gets the glory.

***

THE TRUTH IS, YOU DON'T HAVE A THING THAT HE DIDN'T GIVE TO YOU—AND THAT WILL NEVER CHANGE. (SEE DEUTERONOMY 8:17-18.)

JULY 29

Others May Not Notice, But God Does!

He will not forget your work and the love you have shown...

(Hebrews 6:10 NIV)

Thank you! Two simple words, but oh, how much they mean. Has it been a while since you heard them? You do so much for so many; now you just want a little appreciation in return.

Others may neglect to thank you, but know this—your Heavenly Father appreciates all you do and all you are. He has put you exactly where He needs you, and you are fulfilling His purpose every day!

When you understand that, you'll begin to find meaning in everything you do. He is the reason—*others* are just the beneficiaries!

Don't let somebody else's response decide the level of your joy! They may not notice, but God does. He records, and He rewards. Count on it!

If you feel unappreciated today, stop and read these words carefully: "Whatever you do, whether in word or deed, do it all in the name of the Lord..." (Colossians 3:17 NIV). *That's it—do it for Him!*

Why don't you pray this prayer: "Lord, all that I do today, I do for You. I know that You appreciate me—look at all the gifts that You have given me.

***

"IN RETURN I WILL PRAISE AND HONOR YOU THROUGHOUT THIS DAY, BY MY THOUGHTS, MY WORDS, AND MY ACTIONS. AMEN."

JULY 30

How to Make Things Turn Out Right

Whether we like it or not, we will obey the Lord our God.... For if we obey him, everything will turn out well for us.

(Jeremiah 42:6 TLB)

Many of us are "cafeteria Christians." We walk down the line and decide what we like and don't like. We pick some things and leave the rest. But it doesn't work. Listen: "Whether we like it or not, we will obey the Lord our God."

If you're a parent, you know that your job is not to make your children *happy,* but to make them obedient—for obedience brings happiness, while disobedience brings trouble. For example, if you let your children play with matches you may make them happy for a while, but only until they burn the house down! Breaking the speed limit may bring happiness to an immature teenager, but when it lands him in court, or in a car wreck, he'll change his mind in a hurry.

It was *after* David had been chastened that he wrote, "Your laws are my guide. I used to wander off until you punished me; now I closely follow all you say" (Psalm 119:66-67, TLB).

***

GOD'S PROMISE TO YOU TODAY IS THAT IF YOU WILL WALK IN OBEDIENCE, EVERYTHING WILL TURN OUT WELL FOR YOU.

JULY 31

Take the Time

To every thing there is a season ... a time to laugh ... a time to dance ... a time to love...

(Ecclesiastes 3:1-8)

When did you last take time to do these things that Solomon mentions? Can you even remember? Virginia Frazier writes: "This is the age of the half-read page. The quick hash and the mad dash. The bright night with the nerves tight. The plane hop and the brief stop. The lamp tan in a short span. The big shot in a good spot. The brain strain and the heart pain. The catnaps till the spring snaps. And the fun's done!"

Sobering! But does it really have to be like that? If it does, it's because you make it that way—and you are the only one who can change it. I know you're busy—we're all busy! But who says you can't have fun and enjoy life, even when the pace picks up?

Chuck Swindoll writes, "I refuse to force hilarity into the back seat every time responsibility takes the wheel. If the fun's gone, it's because we didn't want it around—not because it didn't fit."

I don't care if your "to do" list is as long as the horizon, you need to get back in balance and take

the time ... to laugh ... to love ... and to live. Why?
Because the Bible says so!

* * *

YOUR FAMILY AND FRIENDS WILL ENJOY YOU A LOT
MORE WHEN YOU DO!

AUGUST 1

Ditched!

Remember ye not the former things, neither consider the things of old. Behold, I will do a new thing.

(Isaiah 43:18-19)

After helping a lady whose car was in a ditch, I asked her what happened. She said, "I was looking in the rearview mirror instead of looking at the road ahead." What a thought! *There is no way to go forward if you're focused on what's behind.* You'll end in a ditch! Disconnect from the past, focus on the future, and move on with God. Give up all hope for a better yesterday. You can't change the past. You can only obsess over it and run from it—or accept it and be wiser.

There are over 500 Scriptures that tell us God is merciful and forgiving. But none of them are worth anything unless you accept His forgiveness—and then forgive yourself. Listen: "I, even I, am he that blotteth out thy transgressions for mine own sake, and will not remember thy sins" (Isaiah 43:25). God says *He* has forgiven and forgotten your sins, therefore *you* must—otherwise you make yourself better than God. That's spiritual pride in its worst form. The enemy can hurt you every day of your life if you don't forgive yourself, and let the past be the past. Child of God, take that weapon out of his hands today.

***

GOD WANTS TO DO A NEW THING IN YOUR LIFE—LET HIM.

AUGUST 2

You'll Find Him Where You Left Him

But they, supposing him to have been in the company, went a day's journey; and they sought him among their kinsfolk and acquaintance. And when they found him not, they turned back again to Jerusalem, seeking him.

(Luke 2:44-45)

It happens so easily. We get so busy with our battles, our projects, our ministries, and 101 other things that we fail to notice that Jesus is not with us. Jesus' parents returned to where they had last seen Him, *and so also must we.*

To renew us, God brings us back to our most recent encounter with Him. Back to basics. Yesterday's anointing will not sustain us in today's battles. David cried, "I shall be anointed with fresh oil" (Psalm 92:10). God sent manna to His children in the wilderness *each day.* Jesus taught His disciples to pray, "Give us this day our daily bread" (Matthew 6:11). Have you gathered your manna today? Have you eaten your *daily bread?*

In the world of banking we know that if you give out more than you take in, you'll end in bankruptcy. Are you on the verge of burnout and bankruptcy? If so, you need to move from being a Martha to being a Mary and sitting at His feet.

***

CHILD OF GOD, MAKE SURE HE'S WITH YOU.

AUGUST 3

Lord, Teach Me How to Live!

Teach us to make the most of our time...

(Psalm 90:12 NLT)

Last Christmas a neighbor of ours in his early forties was killed in a terrible accident. He and his wife had two teenagers. They'd also just built their dream home. The day it happened, another neighbor who happened to be in our home said to me, "I think I'll go home and hug my wife and kids." So often it takes tragedy to remind us of what *really* matters! It shouldn't, but it does!

When I hear of such things I wonder, *Did they live well? If they could come back for even a week, what would they do differently?*

None of us has any idea how long we have to live. Yet we act as if we're going to be here forever. We postpone things that deep down we know we want to do, and devise elaborate reasons for doing things that really aren't important.

The philosopher Henry David Thoreau wrote, "...I wished to live deliberately ... and not, when I came to die, discover that I had not lived...." What a wonderful outlook!

Paul could say, "I have fought a good fight, I have finished my course, I have kept the faith: Henceforth there is laid up for me a crown of righteousness, which the Lord, the righteous judge, shall give me at that day" (2 Timothy 4:7-8).

***

LIVE EACH DAY AS IF IT WAS YOUR LAST—FOR SOONER OR LATER, IT WILL BE!

AUGUST 4

Setting Boundaries

I will establish your borders.

(Exodus 23:31 NIV)

You won't know what your inheritance is if you don't learn to set boundaries. How far? How wide? Where's the fence line? You'll never enjoy or protect your inheritance without clearly defined boundaries. People (even well-meaning ones) will violate them, and walk "roughshod" through your life. In the Old Testament, Shammah fought for a tiny lentil patch, and the Bible recorded it. Why? Because that lentil patch was an *inheritance* from his father—it put food on his family's table, and guaranteed his children's future. Listen: "Shammah took his stand in the middle of the field ... and the Lord brought about a great victory" (2 Samuel 23:12 NIV).

Your boundaries are your values. What's important to you defines who you really are. Recently, a friend of mine told some people she worked with, *"When you violate my boundaries, you force me to make a decision, and you may not like that decision. I know where I got my boundaries from, and you wouldn't like me without them. That 'old me' was not a nice person. My Father is pleased with me the way I am, and you are the beneficiary of that. So please, respect my boundaries, and we'll get along just fine."* Like Shammah, she took her stand and established boundaries.

There are areas of your life that belong to God alone, and no one else should be allowed access to them.

***

SO, THE WORD FOR YOU TODAY IS "ESTABLISH YOUR BOUNDARIES."

AUGUST 5

Wounded Healers

And with his stripes we are healed.

(Isaiah 53:5)

Because Jesus was wounded, He received authority to bring healing to you and me. Out of His brokenness, others were made whole. Child of God, there's purpose to the pain. *Only the broken become masters at mending.* Paul said that God "comforteth us in all our tribulation, that we may be able to comfort them which are in any trouble, by the comfort wherewith we ourselves are comforted of God" (2 Corinthians 1:4).

Find God's purposes in the reversals of your life, and you'll turn them into stepping-stones to blessing. God doesn't waste experience. All of us have gone through things that we never imagined could have happened to us—but they did. The problem is, the same sunshine that melts the butter hardens the clay. Experience can make us hard and cold, or drive us into the arms of Jesus, where we find answers and compassion.

Today, you're going to meet people who are hurting. They'll relate to your *experience,* not your *theories.* Most won't even listen unless you've been there.

***

LET GOD USE YOUR WOUNDS AND YOUR PAIN TO MAKE YOU AN INSTRUMENT OF HEALING WHEREVER YOU GO.

AUGUST 6

God's Strange Choices

God hath chosen the foolish things ... weak things ... base things ... and things which are not ... that no flesh should glory in his presence.

(1 Corinthians 1:27-29)

God wants you to see things as He sees them. He wants you to look beyond the *obvious* and see the *actual.* Five loaves and two fish were just enough to feed one small boy for a day, but when he put it into the hands of Jesus, it fed 5,000 with plenty leftover.

When Mary and Joseph brought the baby Jesus into the Temple, Simeon saw in that small child God's salvation for the whole world (see Luke 2:28-30). May God help you today to see in what you've got, the potential to make a difference in this world around you. Listen: "Though thy beginning was small, yet thy latter end should greatly increase" (Job 8:7).

God's not looking for ability—He's looking for availability. If you've grown up believing that you're "less than," or that you don't "measure up," then it's time to renew your mind with the Word. God can take a tiny acorn and produce a mighty oak. He can take a tiny seed and produce a great harvest. He can take one surrendered, dedicated life and affect a whole family and its generations.

***

ASK THE LORD TO USE YOU TODAY. THEN GO OUT EXPECTING HIM TO DO IT!

AUGUST 7

Struggling to Believe

Lord, I believe; help thou mine unbelief.

(Mark 9:24)

The father in our story asked Jesus to heal his son, and Jesus told him to believe. His answer is worth noting: "Lord, I believe; help thou mine unbelief." We've all been there. We've reached inside ourselves to find a faith that wasn't there. If you find yourself in this position today, then there are some things you need to do.

First, get into the Word of God. Listen: "So then faith cometh by hearing, and hearing by the word of God" (Romans 10:17). The Bible is faith food, and as you read it faith will begin to grow inside you.

Next, bring people with faith into your life. Multiply your faith with the faith of others, and make your prayer a faith offering to God. Jesus said, "If two of you shall agree on earth as touching any thing that they shall ask, it shall be done for them of my Father which is in heaven" (Matthew 18:19).

Finally, remember that you're not coming to an auditor who's examining your books. You're coming to a loving Heavenly Father who knows your struggles.

***

WHEN YOU'VE REACHED UP AS FAR AS YOU CAN,
HE'LL REACH DOWN THE REST OF THE WAY.

AUGUST 8

The Rope Holders

They risked their lives for me.

(Romans 16:4 NIV)

When Paul was saved, word spread like wildfire. Religious leaders hired assassins to kill him. But some Christians took him by night to the top of the city wall and, using ropes, lowered him over the side in a basket. He escaped and went on to write epistles, build churches, and change history. The Bible doesn't tell us who these Christians were, but we know that had they been caught, it would have cost them their lives.

In Romans 16, Paul writes a doxology to the rope holders who risked their lives for him. They waved no banners, blew no trumpets, and demanded no applause. But without them the work of God would never have been accomplished.

Child of God, you may never be a preacher, or a singer, or a missionary; but by your prayers, your words of encouragement, and your financial support, you can *hold the rope* for those who are. The Day of Judgment will be a day of surprises. Many who have enjoyed the limelight will get little reward—for God saw their hearts and their selfish motives. And many others who seemed so unimportant, will be called to the frontline to hear the words, "Well done, good and faithful servant" (Matthew 25:21).

***

IF GOD HAS MADE YOU A ROPE HOLDER, HE HAS GIVEN YOU A PLACE OF HONOR IN HIS KINGDOM.

AUGUST 9

God Hears and Answers Prayer

I cried unto the Lord with my voice, and he heard me.

(Psalm 3:4)

A pastor friend once told of a lady who came for prayer at the end of one of his services. When he invited her to pray with him, she said, "No, it wouldn't do any good. I just don't think God hears me." He looked at her and said, "Would you mind saying a few curse words?" Greatly offended, she said, "No!" He said, "But why not?" "Because God would hear me!" she said. He replied, "So what you're telling me is God hears you if you *curse,* but He doesn't hear you if you *pray?"* She got the point!

Have you been feeling like that lately? Maybe you've even given up praying altogether, because you feel like it just doesn't work for you. Nothing could be further from the truth. Listen to His promise: "Call unto me, and I will answer thee, and shew thee great and mighty things, which thou knowest not" (Jeremiah 33:3).

One of the keys to answered prayer is to center your life around Christ. David said, "Delight thyself also in the Lord; and he shall give thee the desires of thine heart" (Psalm 37:4). Don't go to Jesus for a miracle—go to Him for a relationship. Once you have a relationship with Him, then you can have a miracle every day of your life.

***

TAKE TIME TODAY TO WORK ON YOUR RELATIONSHIP WITH HIM.

AUGUST 10

Free From the Opinions of People

It matters very little to me what you think of me.... The master makes that judgment.

(1 Corinthians 4:3-4 TM)

If you let it, criticism will ... steal your individuality ... rob you of your creativity ... and keep you from fulfilling your destiny. Insecure people will always criticize when your choices are different from theirs. Why? Because they're uncomfortable with things that don't conform to their way of thinking.

On the other hand, secure people can handle going out on a limb to do something. They allow others the freedom to be different and to make their own choices. Why? Because they're secure in who they are. I once saw a refrigerator magnet that said, "I'm okay with me. I don't have to make you wrong." Can you say that?

Listen: "[He] made himself of no reputation" (Philippians 2:7). Jesus wasn't concerned about what others thought of Him. He had a goal—to do the Father's will—no more and no less. He also knew that to do it, He had to be free from others' opinions!

To me the greatest tragedy in life would be to grow old and know that somewhere along the way I had "lost myself," that I had never succeeded at being who God called me to be. Paul says it this way: "It matters very little to me what you think of me, even less where I rank in popular opinion.... The master makes that judgment" (1 Corinthians 4:3-4 TM).

***

CAN YOU SAY THAT TODAY?

AUGUST 11

A Warning and a Promise

And some who are most gifted in the things of God will stumble in those days and fall, but this will only refine and cleanse them and make them pure.

(Daniel 11:35 TLB)

In the Bible the Holy Spirit reveals the mistakes of some of God's most gifted leaders in both the Old and New Testaments. And there are reasons. One is to let you know that there are *none* of us so strong as to be incapable of falling. President Kennedy once said, "If we don't learn from the past, we are doomed to repeat it." Paul said, "All these things happened to them as examples—as object lessons to us—to warn us against doing the same things" (1 Corinthians 10:11 TLB).

If you are suffering today because of mistakes you made yesterday, God says, "This will only refine you, cleanse you, and make you pure." David wrote his greatest psalms *after* his encounter with Bathsheba.

The Bible says, "And the word of the Lord came unto Jonah *the second time*" (Jonah 3:1). He's the God of the second chance. Today, He will pick you up where you have fallen and restore you by His grace.

***

AND REMEMBER, WHEN GOD RESTORES SOMETHING,
IT'S NOT SECONDHAND—IT'S BRAND NEW!

AUGUST 12

Love

Love is the fulfilling of the law.

(Romans 13:10)

In his famous little book, *The Practice of the Presence of God,* Brother Lawrence points out, "When you truly love God and your neighbor, you will go through life keeping the Ten Commandments." After all, if you really love the Lord you won't take His name in vain, and you won't put anything or anyone before Him. On the other hand, when you truly love your neighbor you would never dream of stealing from him, committing adultery with his wife, or envying anything he had; certainly you would never want to kill him. So when you *truly* love, you will fulfill all the demands of the Law, and it will become a lifestyle instead of a set of rules.

You may ask, "How is such love possible?" I only know one answer. Paul said, "The love of God is shed abroad in our hearts by the Holy Ghost" (Romans 5:5). If you're having trouble loving your husband, your wife, your children, or those you live and work with, get into the presence of God and ask Him to fill you with His Spirit. You will discover that the Holy

Spirit will do *through* you and *for* you what you could never do by yourself.

***

FROM THAT POINT ON, YOU WILL FIND IT EASIER TO TRULY "WALK IN LOVE."

AUGUST 13

Lessons from the Storm

And straightway he constrained his disciples to get into the ship, and to go to the other side.

(Mark 6:45)

He'll never send you on a trip that you can't make. That doesn't mean it will be easy, or that you won't be frightened by the waves. Remember Psalm 23: "Yea, though I walk through the valley of the shadow of death, I will fear no evil: for thou art with me" (Psalm 23:4). He doesn't *send you*—He *leads you* and *sustains you.* How reassuring!

When you can't see Him, He's still watching over you. Jesus was on a mountain praying to the Father, but the Bible says "He saw them [the disciples] toiling in rowing" (Mark 6:48). He sees your toil and your tears today. As Ethel Waters once sang, "His eye is on the sparrow, and I know He watches me."

He's the Master of the wind and the waves. There's no situation He can't handle. Listen: "And the Lord, he it is that doth go before thee; he will be with thee, he will not fail thee, neither forsake thee" (Deuteronomy 31:8).

Finally, before the storm's over God will be glorified in it, and your faith will grow stronger. Remember, your Father is a lot more interested in your *character* than He is in your *comfort.*

***

SO REJOICE TODAY; HE'S GOING TO BRING YOU THROUGH!

AUGUST 14

Share Your Testimony With Someone

Tell them how much the Lord has done for you.

(Mark 5:19 NIV)

The most powerful testimony on Earth is a life that can't be explained outside of God! People may deny your doctrine and attack your church, but your testimony is something else! Six different times Paul stood before hostile audiences, and each time he gave his personal testimony. No arguing, no debating—just his testimony.

David Yong-gi Cho, pastor of the world's largest church, was won to Christ by the testimony of a lady he only met once. She shared it, disappeared, and he's never seen her since.

Your testimony's an awesome thing when it's supported by your lifestyle! People who wouldn't listen to others will listen, relate, and respond to you, if you'll simply share your story with them. But when you do, please remember four things:

(1) *Keep it interesting.* Give them the short version. Jesus is exciting—don't bore people when you talk about Him! (2) *Be specific.* Think in three phases:

(a) how it used to be; (b) how you met Jesus; (c) how it is now. (3) *Be honest.* Don't say, "All your problems will vanish when you become a Christian." It's a battlefield, not a playground; so let others know that you still have struggles, but that you're no longer alone. Remember: "Greater is he that is in you, than he that is in the world" (1 John 4:4). (4) *Be warm.* Don't try to arm-wrestle them into the Kingdom.

***

JUST SMILE, SOW THE SEED, AND LEAVE THE HARVEST TO GOD!

AUGUST 15

Who Are You Kidding?

Even while they were in their kingdom ... they did not serve you.

(Nehemiah 9:35 NIV)

So, you think that if your life was easier, you'd be a better Christian? If you had more money you would tithe? Well—think again! Ninety million Americans go to church regularly, yet only 3 to 5 percent of them tithe. We live in the most affluent society in history, but in our quest to make sure our kids have the things we didn't have, we forget to give them the things that matter most. Things like values they can live by when they face temptation. Things like knowing the difference between getting ahead or going on with God.

Nehemiah tells us that the Israelites enjoyed God's great blessings, but they did not serve Him or turn from their evil ways. Think about it! *The very things that are supposed to bless us, burden us to the point that we can't give God His rightful position—first place in our lives.*

If you can't give God $1 when you have $10, you wouldn't give Him $100 if you had $1,000. The mortgage on a bigger home, the payments on an extra car, and the need to put more aside for retirement would push Him to the end of the line. Listen, your Father longs to bless you, but if He's crowded out by the things you already have, can you imagine what would happen if He gave you *more?*

***

PERHAPS YOU NEED TO GET BACK INTO GOD'S PRESENCE AND DISCUSS ALL OF THIS WITH HIM. WHAT DO YOU THINK?

AUGUST 16

A Look at Rejection

The stone which the builders rejected, the same is become the head of the corner: this is the Lord's doing, and it is marvellous in our eyes.

(Matthew 21:42)

Do you realize that the rejection of men can actually be "the Lord's doing"? After Joseph had been rejected by his brothers, he said, "Ye thought evil against me; but God meant it unto good" (Genesis 50:20).

How many times have things happened that you later realized were necessary? If you hadn't sustained that loss, or walked through a difficult time, you wouldn't be ready for the blessing you're now enjoying, or the assignment you're now fulfilling. When you begin to see the hand of God in it, it becomes "marvellous" in your eyes!

To be "more than a conqueror," means you stand up and say, "Here's how I see it. It took all I've been through to make me who I am today, and to teach me what I know. I choose to be better—not bitter! I trust the faithfulness of God more today than ever before. If faith doesn't remove the mountain today, it will give me strength to endure until tomorrow. If it's not gone by tomorrow, I'll still believe He is able, and trust Him until the mountain is gone." Your steps are being arranged by God, and they're also being observed by Him!

$$***$$

REJECTION BRINGS NEW DIRECTION—AND IT CAN BECOME "MARVELOUS IN YOUR EYES" WHEN YOU SEE IT FROM GOD'S PERSPECTIVE.

AUGUST 17

To Nurture or Neuter

"...Didn't you sow good seed in your field? Where then did the weeds come from?" "An enemy did this," he replied.

(Matthew 13:27 NIV)

Unless you want your future to be a second helping of your past, stop nurturing what needs to die. If you don't, it'll continue to live off your strength and suck up all your joy, like the hungry mouth of a nursing child.

Neuter it! Anything that's neutered loses its ability to threaten you or to reproduce itself in your life. "But how?" you ask. By forgiving, "...as God for Christ's sake hath forgiven you" (Ephesians 4:32). That means forgive—and keep on forgiving, until it loses its power to infect your words or influence your thoughts.

God says, "Remember ye not the former things, neither consider the things of old. Behold, I will do a new thing..." (Isaiah 43:17). God doesn't just command this—He enables you to do it! He says you can start again. You can nurture your problem child through this crisis, or your partner through this illness, or your part-time job into a full-time, executive position.

The reason you can neuter a bad past and nurture a great future is because, "Greater is he that is in you, than he that is in the world" (1 John 4:4).

***

TODAY, NEUTER WHAT NEEDS TO DIE, AND START NURTURING WHAT NEEDS TO LIVE!

AUGUST 18

According to What?

But my God shall supply all your need according to his riches in glory by Christ Jesus.

(Philippians 4:19)

His riches. Think about it; who else would tell a prophet in the middle of a famine to go sit by a stream in the mountains, and birds would show up every evening with fresh meat? Who else would tell exhausted fishermen who had "fished all night and caught nothing," to cast their nets on the right side? Or how about filling pots with water and pouring it into the wineglasses of guests, believing that what went in as water, would come out as wine? How about manna from heaven? Or blessings that pursue you until they overtake you? These things can only be found in God's storehouse. When God says He'll meet *all* your needs *according to His riches,* He's saying your job is not your source, and your bank account is not your security.

Do you really believe the Bible, or are you just reading stories? Isn't it time you made up your mind that the God who did all these things for His people in Bible days is willing, waiting, and wanting to do them for you, too? Go ahead, place your needs beside

His riches, and you'll see just how well off you really are.

*** ***

THEN, SAY WITH DAVID, "THE LORD [THE ONE WHO'S IN CHARGE OF EVERYTHING] IS MY SHEPHERD; I SHALL NOT WANT [FOR ANYTHING]" (PSALM 23:1). WHAT A WAY TO LIVE!

AUGUST 19

Blessed for a Purpose!

And afterward they will come out with great possessions.

(Genesis 15:14 NIV)

God transferred wealth from one group of people to another overnight. Why? Because they had been called to fulfill His purposes in the Earth. After ten generations of making bricks, polishing brass, and sweeping floors, God said, "It's payday! All that stuff you've been scrubbing and shining is going to be yours!" The greater the affliction, the greater the abundance!

Money's not offensive to God—the misuse of it is! Brian Houston says, "Money speaks; it says to *land,* 'I can own you.' It says to *buildings,* 'I can build you.' It says to *vision,* 'I can fulfill you.' It says to a *missionary,* 'I can support you.' It says to *poverty,* 'I can feed you.' It says to *opportunity,* 'I can accept you.'"

Why did Pharaoh pursue the children of Israel? To get back the wealth of Egypt. Think about that! *The enemy doesn't care who gets it, as long as it doesn't go to God's people or fulfill His purposes!* He dreads the thought of a mature, prosperous you committed to the purposes of God. That's why he'll keep you living in ignorance if he can.

***

TODAY, GOD WANTS TO LIBERATE YOU FROM ANYTHING THAT KEEPS YOU FROM FULFILLING YOUR DESTINY!

AUGUST 20

Protection and Correction

Thy rod and thy staff they comfort me.

(Psalm 23:4)

The tall staff with the crook was what the shepherd used to slip around the neck of a sheep that had wandered off and fallen into a ditch. He'd gently reach down, lift it up, hold it in his arms, and comfort it.

The rod had a different purpose. It was a weapon used to drive off the wolves lurking in the shadows. Even though the sheep couldn't see the danger, the shepherd could. At times, he'd also use the rod to prod a wayward sheep back onto the path, or a reluctant one to go forward.

If the pattern of your Christian life these days seems to be a blessing and a beating, it's because your Shepherd knows that some days you need the rod of correction, and other days you need the staff of protection. Either way, isn't it comforting to know that He will take care of you and lead you safely home? Has He been prodding you lately? Has He lifted you out of any ditches?

***

REMEMBER, AS LONG AS YOU'RE FOLLOWING THE SHEPHERD, NOTHING CAN GET TO YOU WITHOUT FIRST COMING THROUGH HIM.

AUGUST 21

He's Not Sending You; He's Leading You

He leadeth me.

(Psalm 23:2)

Aren't you glad He didn't redeem you and leave you on your own? If He had saved you and said, "Here's a road map; see you in Heaven someday," you would never make it. Listen to this promise: "He leadeth me beside the still waters" (Psalm 23:2). Why? To *restore* you when life is too much. Sometimes we get so busy that we don't take time to read His Word, talk to Him in prayer, or wait quietly in His presence for the strength we need. As a result, we finish up running on empty. At times like this, *He'll make you lie down,* while He does a work of restoration in you. Remember, He's much more interested in what you *are* to Him, than what you *do* for Him.

Listen again: "He leadeth me in the paths of righteousness" (Psalm 23:3)—the right direction for my life. As I look back at the problems and painful situations I've been in, I confess that it was my best thinking that got me there. So I need His guiding, protecting hand in my life every day. How about you?

Child of God, your Shepherd knows where the wolves are lurking, where the poison pasture is waiting, or how close you are to the ditch. You don't.

***

SO TRUST HIM, FOLLOW HIM, COMMIT EVERYTHING TO HIM, AND HE WILL TAKE CARE OF YOU.

AUGUST 22

The Days of Time and Chance

Time and chance happeneth to them all.

(Ecclesiastes 9:11)

Live every day like there was no tomorrow. Speak that kind word, send those flowers, make that phone call, spend time with your children or grandchildren, volunteer to teach that class, visit that shut-in. Stop merely *thinking* about it, and start *doing* it.

A pastor once ministered to a man in his mid forties. The pastor had just preached at the funeral of the man's father. Twenty years before, father and son had a bitter argument, and apart from exchanging pleasantries at family gatherings, not a word had been spoken between them since. They were both stubborn, and neither of them would give in. Now at the grave side, this successful young executive collapsed into the pastor's arms weeping, and said, *"I loved him so much, but somehow I could never tell him ... and now I'll never have a chance to."*

You have better perspective at a funeral than you do at a party. In your autumn years, you find yourself thinking a lot about the seasons of your life, and about what is really important. Were you so busy paying the mortgage that you didn't get to enjoy the house? Did you put your career ahead of your loved ones and now there's so little time left to enjoy them?

***

WHEN YOU REACH THE END, WHAT WILL YOU WISH YOU HAD DONE IN THE DAYS OF "TIME AND CHANCE"?

AUGUST 23

The Harvest Law

But remember this—if you give little, you will get little.

(2 Corinthians 9:6 TLB)

God operates according to set laws. One of them is sowing and reaping. Listen: "A farmer who plants just a few seeds will get only a small crop, but if he plants much, he will reap much" (2 Corinthians 9:6 TLB).

The most sensitive nerve a man has is the one connected to his pocketbook! Money represents time, security, and hard work; so when God talks to us about sowing some of it, we usually *bargain,* because we're used to giving at a certain level. But if God talks to you about planting a *bigger seed,* it's because He has a *bigger harvest* in mind. If God's telling you to *sow* at a higher level today, it's because He wants you to *reap* at a higher level, and you'll never break out of your present circumstances until you take that step of faith.

Maybe you say, "Someday, when things get better, I'll try it." However, since your seed is the door to your harvest, that day may never come. God said in Malachi, "Prove me now" (Malachi 3:10), and He's saying the same thing to you today. If you want to know what God can do, give Him something to work with. And remember, every seed produces a harvest, but your faith is the magnet that pulls it into your life.

***

TODAY, GOD WANTS TO TALK TO YOU ABOUT GIVING—ARE YOU LISTENING?

AUGUST 24

Hammered by the Word

Is not my word like as a fire? saith the Lord; and like a hammer that breaketh the rock in pieces?

(Jeremiah 23:29)

What you hear often enough you eventually believe. And what you believe determines your direction, your decisions, and your destiny. Paul told the Philippians, "I never get tired of telling you this, and it is good for you to hear it again and again" (Philippians 3:1 TLB).

How often do you have to listen before you really hear? How often do you have to hear before you start putting it into practice? Someone suggested that when you put something into practice consistently for thirty days, it becomes part of you. Now, not every page in this devotional may be just what you need; but when you find one that is, read it over and over until it becomes part of you.

Jesus said, "The flesh profiteth nothing: the words that I speak unto you, they are spirit, and they are life" (John 6:63). First, His words enter your *spirit,* and then they become part of your *life.* Otherwise you're simply going through the motions. The point is, you need to be hammered continually by the Word until your carnal nature has been crushed and broken. Then you can start getting somewhere with the Lord.

***

ARE YOU LETTING THE WORD WORK IN YOUR LIFE TODAY?

AUGUST 25

Do It Now!

You are just a vapor that appears for a little while and then vanishes away.

(James 4:14 NAS)

Redwood trees last for about a thousand years. Some other things go relatively fast. For instance, a face lift lasts only six to ten years. A dollar bill lasts for about a year. The painted white lines on the road last only about four months. A tornado lasts for just a few minutes.

You ask, "What about me?" Well, the average life span of a human being is now between seventy-five and eighty years. That sounds pretty good—*if you're still young!*

The Bible says your life is like a vapor, and vapors aren't known for their longevity—a puff of smoke, and they're gone! So why are you still waiting? It could be now or never; you don't have forever, so get busy!

Have you always wanted to play the piano? Start taking lessons! Have you dreamed of taking a trip to the Holy Land? Call a travel agent! Do you hate your bathroom wallpaper? Scrape it off, and repaint! Do you feel better when you exercise? Stop talking and start jogging! Do you enjoy the taste of homegrown tomatoes? Plant some! Are you upset about the pot-holes in your street? Go to your next town meeting! Whatever you've been postponing—do it now. Tomorrow may be too late!

You think you're too old? Not a chance—the older the fiddle, the sweeter the tune!

***

PUT YOUR LIFE INTO GOD'S HANDS TODAY, AND LET HIM SHOW YOU WHAT HE CAN DO WITH IT!

AUGUST 26

Your Reward

Your labour is not in vain.

(1 Corinthians 15:58)

It's easy to forget that this world is not your home! You're going to spend eternity with Christ in a place prepared especially for you (see John 14). You'll also be rewarded for the job you've done. The Bible not only supports that idea, it spells out some specifics. Here are three you need to know about today:

1) *Most of your reward will be received in Heaven—not on Earth!* There are earthly rewards (see Mark 10:30), but God reserves special honors for the day when "each man's work will become evident," and "he will receive a reward" (1 Corinthians 3:13-14 NAS). Your service now will determine your status then.

2) *Rewards will be based on quality, not quantity!* We're impressed by size, volume, noise, and numbers. But God has His eye on motive. His rewards are based on what you do with what you have, and the "heart" you put into it. He's an Equal Opportunity Employer when it comes to rewards.

3) *Your reward may be postponed, but it'll never be forgotten!* When you've done what was required, yet are ignored and misunderstood, remember, "Your labor is not in vain." When you've done the right thing, and receive neither credit nor acknowledgment, remember, "Your labor is not in vain." When you've served, given, sacrificed, and willingly stepped aside in order for God to get all the glory, remember, "Your labor is not in vain."

***

WHAT AN ASSURANCE!

AUGUST 27

Heartburn

Did not our heart burn within us, while he talked with us by the way, and while he opened to us the scriptures?

(Luke 24:32)

On the Emmaus Road a man and his wife walked in silence and despair. Jesus was dead! Their hopes had been destroyed! We've all been on the Emmaus Road. Maybe that's where you are today. *But suddenly Jesus came!* Don't you love those words? They didn't know it was Him—they thought He was a stranger. On resurrection morning, Mary thought He was the gardener; and on the Sea of Galilee the disciples thought He was a ghost.

The Bible says, "Some have entertained angels unawares" (Hebrews 13:2). Keep your eyes and your heart open, and before the day is through you might be saying, "It's Him! It's His voice! He's here." In that moment, you can reach out and touch Him and be made whole.

You ask, "How will I know it's Him?" *Heartburn!* Listen: "Did not our heart burn within us, while he talked with us by the way?" You'll know it's Him, all right. There's no voice like His. No touch like His. No peace like His. As you open the pages of your Bible, He'll open your understanding.

***

WHEN HE DOES, YOUR HEART WILL BURN, AND YOU'LL FEEL THE WARMTH AND GLOW OF HIS PRESENCE. THERE'S NOTHING LIKE IT!

AUGUST 28

A Timely Warning

Though ... riches increase, do not set your heart on them.

(Psalm 62:10 NIV)

If God can trust you, He'll bless you materially as well as spiritually (2 Corinthians 9:6-11 NIV). But with His blessings come conditions. Here are four that you need to honor:

1) *Don't claim the credit!* Listen: "You may say to yourself ... 'My hands have produced this wealth for me.' But remember the Lord your God, for it is he who gives you the ability to produce wealth.... If you ever forget [that] ... you will surely be destroyed" (Deuteronomy 8:17-19 NIV).

2) *Don't forget others!* Listen: "Command those who are rich in this present world ... to put their hope in God, who richly provides us with everything for our enjoyment. Command them to ... be rich in good deeds ... generous and willing to share. In this way they will lay up treasure..." (1 Timothy 6:17-19 NIV).

3) *Don't become arrogant.* Listen: "Let not the wise man boast of his wisdom or the strong man ... of his strength or the rich man ... of his riches,

but let him ... boast ... that he understands and knows me..." (Jeremiah 9:23-24 NIV).

4) *Don't allow anything to replace God!* Listen: "Give me neither poverty nor riches, but give me only my daily bread. Otherwise, I may have too much and disown you and say, 'Who is the Lord?'" (Proverbs 30:8-9 NIV). Remember that you don't own anything—you're just the administrator of His estate and the executor of His will.

***

SO TODAY, MAKE SURE YOU DO A GOOD JOB WITH IT!

AUGUST 29

Are You Washing Your Nets?

He noticed two empty boats standing at the water's edge while the fishermen washed their nets.

(Luke 5:2 TLB)

Why would fishermen wash nets that hadn't been used? Nets that hadn't caught fish? The answer is—they were quitting because of an overnight problem. Listen: "We have fished all night and caught nothing" (see Luke 5:5). Don't you know how that feels? They believed that the way things were, was how they would always be. They were beaten. And that's when Jesus loves to show up! He walked right into the middle of their problem with a solution.

First, He asked them for their boat (their business), and used it to preach to the crowd. Turn it all over to Him—all you have and all you'll ever be—and let Him use you for His highest purposes.

Next, He gave them a word that only faith could receive: "Launch out into the deep, and let down your nets for a draught" (Luke 5:4). Can you see why He has to wait until you've done everything you know to do? Only then are you ready to listen and obey without question.

You may be washing your nets today, but it's not over! Who told you God wasn't going to bless you again? Who told you He wasn't going to bring victory out of the ashes?

***

IF HE CAN FILL EMPTY NETS FOR DISCOURAGED DISCIPLES, THEN YOU DON'T HAVE A PROBLEM THAT HE CAN'T SOLVE!

AUGUST 30

The Cure for Depression

O my God, my soul is cast down within me: therefore will I remember thee.

(Psalm 42:6)

The Message says, "When my soul is in the dumps, I rehearse everything I know of you." David talked to himself—and you've got to learn to do that, too! Listen: "Bless the Lord, O my soul, and forget not all his benefits: Who forgiveth all thine iniquities" (Psalm 103:2-3). The charges against you have all been dropped. It doesn't matter how many court records there are, or how many fingers point in accusation. John wrote, "He is faithful and just to forgive us our sins, and to cleanse us from all unrighteousness" (1 John 1:9).

Read the rest of Psalm 103:3: "Who healeth all thy diseases." Has He ever healed you? Or better yet, has He *kept you healthy?* Isaiah says, "The Lord will guide you continually, and satisfy you with all good things, and keep you healthy too" (Isaiah 58:11 TLB). If you can *speak,* praise Him! If you can move, lift up your hands and exalt Him! If you can *think,* rehearse His goodness to you!

We forget so easily. Before we know it we're complaining about things that don't amount to a hill of beans. Come on, it's time for a rehearsal. David said, "Let the redeemed of the Lord say so, whom he hath redeemed from the hand of the enemy" (Psalm 107:2).

***

TRY IT! IT'S THE BIBLICAL CURE FOR DEPRESSION!

AUGUST 31

The Power of Purpose

And we know that all things work together for good to them ... who are the called according to his purpose.

(Romans 8:28)

Before you ask for prosperity, ask for purpose. Before you ask for relationships, ask for direction. When it comes to people, the right ones add to you and the wrong ones subtract from you. If God doesn't send them, you don't need them!

The Bible says, "There was a man sent from God, whose name was John" (John 1:6). God can send people into your life. Ask the widow of Zarephath. When she was willing to put God first, she prospered in the middle of a famine. (See 1 Kings 17:9-24.) She could have held on to what little she had. But she knew that as long as it was in her hand, one meal was all it would ever be. In God's hand, however, it could start a harvest that would last seven years. When what you have is not enough, make it a seed for the harvest you need.

Success is not found at the top of the corporate ladder, or pastoring the biggest church in town. It's not being married to a "10," or driving a Rolls Royce.

No! Success is being in the middle—right in the center—of God's will for your life.

***

WHEN YOU'RE THERE, YOU KNOW THAT ALL THINGS ARE WORKING TOGETHER FOR YOUR GOOD.

SEPTEMBER 1

A Message to the "Me" Generation

Regard one another as more important.

(Philippians 2:3 NAS)

Here are words to keep you on your toes—and knees! "Do nothing from selfishness or empty conceit, but with humility of mind ... regard one another as more important than [yourself]; do not merely look out for your own personal interests, but also for the interests of others. Have this attitude ... which was also in Christ Jesus" (Philippians 2:3-5 NIV).

That's how Jesus lived, and you should strive to live that way, too. I say, "strive" because it's contrary to your carnal nature. Because you were gracious yesterday is no guarantee you'll be the same today. Grace is like a garment—you've got to practice putting it on every morning.

"But how can I live like that?" you ask. By putting others first! By looking for ways to support and encourage them. Everybody you'll meet today is fighting a battle of some kind, and you may be the only person capable of speaking a healing word to him or her (see Proverbs 16:24 NLT). Don't let them down!

Humility's an attitude! It determines ahead of time: "I care about those around me. I don't *always* have to be first. I'm going to help somebody else to win." It prays, "Lord, help me curb my fierce competitive tendencies, and turn them into loving and lifting at least one other person today.

***

"SHOW ME HOW YOU WOULD DO IT; THEN HELP ME TO DO IT IN YOUR NAME. AMEN."

SEPTEMBER 2

Be Christ-Like and Stay in Touch

Better a neighbor nearby than a brother far away.

(Proverbs 27:10 NIV)

A few winters ago in Sweden, an eighty-four-year-old woman sat for two months on her balcony before neighbors discovered she was dead. They realized something was wrong when they saw her sitting there around the clock, despite freezing temperatures. One neighbor said, "I feel terrible. I hope this makes us stop and think more about one another."

Doctor Philip Zimbardo writes in *Psychology Today:*

I know of no more potent killer than loneliness. It's the central agent in depression and suicide. It's the devil's strategy for isolating us from one another, while creating the delusion that the reasons are ... time-pressures ... work-demands ... or anxieties created by economic uncertainty.

Jesus heard cries that nobody else heard. He noticed people whom others had no time for. When the disciples tried to silence blind Bartimaeus, Jesus stopped them and restored his sight. He walked for days to meet with a hurting woman whose heart was as empty as her water pots (see John 4). He's the Shepherd who left ninety-nine sheep in the fold to look for the one that was lost. Do you want to be more like Him?

***

CARE ABOUT PEOPLE—LET HIM LOVE A HURTING WORLD THROUGH YOU!

SEPTEMBER 3

Who's on Your Wheel?

...The potter ... made it again another vessel ... as seemed good to the potter.

(Jeremiah 18:4)

Whom do you have on your potter's wheel? Do yourself a favor—take them off and give them to God, because He's the potter, not you!

One reader writes: *"For years I tried to change my family, and almost drove them away. Finally, I turned them over to God. The amazing thing is, He either fixed them or He fixed me, because now I like them the way they are. Without my even knowing how, God took care of the problem."*

Jesus said, "...Whatsoever thou shalt loose on earth shall be loosed in heaven" (Matthew 16:19). Think; through prayer you can enter any situation, declare God's will to be done in it, and bring about change. God says when you do that on Earth, He'll back you up in Heaven. Consider these three things:

1) *People can't change other people; only God can.* Until you pray and involve Him, you won't get the results you want.

2) *God allows certain situations to build character in us.* Until you first pray and allow Him to deal

with the things that are wrong in you, nothing will change.

3) *In prayer God can take you beneath the surface and show you the real problem.* When that happens, attitudes change and answers come.

***

PRAYER—WHAT A PRIVILEGE!

SEPTEMBER 4

When the Giver Delights in His Giving

God loves it when the giver delights in the giving.

(2 Corinthians 9:7 TM)

Have you ever been in church when a special offering was being taken and thought, *I've given a lot this month, and financially I'm tapped out. Let somebody else do the giving tonight?* But do you realize that if somebody else does your sowing, somebody else will do your reaping—is that okay with you?

Paul said, "Let us not be weary in well doing: for in due season we shall reap, if we faint not" (Galatians 6:9). Did you hear that? There is a date scheduled for your harvest. The only thing that will keep you from reaping is if you *get cynical, discouraged,* or *impatient.* When someone has a need, or a letter arrives asking for your help, ask yourself, *Could this be God giving me a chance to schedule another harvest?* Offerings are not how God gets money from you; they're how He gets blessings to you! As Paul said to the Corinthians, "Take plenty of time to think it over, and make up your own mind what you will give. For

God loves it when the giver delights in the giving" (2 Corinthians 9:7 TM).

**

REMEMBER, YOUR GIVING IS THE BRIDGE TO YOUR FUTURE!

SEPTEMBER 5

Take No Thought

Take therefore no thought for the morrow.

(Matthew 6:34)

Somehow we've picked up the idea that *we're* in control of our lives. Satan told Eve, "In the day you eat ... you will be like God" (Genesis 3:5 NAS). What a deal—you'll be in control! Then we get ambitious and try to control the lives of others. When things don't go the way we think they should, we feel like we've let ourselves and everybody else down, and we worry ourselves sick.

Then someone says to us, "Only believe." So we stock up on tapes and books, and we start naming and claiming things—but still nothing happens. Then someone else tells us we don't have enough faith, or we're not worthy. So we try going through some messenger of God, hoping they can get it for us.

Finally, in despair, we turn to God and say, "I just can't *think* anymore—it's all Yours!" And God smiles and says, "That's what I've been trying to tell you all along: *take no thought.*" When we take thought, we take charge, and you know where that gets us. When we take thought, we take stock, and we look at what we've got instead of what *He's* got. So today, stop thinking and start trusting!

***

PUT IT ALL INTO GOD'S HANDS—AND DON'T TAKE IT BACK!

SEPTEMBER 6

It Won't Be Taken Away!

...That your fruit should remain...

(John 15:16)

The morning after Jacob had been visited by God, he said, "...Surely the Lord is in this place; and I knew it not" (Genesis 28:16). Imagine, blessed but unaware of it! Is that where *you* are today? Asking, "How can I be so blessed, yet feel so bland?" It could be that the defenses you've built up to protect yourself from being hurt again, are stopping you from enjoying the blessings God has given you. You see, success doesn't feel like success when you still have the taste of pain in your mouth. It cost you so much to get to where you are that spiritually speaking, you're still in shock; and shock causes us to shut down and say, "I don't want to feel anything anymore."

"What's the answer?" you ask. Listen: "I have chosen you ... [to] bring forth fruit, and that your fruit should remain" (John 15:16). Note the word *remain.* God is saying to you today, "I'm going to bless you, but it's not going to be like any time in the past. What I'm giving you will remain! You're not going to lose it! You can rest in it! You can hold on to it!

***

"LOWER YOUR GUARD, OPEN YOUR HEART, AND GET READY TO RECEIVE FROM ME!"

SEPTEMBER 7

A Quick Response

When thou sadist, Seek ye my face; my heart said unto thee, Thy face, Lord, will I seek.

(Psalm 27:8)

It's sad to see two people who couldn't wait to be together, reach the place where they treat each other with indifference. There's no unfaithfulness, no fighting—and *no passion.* They park in the same garage and write checks on the same account. But they pass like ships in the night, without closeness, commitment, or communication. Jesus said, "The love of many shall wax cold" (Matthew 24:12). If this is the way things are in your life today, do something about it.

When David heard the voice of God, he responded *immediately,* "Thy face, Lord, will I seek." How's your response time? Do you remember when the slightest tug and the smallest whisper was all you needed? What happened?

Look at the life of Noah. In Genesis 6:9 we read, "Noah walked with God." In Genesis 7:5 we read, "And Noah did according unto all that the Lord commanded him." Finally we read that Noah *got blessed, got busy,* and *got drunk.* Listen: "And Noah began to be an husbandman, and he planted a vineyard: And he drank of the wine, and was drunken; and he was uncovered within his tent" (Genesis 9:20-21). What a progression! *Don't let it happen to you.*

***

YOU CAN SAY AND DO ALL THE RIGHT THINGS, BUT IT MEANS NOTHING UNTIL YOUR HEART SAYS, "THY FACE, LORD, WILL I SEEK."

SEPTEMBER 8

He Knows What You Need

Your heavenly Father knoweth that ye have need of all these things.

(Matthew 6:32)

There's a difference between what outsiders and family members know. Your children know things about you—what you have, what you like, what you do—that outsiders will never know.

And it's the same with God's children. Because we know that our Father is rich and has great plans for us, our expectations of Him are enhanced, and our confidence in Him is strengthened. (See Jeremiah 29:11.)

But just because He has it, doesn't mean He *automatically* gives it to you. No. A good father exercises restraint. He's not only good to his children; he's good *for* them. Often he withholds things for a season in order to temper character and correct behavior. Then, when blessing comes, his children are mature enough to handle it.

When you don't understand this, you can easily become discouraged and turn away from God in anger, because you believed for something that didn't come on time or come at all.

But if your faith in God's wisdom is stronger than your personal agenda, you'll hold on to His promise, trust Him, and wait patiently for the blessing to come. Why?

***

BECAUSE YOU UNDERSTAND THAT YOUR HEAVENLY FATHER KNOWS WHAT YOU NEED!

SEPTEMBER 9

When a Tree Falls

If you think you are standing strong, be careful, for you, too, may fall.

(1 Corinthians 10:12 NLT)

When I was growing up, a big oak tree in the local park fell across the main road, stopping all the traffic. It looked like a strong, healthy specimen—the last one you'd expect to go. But as workers hauled it off, it became clear that it had rotted from the inside. Thus, a minor storm that wouldn't even have threatened a scrub oak, felled this giant.

The fall seemed sudden, but it had been in the works for years. And when it fell, it took others with it. What a lesson!

Saul, Israel's first king, started on Mount Mizpah, which means "humility." Tragically, he later died on Mount Gilboa, which means "pride." At the beginning we read, "Do you see him whom the Lord has chosen? Surely there is no one like him" (1 Samuel 10:24 NAS). At the end we read, "How have the mighty fallen" (2 Samuel 1:25 NAS).

(1) *A good start doesn't guarantee a strong finish.* Your daily habits determine that. (2) *You can look good outside, yet be in trouble inside.* Attend to what's

not seen; your strength comes from within. Listen: "With joy shall ye draw water out of the wells of salvation" (Isaiah 12:3). It's an "inside job." (3) *Never try to convince yourself that your fall won't hurt others.* More people than you know admire and trust you. If you collapse, they'll be injured.

***

PLEASE DON'T LET THEM DOWN!

SEPTEMBER 10

A Friend Who Sticks

There is a friend that sticketh closer than a brother.

(Proverbs 18:24)

A relationship is like riding a bus—you have to move over and make room for somebody else and their baggage. Your willingness, not your words, is what sustains real friendship. Willingness to forgive. Willingness to adjust. Willingness to believe the best.

The pastor of one of the largest churches in America once said to me, "I don't have *one* real friend. I trust nobody." He's a prisoner of his own image and other people's expectations. He can't show his humanity in case they reject him. What a terrible way to live.

So often we discard a good person because he made a mistake. We forget all the good and dwell on only the thing he did to hurt us. Would you throw your car away because of a bad battery? Is there any possibility of repair? You say, "No." Then how does God ever love you? If He forgave *you your* debts in the same way that you forgive your debtors, could you stand?

***

TODAY, ASK GOD TO MAKE YOU A FRIEND WHO STICKS.

SEPTEMBER 11

When You're Treated Unfairly

If you suffer for doing good and you endure it, this is commendable before God. (1 Peter 2:20 NIV)

Just about everybody you admire in the Bible was treated unfairly! And God permitted it! Think about Daniel, thrown to the lions, and Joseph, locked in prison. What did they do to deserve it? Nothing! Listen: "If you suffer for doing good and you endure it, this is commendable ... to this you were called" (1 Peter 2:20-21 NIV). Imagine—it's your calling!

There's purpose in your pain. Everything that touches you today has first passed through God's hands and bears His fingerprints! He anticipated and approved it. What you're going through right now is preparing you to serve Him more effectively. Paul said, "At my preliminary hearing no one stood by me. They all ran like scared rabbits. But it doesn't matter—the Master stood by me and helped me spread the Message" (2 Timothy 4:17 TM). Paul didn't see it as enduring; he saw it as advancing!

Today you're growing in grace (becoming more gracious), and in the knowledge of the Lord (see 2

Peter 3:18). You're in the preparation process. You say, "But I don't understand." Listen to Joni Erickson Tada: "If God's mind was small enough for me to understand, He wouldn't be God. Sometimes I can't stand being in this wheelchair, but *there* God's grace takes over. Even in my handicap, God has a plan and purpose for my life."

***

WHETHER GOD BRINGS YOU OUT OR THROUGH, TRUST HIM TO WORK FOR YOUR GOOD!

SEPTEMBER 12

Make Sure the CaptainIs on Board

Take fast hold of instruction; let her not go: keep her; for she is thy life.

(Proverbs 4:13)

A young ensign was given an opportunity to display his ability at getting the ship out of port. He had the decks buzzing with men, and soon the vessel was steaming out of the channel. He actually set a new record for getting the destroyer under way, and was feeling good until he received a radio message from the captain that said, "My personal congratulations on completing this exercise according to the book, and with amazing speed. However, in your haste you overlooked one unwritten rule—*make sure the captain is on board!*"

Before you make that important decision about your family, your job, or your life's goals, take time to read your Bible. Jesus said, "The words that I speak unto you, they are spirit, and they are life" (John 6:63).

***

REMEMBER BEFORE YOU LAUNCH OUT TO MAKE SURE
THE CAPTAIN IS ON BOARD!

SEPTEMBER 13

A Word About Values

For the Lord is a God of knowledge, and by him actions are weighed.

(1 Samuel 2:3)

Before you set your *goals,* determine your *values.* If you don't, your gift could carry you to heights at which your character can't sustain you. Before you tell others how to live, determine what you really believe yourself.

It's possible to be in ministry a long time before learning how to be a real Christian. You can spend a lot of time developing your skills, but not enough developing a relationship with the Lord. Your ministry is not where you draw strength from in the hour of testing. That comes from your *relationship* with God.

A pulpit is a two-edged sword. First, it introduces us to men and women of God who bless our lives. However, if you haven't heard clearly from God for yourself, it can pressure you into thinking, *Wouldn't it be wonderful to be up there with them?* But if God didn't tell you to do it, you're setting yourself up for disappointment. Jesus said, "I have finished the work which thou gavest me to do" (John 17:4). What has God told *you* to do? If you don't get a vision for your own life, you'll probably spend it helping somebody else fulfill his.

***

TODAY, ASK YOURSELF: DO I REALLY KNOW WHAT I BELIEVE? DO I HAVE A CLEAR SENSE OF HIS LEADING IN MY LIFE?

SEPTEMBER 14

The Giving Tree

Every time I think of you, I give thanks to my God."

(Philippians 1:3 NLT)

A young boy swung from a tree's branches, ate its apples, and slept in its shade. The tree loved him and was happy. But the boy spent increasingly less time with the tree. "Let's play," said the tree. But now the young man's interests lay in making money. "Take my apples and sell them," said the tree. He did, and the tree was happy. The young man left and didn't return for a long time. When he finally passed by one day, the tree smiled and said, "Come on, let's play." But now the man was tired of his world and wanted to get away from it all. "Use my trunk to build a boat; then you can sail away," said the tree. He did, and the tree was happy. Many seasons passed—and the tree waited. Finally, an old man returned, too tired to play, pursue riches, or sail the seas. "I still have a good stump left," said the tree. "Sit and rest." He did, and the tree was happy.

How many "giving trees" have there been in your life? People who've sacrificed so that you could grow and accomplish your goals. If you're like me, you've thought about them a thousand times, but never told them once. Don't leave it unsaid! Find a way—a card, a call, an e-mail, a visit! Let them know you appreciate them. Paul dedicated an entire chapter to it (see Romans 16).

***

I COULD, TOO—HOW ABOUT YOU?

SEPTEMBER 15

For Men Only

Husbands, love your wives, just as Christ loved the church.

(Ephesians 5:25 NIV)

How did Jesus love the Church? Let me tell you:

He always put it first. This calls for the death of self-serving, self-seeking, and self-centered living. That's hard!

He lived to develop it. Jesus spent most of His ministry grooming twelve men to be world-changers. Their success didn't threaten Him; it thrilled Him. Sadly, some men are happy to have a wife who is a good mother, a good cook, and a good entertainer. But if God calls her to ministry, they feel they have to blow her light out to let their own light shine. However, a secure man will rejoice in her calling.

He was patient and loving toward it. One of His disciples denied Him, one of them doubted Him, and some others wanted to call down fire upon those who disagreed with them. What a bunch! But He poured His life into them anyhow.

So there you have it, guys! *That's* how Christ loved the Church—and that's how *you're* supposed to love your wives!

***

ISN'T THAT ENOUGH TO GET ANY MAN ON HIS KNEES?

SEPTEMBER 16

One Who Stands Beside to Help

The Comforter [paraclete], which is the Holy Ghost ... shall teach you all things.

(John 14:26)

Recently I read about a man who underwent open-heart surgery. He said, "The day before my surgery, a lovely nurse came into my room. She took my hand and said, 'During the surgery tomorrow you'll be disconnected from your heart and kept alive by machines. When the operation's over you'll waken in the recovery room, but you won't be able to move for about six hours. You won't be able to speak, or open your eyes, but you'll be completely conscious. You'll hear and know everything that's going on. That can be frightening, so during those hours I'll stay by your side and hold your hand, just like I'm doing now. I'll stay with you until you're fully recovered. *If you become anxious or afraid, just feel the touch of my hand on yours, and know that you're not alone. I won't leave you.'*

"It happened exactly as she said. I awoke, and even though I was totally immobilized—the touch of her hand made all the difference!"

What a picture! Jesus' favorite word for the Holy Spirit was *Paraclet*—"one who stands beside to help." Engrave those words on your mind today until they're such a part of you that regardless of what you're going through, you'll always know with certainty that God's Spirit is surrounding you, sustaining you, and strengthening you.

***

YOU'RE HIS CHILD, AND THAT'S HIS PROMISE TO YOU!

SEPTEMBER 17

Mending and Resetting

If someone falls into sin, forgivingly restore him, saving your critical comments for yourself. You might be needing forgiveness before the day's out.

(Galatians 6:1 TM)

Geoff Jackson, a Greek scholar, says the word *restore,* in original Greek, paints two pictures: first, fishermen mending their nets; second, a doctor resetting a dislocated bone. What insight! A broken net can't catch fish, so it must be taken out of service and repaired. And what about the doctor who resets a broken bone? He'll set it in a cast for several weeks, and tell you not to use it.

Forgiveness and restoration are first cousins—but with one big difference. Forgiveness can happen in an instant; restoration often requires time. The good news is that our God is in the business of resetting and restoring. Doctors who reset broken bones tell us that once they're truly healed, they're stronger than the original.

He can do that for you. Don't be afraid of time out and time alone with Him. Jeremiah was told to go down to the house of the potter, and watch him take a broken vessel and skillfully work with it until it was beautiful once more.

***

TODAY, THE POTTER WANTS TO PUT YOU BACK TOGETHER AGAIN.

SEPTEMBER 18

Looking at a Different Pile of Stones

That all the people of the earth might know the hand of the Lord, that it is mighty.

(Joshua 4:24)

Jericho was too big, so God gave His people an interesting plan. He told them to walk around its walls once a day, and then come back home each evening to Gilgal. From there they could see the River Jordan and a monument of stones erected to commemorate the day that God miraculously dried up its waters. (God's people were circumcised at *Gilgal,* so it also represents putting away the flesh.) The plan was this: don't look at Jericho through the eyes of the flesh, for that only frames it in fear. No! We've circumcised our hearts. We're walking in faith. We're looking at it through the eyes of our spirit, and we're getting stronger each day. *We're looking at a different pile of stones.*

Jericho represented what men could do. Jordan's monument represented what God could do. Before you face tomorrow, check with yesterday. Surely! Surely! Surely! Keep saying it until you believe it.

"Surely goodness and mercy shall follow me all the days of my life" (Psalm 23:6). Come on, child of God, He has promised to bring down those walls in your life. The pile of stones that stood between Israel and the Promised Land was flattened when God's people stepped out in faith and obeyed His Word.

***

TODAY, START LOOKING AT WHAT GOD CAN DO!

SEPTEMBER 19

The Reason for the Test

These trials are only to test your faith....

(1 Peter 1:7 NLT)

Tests cause both strengths and weaknesses to surface in us. The "refiner's fire" in Malachi 3:3 is not associated only with the *negative* qualities God wants to remove. That's just part of it. You also have inner strengths and gifts you're not yet aware of, because no demand has ever been placed on them.

In 1 Kings 17, when the widow met Elijah, *both* were in the middle of a famine. Yet he asked her for her last meal! You may be thinking, *Typical preacher!* But don't be too hasty! *The best day of her life came when someone placed a demand on her faith!* Her response changed her future, blessed her family, and made her famous.

When you're faced with a need, how do you respond? Do you withdraw? Withhold? Give only out of obligation? Or do you see it as an opportunity to change your future? (See 2 Corinthians 9:6-11.) *You can actually give your way out of trouble!*

Before God sent Moses to Pharaoh, He told him, "The king of Egypt will not let you go unless a mighty hand compels him" (Exodus 3:19 NIV). Sometimes

God permits the enemy to come against you: (1) to demonstrate that He's strong on your behalf; (2) to reveal how you'll perform under pressure; and (3) to find out whom you'll believe when God says, "I'll bring you out with a mighty hand," while the enemy says, "I won't let you go."

**

THAT'S WHAT THIS TEST IS ALL ABOUT!

SEPTEMBER 20

Don't "Take It Easy"!

You will come to the grave in full vigor.

(Job 5:26 NIV)

Norman Cousins said, "No disease is more lethal than the boredom that follows retirement." The other day I heard about a woman in her eighties who was being examined by her doctor. He asked her if she stayed pretty active. With a smile, she said, "I walk about four or five miles every day." Surprised, he told her that she didn't need to overdo it. "Take it easy," he suggested.

She took his words to heart and decided to slow down. She reduced her brisk walks to a stroll and cut back to three days a week. She died in less than a year! The doctor who had given her the advice sadly told a friend, "Never again will I tell a patient who's doing so well to take it easy."

The Bible is filled with people who lived on because they had something to *live for!*

Remember Caleb? At eighty-five he attacked giants in the hill country, drove them out, and became a land developer (see Joshua 14). And how about Noah, who began building an ark when he was 500, and helped to start the world over again at 621?

Age means nothing—unless you're cheese! Wrinkles, gray hair, and age spots mean less than nothing. If God chooses to leave you on this Earth, then don't just exist—live! Keep dreaming! Accept new challenges.

***

AND WHATEVER YOU DO—DON'T TAKE IT EASY!

SEPTEMBER 21

God Didn't Call You to Fight Every Battle

The battle is not yours, but God's.

(2 Chronicles 20:15)

Some battles are not yours—they're God's! Listen: "Ye shall not need to fight in this battle: set yourselves, stand ye still, and see the salvation of the Lord" (2 Chronicles 20:17). What a relief! Now, if the battle is the Lord's, guess who chooses the weapons, the battlefield, the strategy, and the timing? That doesn't mean we don't have anything to do. God's people were told to "stand ye still" and trust in His unfailing faithfulness. Never discuss your problems with people who are incapable of solving them. Give them completely to the Lord, then begin to praise Him for victory.

God told His people to put the choir in front of the army and have them march out to meet the enemy. Can you imagine their reaction? *But praise moves God!* It brings Him into your circumstances. While the choir sang, God moved among the enemy and they began to fight each other. Israel never fired a shot, they never sustained a casualty, and the victory they won was so great that it took three days to pick up the spoils of battle. Today "the battle is not yours, but God's."

***

TRUST HIM AND PRAISE HIM FOR THE VICTORY THAT HE IS GOING TO GIVE YOU.

SEPTEMBER 22

Under Attack!

When the enemy shall come in like a flood, the Spirit of the Lord shall lift up a standard against him.

(Isaiah 59:19)

Your biggest mistakes usually happen during the first moments of any attack. Surprise is the enemy's great strategy. If you're under attack today, here are four things you need to know.

First, don't panic! Listen: "Be still, and know that I am God" (Psalm 46:10). That means He's present ... He's in charge ... and He has a solution! Stop and listen carefully to the inner voice of His Spirit (see John 16:13). Time is your friend. Remember, patience is the weapon that causes motives to surface.

Second, analyze it! Solomon said, "In the day of prosperity be joyful, but in the day of adversity consider..." (Ecclesiastes 7:14). A crisis is merely concentrated information. Take time to analyze it and you'll benefit.

Third, seek worthy counsel! Listen: "Where no counsel is, the people fall" (Proverbs 11:14). Ignorance is deadly. Don't risk it! Somebody knows something you need to know—something that can help you survive, and even succeed, in the most painful chapter of your life. Reach out to them!

Fourth, expect God to move! Listen: "When the enemy shall come in like a flood, the Spirit of the Lord shall lift up a standard against him" (Isaiah 59:19). Adversity is just the enemy's reaction to your progress. Rejoice! The eyes of your Father are upon you.

***

HE'S GOING TO MAKE YOU VICTORIOUS!

SEPTEMBER 23

Where There Is Unity, God Commands His Blessing

Behold, how good and how pleasant it is for brethren to dwell together in unity ... for there the Lord commanded the blessing.

(Psalm 133:1, 3)

When God sees us working together in unity and love, He *commands* His blessing upon us. Since we know that, why don't we work harder for unity? One word that comes to mind is *striving.* Listen: "An argument started among the disciples as to which of them would be the greatest" (Luke 9:46 NIV). Jesus had to deal with the spirit of striving among His disciples. Someone has wisely said, "There is no limit to what can be accomplished if nobody cares who gets the credit."

Another reason for lack of unity is our *failure to walk in love.* We are unwilling to accept people as they are, to love them, and to let the Holy Spirit change them.

Sadly, some of those who are most guilty can be found in the pulpit. They are only interested in protecting their reputation, their influence, and their turf.

Today, you need to pray that God will help you transcend the spirit of striving, pettiness, and selfishness, and to reach out to others in love. Only a united Church can bring healing to a divided world.

***

IF IT DOESN'T WORK FOR US, HOW WILL IT EVER WORK FOR OTHERS?

SEPTEMBER 24

If You Don't Accept God's Messenger, You Won't Receive God's Message

He that receiveth whomsoever I send receiveth me.

(John 13:20)

When God gets ready to bless you, He usually sends a person to do it. It may take the form of correction, stretching your faith, or deepening your devotion to the Lord. If you want to take big steps, follow in the footsteps of big people. Who inspires you? Whom do you read? Timothy was an apostle by the time he reached seventeen, because he had spent much of his life under the influence of Paul. Elisha was influenced by Elijah, and he did twice as many miracles as his teacher before him.

The greatest man I ever knew was my pastor. I spent months in his home and years in his company, listening to every word and opening my life to his counsel. God never meant you to go it alone. Solomon said, "Two are better than one.... For if they fall, the one will lift up his fellow: but woe to him that is alone when he falleth; for he hath not another to help him up" (Ecclesiastes 4:9-10). Jesus sent His disciples out in companies *of two.* Today ask God to give you the humility and hunger to open your life to those whom God sends, and to give you a willingness to listen to them.

***

AFTER ALL, YOUR DESTINY DEPENDS ON IT.

SEPTEMBER 25

Are You Really Serious?

Wilt thou be made whole?

(John 5:6)

A pastor friend once shared with me three questions he asks every person seeking counseling. By the time they've answered them honestly, over 75 percent discover they don't need counseling after all, because they've gotten a handle on the situation themselves. He asks them to write down their answers, which is always a big step toward solving any problem.

Here are the questions:

1. *What exactly is the problem?* We get so bogged down in our feelings, circumstances, and excuses that we lose sight of the real problem. Just writing it down for the first time can change our whole perspective.

2. *What have you already done to solve this problem?* What steps have you already taken? What does the Word say about it? What Scriptures are you standing on?

3. *What do you think we can do for you that you cannot do for yourself?*

By asking these questions, you'll discover whether someone's looking for *solutions or sympathy, answers* or *attention.* These questions, when honestly answered, bring to the surface such things as blame-shifting, making excuses, unwillingness to change, and dishonesty. Either way, you'll get to know what you're dealing with, and have the option of solving it and moving on, or remaining stuck.

***

WHICH OPTION ARE YOU TAKING?

SEPTEMBER 26

God Has It All Figured Out

Having predestinated us ... according to the good pleasure of his will.

(Ephesians 1:5)

God's plan for your life is set. It can't be edited or changed any more than His character can be changed.

"But what about the sin of Adam and Eve—was that His plan, too?" you ask. No! Satan created a dilemma when Adam sinned; he took what God loved and seduced it into doing what God hated. The idea was to hand God a problem He couldn't solve. For God to kill what he hated—sin—He'd also have to destroy what He loved—man.

But God had a strategy in place long before Satan ever created the dilemma. Jesus was "...the Lamb slain from the foundation of the world" (Revelation 13:8). Before there was ever a sinner on Earth, there was a Savior in Heaven. That means that nothing the devil can throw at you will ever thwart the purpose of God for your life!

Think of it this way: The script is already written before the actor arrives on stage. All he has to do is play the role assigned to him and follow the director.

You say, "You mean I've no choice?" Yes, you do: submit and be blessed, or rebel and be sorry. That's it!

***

TODAY, GOD ALREADY HAS IT ALL FIGURED OUT "...ACCORDING TO THE GOOD PLEASURE OF HIS WILL."

SEPTEMBER 27

You Can Start Again

You will give me added years of life, as rich and full as those of many generations, all packed into one.

(Psalm 61:6 TLB)

I once saw a bird's nest lying on the ground. It had been destroyed by a storm. I thought sadly of the time and work it must have taken to build it, when suddenly my thoughts were interrupted by a bird singing. When I looked up into the tree, I saw a wonderful sight—the little bird was busy building another nest.

You can't go back. You can't rewrite the past. But you don't have to wallow in regret or remorse. Your experiences have made you the person you are today, and if you're still breathing, then you can start your life over again, beginning right now. David's mistakes were bigger than those of most people. But he decided not to be a prisoner of his past. Listen: "You will give me added years of life, as rich and full as those of many generations, all packed into one."

Everything begins with a decision—decide to live again! All of us have things we wish we had done differently or hadn't done at all. What's past is past.

Rearview mirrors were made to glance at, not stare into! Put your past under the blood and move on!

***

YOUR BEST DAYS ARE AHEAD—IF YOU ACCEPT GOD'S PROMISE AND ACT ON IT.

SEPTEMBER 28

Longing for God

As the deer pants for streams of water, so my soul pants for you, O God.

(Psalm 42:1 NIV)

Something deep within me understands David's heart's cry for the presence of God. It's a thirsting and a longing that nothing else will satisfy. When I've been in God's presence I'm different! I'm confident about the future, I'm sensitive to the needs of others around me, and I'm definitely more loving and long-suffering. Isn't it that way in your life, too?

Some animals can go for days and weeks without water, but not the deer. He must drink from the stream every day. The New Testament believers were like that, too. When the business of the Church became too demanding, they refused to let anything take the place of fellowship with God, and studying His Word. Listen: "We will give ourselves continually to prayer, and to the ministry of the word" (Acts 6:4). The original Greek word for "give" is *addict.* Did you hear that? They were addicted to the Word of God and prayer. What a way to live!

Hind's feet belong in *high* places! Others may live in the valleys or on the plains, but the deer was born to live in high places—and so were you!

***

GET INTO GOD'S PRESENCE TODAY, AND LET HIM WATER YOUR SOUL.

SEPTEMBER 29

How Well Do You Know the Holy Spirit?

...The Holy Spirit, whom the Father will send in my name...

(John 14:26 NIV)

You ask, "Why's that important to me?" Well, here are a few reasons:

1) *The Holy Spirit determines what gifts and skills you receive.* "It is the one and only Holy Spirit who distributes these gifts. He alone decides which gift each person should have" (1 Corinthians 12:11 NLT). If you feel like a square peg in a round hole, ask Him to show you what your gifts are and to open doors and give you favor with the right people.

2) *The Holy Spirit knows where you belong.* Listen: "So they, being sent forth by the Holy Ghost, departed unto Seleucia" (Acts 13:4). Where you are matters! If you're a whale—you'd better be in the ocean! But if you're a bird—you were born to be in the air. During a famine God sent Elijah to the brook Cherith, saying, "I have commanded the ravens to feed thee there" (1 Kings 17:4).

Had Elijah decided to stay where he was, he'd have starved. Why? Because you don't have to do anything to get God's love, but you do have to do certain things to obtain His blessing.

3) *The Holy Spirit can be offended.* Listen: "Do not grieve the Holy Spirit..." (Ephesians 4:30 NIV). A dove returning to its nest won't land if the nest's in disorder. What a lesson!

***

ASK GOD TO MAKE YOU CONSCIOUS OF THE HOLY SPIRIT'S PRESENCE, AND MAKE YOUR HEART A PLACE WHERE HE WILL ALWAYS FEEL AT HOME!

SETEMBER 30

We're Not Ornaments – We're Vessels

I must be about my Father's business.

(Luke 2:49)

Somehow we've picked up the false notion that we can have Jesus as Savior without having Him as *Lord.* Sometimes when we need others to help with God's work, we're almost afraid to ask. We say, "If you have the time." Or, "Would you please consider?" But Jesus said, "I must be about my Father's business." Paul cried, "The love of Christ constraineth [me]" (2 Corinthians 5:14). One translation reads, "The love of God leaves me no choice."

Service is not an option; it's an obligation. You're not just a son or daughter; you're a servant. If God has given you a voice to sing, you shouldn't have to be coaxed; you should volunteer. If God has blessed you with money, remember that you're not its owner; you're simply the administrator of God's estate in your life. Listen to these words: "Everything comes from you, and we have given you only what comes from your hand" (1 Chronicles 29:14 NIV).

Are you getting the message? Listen again to the words of Jesus in Matthew 21:28: "Son, go and work today in the vineyard."

***

IT'S NOT JUST A SUGGESTION; IT'S AN ORDER—AND IT'S YOUR CALL TO SERVICE TODAY.

OCTOBER 1

Deal with It Today!

If I regard iniquity in my heart, the Lord will not hear me.

(Psalm 66:18)

After a historic victory at Jericho, Israel was defeated by a handful of villagers at the town of Ai. Joshua was so distressed that he fell weeping before God. But God said, "Get thee up; wherefore liest thou thus upon thy face? Israel hath sinned ... therefore the children of Israel could not stand before their enemies..." (Joshua 7:10-12). There's a time to pray, and a time to stop praying and go deal with the problem. If you're hoping God will give you an easier option—forget it!

After David sinned with Bathsheba, he wrote, "There was a time when I wouldn't admit what a sinner I was. But my dishonesty made me miserable ... until I finally admitted all my sins to you ... [now] all my guilt is gone" (Psalm 32:3-5 TLB). Nothing will change for you until you decide to deal with the situation and make things right.

Susanna Wesley, mother of John and Charles Wesley, said, *"Whatever weakens your reason, impairs the tenderness of your conscience, obscures your sense of God, or removes your desire for spiritual things—that is sin to you."* Let others argue over what sin is and isn't. You know in your heart of hearts if there's something standing between you and the Lord.

***

DEAL WITH IT TODAY, AND GET BACK INTO A RIGHT RELATIONSHIP WITH GOD.

OCTOBER 2

Postage Stamp Christians

Let us throw off everything that hinders and the sin that so easily entangles, and let us run with perseverance the race marked out for us.

(Hebrews 12:1 NIV)

Author John Mason tells of a tree called the Chinese Bamboo. During the first four years they water and fertilize the plant with seemingly little or no results. Then, in the fifth year, as they continue to apply water and fertilizer, *in five weeks time* the tree grows *ninety feet tall.* The question is: Did the tree grow ninety feet in five weeks, or did it grow ninety feet in five years? The answer is, it grew ninety feet in five years. Because if at any time during those five years people had stopped watering and fertilizing the tree, it would have died.

Perhaps your dreams and plans don't seem to be succeeding, and you're tempted to give up. Don't do it! Continue to water and fertilize them. Charles Spurgeon said, "By perseverance the snail reached the ark." Perhaps you've failed and feel discouraged. Remember, failure isn't fatal! Mistakes aren't final! Paul said, "We get knocked down, but we get up again and keep going" (2 Corinthians 4:9 TLB). Get back up! Josh Billings said, "Consider the postage stamp. Its usefulness consists in its ability to stick to something until it gets there!"

***

STICK WITH IT, AND BY GOD'S GRACE YOU'LL MAKE IT!

OCTOBER 3

Have You Discovered Your True Calling?

For God's gifts ... can never be withdrawn.

(Romans 11:29 TLB)

Some people live and die without ever discovering their gifts, while others spend a lifetime trying to *change* theirs. Today, you need to get into God's presence and ask Him to clearly show you your gifts and strengths, and then start building on them. Even if you've never done anything with them before, or if you've failed time and time again, God's gifts are still resident within you. *His call can never be withdrawn.*

If you choose not to use the talents He has given you, you'll probably spend your life helping others reach their goals, because most people let others control their destiny. Don't do it! Don't allow anyone to take over the driver's seat in your life. Fulfill your own dreams, and determine your own life's course.

Remember, there are people whose lives are waiting to be touched by what God has placed within you.

***

ASK GOD TO SHOW YOU THE GIFTS HE HAS PLACED
WITHIN YOU. THEN START USING THEM!

OCTOBER 4

The Hitchhiker

He orders his angels to protect you wherever you go.

(Psalm 91:11 TLB)

Late one evening a missionary asked God to help him stay alert as he drove through the night to speak at a church. Just then he saw a hitchhiker in the rain and picked him up. As they talked, he discovered that the stranger was a believer, and they had many of the same friends. They laughed, shared stories, and before they knew it dawn was breaking, and the hitchhiker was saying, "Here's where I get out." Before they parted, they had a cup of coffee at a roadside café, and they each promised to pray for each other.

By now the rain had stopped and it was morning. Just down the road, the missionary realized that he hadn't gotten the man's phone number, so he returned to the café hoping to catch him. But there was no sign of him. When he asked the cook which way the man had gone, he looked surprised and said, "Who? You came in alone! I wondered why you ordered two cups of coffee." The missionary glanced at the table where they'd sat, and sure enough, the hitchhiker's cup was still full to the brim—and cold! Then suddenly he remembered that when he'd picked the man up the night before in the pouring rain—he wasn't even wet!

***

JUST WHEN YOU NEED THEM MOST, "HE ORDERS HIS ANGELS TO PROTECT YOU WHEREVER YOU GO" (PSALM 91:11 TLB).

OCTOBER 5

The Discipline That Endures

He endured, as seeing him who is invisible.

(Hebrews 11:27)

The life of Moses is described in two words—"He endured." He endured despite the contempt of Pharaoh, the mightiest monarch on Earth. He endured despite the stubbornness of the Hebrews, who grumbled, blamed, and rebelled. He endured despite the criticism of Miriam and Aaron in his own family. Their words cut deeply, but he refused to back off. He endured despite the negative report of the ten spies who said, "The giants are too big, and we are too small."

Paul writes, "And having done everything ... stand firm" (Ephesians 6:13 NAS). Stand firm when your enemies seem to prosper. Stand firm when the wicked seem to be winning. Stand firm when big people act small, and little people demand authority they don't deserve. Stand firm when no one would ever know you compromised.

Where are you today? Are you feeling shaky in areas where you once stood strong? Are you giving in to your family, or to the opinions of others, because you're tired of their disapproval?

Moses endured even when he was in his eighties. How? "Because he saw him who is invisible" (Hebrews 11:27 NIV). That's it! He continually reminded himself that his sole purpose in life was to please the Lord ... to obey Him ... to glorify Him ... and to gain His approval at all cost.

***

WHAT MORE CAN BE SAID?

OCTOBER 6

Write and Run

Write the vision, and make it plain upon tables, that he may run that readeth it.

(Habakkuk 2:2)

There is power in putting your dream on paper, because while it's merely in your mind other things can crowd it out. When God wanted to change the world, He wrote a book. He put His heart in writing, and it's been changing lives ever since. Here are four questions to ask yourself, and to help get you up and running:

1. *What would I do if I knew for sure I could not fail?*
2. *What one thing should I eliminate from my life because it's holding me back from reaching my full potential?*
3. *Am I on the path of something marvelous or something mediocre?*
4. *Am I running from something or toward something?*

Note the word *run.* Get going! You've wasted too much time already. Get rid of your excuses for not taking decisive action. If you wait for perfect conditions, you will never get anything done. (See Ecclesiastes 11:4.)

The longer you take to act on God's direction, the more unclear it becomes. Perhaps others have told you that your plans are impossible, or that they will never work. That's what they told Edison, Ford, Columbus, and Paul. Don't listen to them.

***

INVOLVE YOURSELF WITH SOMETHING BIGGER THAN YOU ARE. YOU'LL DISCOVER THAT'S WHERE GOD IS!

OCTOBER 7

Trusting Your Spiritual Intuition

But ye have an unction from the Holy One, and ye know all things.

(1 John 2:20)

How many times have you said to yourself, *I knew I should have done that,* but instead you allowed your head to override that little inner voice? That voice is called "spiritual intuition." Listen: "Your ears will hear a voice behind you, saying, 'This is the way; walk in it'" (Isaiah 30:21 NIV). Listen again: "But ye have an unction from the Holy One, and ye know all things" (John 2:20).

Trusting your spiritual intuition means trusting what you hear, because it'll tell you: (1) what you need to do, (2) which direction you need to take, and (3) what needs to be changed in your life.

What a gift, yet we seldom use it. Why? Because we're afraid we couldn't possibly *know* anything without thinking it through, or because it just seems "too obvious." We think to ourselves, That *can't* be right. Or, I couldn't possibly do that. *We argue for our limitations, and behold—they become our limitations!*

You've got to learn to recognize and trust your spiritual intuition. It's your connection to the greatest source of wisdom—God's wisdom! Don't be surprised if some of what you discern in your spirit sounds like what you've *thought a hundred times before* and then disregarded. Listen again: "It is God who works in you to will and to act according to his good purpose" (Philippians 2:13 NIV).

***

THE NEXT TIME YOUR SPIRITUAL INTUITION TELLS YOU SOMETHING—TRUST IT!

OCTOBER 8

Does Your Countenance Need Help?

I shall yet praise him, who is the health of my countenance.

(Psalm 42:11)

Lighten up! Get a spiritual face lift! Don't just give your children orders; smile while you're doing it. If your husband or wife works in a difficult environment, make sure they don't come home to more of the same. Smiles are like thermostats; they set the temperature and determine the climate around you. Who wants to be around somebody who looks like they'll bite your head off at any moment? Learn to smile. It opens doors and hearts! It causes others to relax and lower their guard. It says, "I'm happy to be with you."

A well-known Bible teacher recently wrote, "One morning in the shower God said to me, I wish you'd smile when you're talking to Me. At 6:00a.m. I didn't feel much like smiling, but I tried it anyway. I thought, I'm glad nobody sees me doing this. But when I did it, I suddenly felt better. Then God reminded me of the words, "...joy cometh in the morning" (Psalm 30:5). In that moment I realized that when my eyes open each morning—joy is right there with me. All I have to do is activate it, and I can operate in it all day long.

***

THE DECISION COMES FIRST—THE FEELING FOLLOWS. THAT'S HOW IT WORKS.

OCTOBER 9

Godly Parents – Ungodly Children

And he did that which was evil in the sight of the Lord.

(2 Kings 21:2)

Hezekiah was one of the most righteous kings in Israel's history. Yet his son, Manasseh, seduced God's people into doing, "...more evil than did the nations whom the Lord destroyed" (2 Kings 21:9). Why? Here are three reasons worth considering:

1) *Good parents sometimes have prodigal children.* (See Luke 15:11.) Don't let anybody "guilt-trip" you about your children. Your example can still influence them, your prayers can still mold them, and your love can still keep the door open for God to work on them.

2) *Bad company can destroy good character!* Manasseh was evidently weak-willed and easily influenced by the wrong people. Teach your children that their company will shape their conduct, their character, and, ultimately, their destiny. (See Proverbs 1:10.)

3) *This father may have been too busy.* While you still have your children under your roof, make time to pray, play, and talk together. "Talk about what?" you ask. Personal responsibility. In an era where "passing the buck" has become an art form, teach them to accept responsibility for their choices. And emphasize "the erosion principle." Explain to them that evil is getting increasingly worse; more cleverly disguised; easier to get into; and harder to get out of.

***

AND WHATEVER YOU DO, NEVER GIVE UP ON THEM!

OCTOBER 10

Desperation

Blessed are they which do hunger and thirst after righteousness: for they shall be filled.

(Matthew 5:6)

My friend David Robinson called me after he had spent the day fasting and praying. He said, "I told my Father that if I cannot walk in the power of the Spirit and see the results He promised in His Word, then I don't want to hang around. He can just take me home." Does that sound extreme? Paul cried, "I could wish that myself were accursed from Christ for my brethren, my kinsmen according to the flesh" (Romans 9:3). Jacob cried, "I will not let thee go, except thou bless me" (Genesis 32:26). Listen to the results: Paul changed history, and Jacob became known as "Israel," a prince with God. *Something happens when we get desperate.* God hates apathy and indifference. Listen: "So then because thou art lukewarm, and neither cold nor hot, I will spew thee out of my mouth" (Revelation 3:16).

God responds to *passion.* He told Jeremiah, "Ye shall seek me, and find me, when ye shall search for me with all your heart" (Jeremiah 29:13). Maybe this sounds fanatical to some, but God can do more with a fool on fire than He can with a scholar on ice! John Knox, the great Scottish reformer, prayed, "God give me Scotland, or I die." That cry was heard, and the fires of revival swept through the land.

***

GOD HAS NOT CHANGED. HE STILL RESPONDS TO THOSE WHO SEEK FOR HIM WITH ALL THEIR HEARTS.

OCTOBER 11

Quick, Cheap, and Not Deep Enough

The stream beat vehemently upon that house, and could not shake it: for it was founded upon a rock.

(Luke 6:48)

Listen to Jesus: "But all those who come and listen and obey me are like a man who builds a house on a strong foundation laid upon the underlying rock. When the floodwaters rise and break against the house, it stands firm, for it is strongly built. But those who listen and don't obey are like a man who builds a house without a foundation. When the floods sweep down against that house, it crumbles into a heap of ruins" (Luke 6:47-49 TLB).

Both houses experienced the same storm, but only one was able to stand. The other fell because it was built *quick, cheap,* and *not deep enough.* Beware of the snare of instant things. Don't seek for an *experience;* seek for a *relationship.* One can be had in a *day*—the other is the product of a *lifetime* of walking with the Lord.

Both houses looked identical. The storm revealed the difference. You can count on the fact that you will go through storms. Paul said, "All that will live godly in Christ Jesus shall suffer persecution" (2 Timothy 3:12). He asked of the Galatians, "Ye did run well; who did hinder you?" (Galatians 5:7). The answer was, they built *quick, cheap,* and *not deep enough.*

***

WILL THE HOUSE YOU'RE BUILDING TODAY
WITHSTAND THE STORM TOMORROW?

OCTOBER 12

Minding Your Own Business

We hear that some among you are ... busy-bodies.

(2 Thessalonians 3:11)

One day Peter said to Jesus, "What about him, Lord?" Jesus rebuked him and said, "What is that to you?" (John 21:21-22 NLT). Now, if *Peter* could get into trouble for meddling, then any of us can. The issue here is not about helping others—it's about knowing when to mind your own business! There's a big difference.

I used to jump in without having been asked and try to solve other peoples' problems. My motives were the best in the world, but my efforts were fruitless—and often resented. Since recovering from the need to be "Mr. Fix-It," my life's a lot simpler. Now that I'm not butting in where I'm not invited, I'm more available to help when I'm needed. Remember, "If it doesn't have your name on it—don't pick it up." It's that simple!

However, minding your own business goes far beyond simply avoiding the temptation to police, enlighten, and "rescue." It includes not eavesdropping, gossiping, or speculating about things that don't concern you. *That got you—didn't it?*

Do you know why we focus so much on the shortcomings of others? You've guessed it—to keep from having to look at our own! The *only* thing you can change about other people is your attitude toward them.

***

THE BIBLE SAYS, "EXAMINE YOURSELVES" (2 CORINTHIANS 13:5). WHAT MORE IS THERE TO SAY?

OCTOBER 13

"Lighten Up!"

These things have I spoken unto you, that my joy might remain in you.

(John 15:11)

Most of us are far too serious. We're uptight about everything—being five minutes late, getting stuck in traffic, somebody giving us a wrong look, waiting in line, overcooking a meal, gaining a pound, discovering a wrinkle, making an honest mistake. You name it—we lose all perspective over it! The problem is, we have unrealistic expectations! Consider that for a minute!

If you want to experience the joy God promises, try these two things: (1) Admit that your anxiety is largely because of the way you have decided life *should be.* (2) Understand that your *expectations* are frustrating you, and that expecting things to *always* be a certain way is keeping you constantly upset.

Here's an idea. Try approaching life today *without* all those expectations and "shoulds." For example, don't expect everyone to be friendly, and then when some people are, you'll be pleased. Don't expect your day to be trouble-free. Instead, when problems come up, say, "Thank You, Lord, for another chance to grow." Go ahead, do it, and you'll see how much better everything is. Rather than always rowing against the current in life, you'll be flowing with it.

***

IF YOU WORK AT THIS, YOU'LL ENJOY LIFE MORE—AND OTHER PEOPLE WILL ENJOY BEING AROUND YOU MORE, TOO!

OCTOBER 14

God Wants You to Prosper

You will be made rich ... so that you can be generous....

(2 Corinthians 9:11 NIV)

How often does God have to say it before you believe it? He wants to empower you spiritually, relationally, and financially! But the following things will always determine your prosperity:

1) *What you sow!* Listen: "...whoever sows generously will also reap generously" (2 Corinthians 9:6 NIV). But you say, "I don't have much." Listen, you always have enough to create what you need. What has God given you? Use it as a seed to begin your next harvest.

2) *The level of your maturity.* It takes character to handle success. God only wants you to prosper "as your soul prospers" (3 John 2, NAS). If your harvest is slow in coming, be patient! God loves you too much to put you in jeopardy by giving you more than you can handle right now.

3) *Your obedience.* Listen: "Do not let this Book of the Law depart from your mouth; meditate on it day and night ... do everything written in it. Then you will be prosperous and successful" (Joshua

1:8 NIV). Obey God's Word. Why? Because God can't bless you beyond your last act of obedience.

4) *Your purpose.* General William Booth, the founder of the Salvation Army, was asked the secret of his success. He replied, "Years ago I decided to give God all of me, and that's no secret. Anybody can do it—if they'll pay the price."

***

WHEN YOU CAN SAY THOSE WORDS, GOD WILL ENTRUST YOU WITH MORE THAN YOU EVER DREAMED POSSIBLE.

OCTOBER 15

Learning to Be Confident

Yet amid all these things we are more than conquerors.

(Romans 8:37 AMP)

You are more than a conqueror when ... you have a sense of victory *before* the battle begins ... you know you have the solution *before* the problem arises ... are you're confident of God's approval *regardless* of who else's rejection you experience.

Sometimes it's the *length,* and not the *strength* of the trial that shakes us up! Is that where you are today? If so, listen: "Do not throw away your confidence ... you need to persevere so that when you have done the will of God, you will receive what he has promised" (Hebrews 10:35-36 NIV).

Confident people get the job done! Yes, they make mistakes. Yes, God has to correct them (see Hebrews 12:6). But isn't that better than always playing it safe and accomplishing nothing?

Understand something: *If you don't believe in yourself, you don't believe in God either. Because, even though He's in you, He can only do through you what you believe Him for.* Think about that for a moment!

You say, "I wish I had your confidence." Listen, confidence is something you *decide* to have. It comes from reading God's Word and *choosing* to believe it. If you do, you'll have confidence. If you don't, you'll continue to live in doubt.

***

SO, THE WORD FOR YOU TODAY IS—"LEARN TO BE CONFIDENT!"

OCTOBER 16

Mature Love

Love never fails.

(1 Corinthians 13:8)

Mature love—the kind that enables two people to go the distance—is spelled out clearly in 1 Corinthians 13. You need to read it regularly. It says:

1) *Mature love is tolerant.* It knows that a relationship is a package deal—you enjoy what's good, and you develop patience by learning to live with what's still under construction.

2) *Mature love is never envious.* It understands that real contentment comes from knowing that God has a plan for each of us—and that what He's got for you, He'll never give to anybody else.

3) *Mature love is courteous.* In a culture where good manners are in short supply, it knows that the value you place on something is evidenced by how you treat it.

4) *Mature love is not touchy.* It knows that if you always wear your feelings on your sleeve, you'll need a steady supply of Kleenex.

Now, listen to how Paul describes mature love in *The Message:* "Love never gives up. Love cares more for others than for self ... always looks for the best, never looks back, but keeps going to the end" (1 Corinthians 13:4-8 TM).

***

TODAY, ASK GOD TO GIVE YOU THAT KIND OF LOVE!

OCTOBER 17

Living Bibles

You are our letter, written in our hearts, known and read by all men.

(2 Corinthians 3:2 NAS)

Bill has wild hair, a T-shirt, torn jeans, and no shoes; it's his complete wardrobe for four years of college. Across the street from campus is a very conservative church, which Bill decides to visit.

In he walks without shoes, wearing his usual get-up, complete with wild hair. The church is packed, and he can't find a seat, so he walks down the aisle and sits on the carpet in front of the pulpit—something you just don't do in this church!

Within seconds everybody is uptight, and the minister stops preaching. Suddenly, an eighty-year-old deacon with a courtly manner, a cane, and silver-gray hair begins to walk slowly toward the newcomer. It takes a long time to reach him, and most of the congregation is sure they know what he's going to do when he gets there—and they don't blame him.

But what happens next stuns all of them and changes their church forever. To their amazement, when the old man reaches Bill, he drops his cane to the floor, and with great difficulty he lowers himself and sits down beside him—so that he won't be alone!

When the pastor regains control, he tells the hushed congregation, *"What I am about to preach, you will never remember. What you have just seen, you will never forget!"*

***

BE CAREFUL HOW YOU LIVE TODAY—YOU MAY BE THE ONLY SERMON SOMEONE WILL EVER SEE!

OCTOBER 18

An End to All Arguments

O taste and see that the Lord is good.

(Psalm 34:8)

Two professors were discussing the ingredients in a barrel of honey, when a little boy standing by stuck his hand in, tasted it, and said, "Suck it and see." That's the bottom line. *Your experience with God is not dependent on someone else's argument.* Remember, it's yours, not theirs! Saul of Tarsus had to be blinded and thrown to the ground in a life-changing confrontation with Jesus. Gideon was hiding in a cave when he met the Lord and heard these words: "Surely I will be with thee" (Judges 6:16). Isaiah had an entirely different experience, "in the year that king Uzziah died I saw also the Lord sitting upon a throne, high and lifted up, and his train filled the temple" (Isaiah 6:1).

Don't try to pour someone else into the mold of your experience. And don't cast doubt on their experience with the Lord because it's different from yours. No two of us are alike—if we were, one of us would be unnecessary! God knows what you need. When John saw the Lord on the isle of Patmos, he "fell at his feet as dead" (Revelation 1:17). Our individual experiences with the Lord will each be different. You don't have to understand somebody else's experience—so long as it produces the fruit of the Spirit and makes Jesus Lord in their lives.

***

THAT'S AN END TO ALL ARGUMENTS!

OCTOBER 19

Getting to Know His Voice

And the sheep follow him: for they know his voice.

(John 10:4)

Recently a tourist in the Middle East paid a local shepherd to exchange clothes with him, to see if this verse is really true. The shepherd dressed like a tourist, and the tourist like a shepherd, and both men went out to call the sheep. As you may have guessed, the sheep *ran to* the shepherd and *ran from* the tourist. Why? Because they had spent enough time with the shepherd to know his voice. What a lesson for us today. The burning desire of your heart, indeed the quest of your life, should be to know His voice—and that takes time spent in His presence. *Nothing else will do.* Listen to what Jesus said: "He calleth his own sheep by name" (John 10:3). He knows your name. He has a plan for your life. He has a destiny that was scheduled before you took your first breath.

Listen again to Jesus: "He leads them out" (John 10:3). That's not easy! Leaving the familiar for the unknown. Learning to stop seeing people as your security. Trusting *Him alone* to meet your every need.

Learning to stop using your *head,* and start using your *faith.* Don't implement your own plan and then ask Him to bless it. Don't kick doors open and try to make it happen! Jesus said, "He goes on ahead of them, and his sheep follow him, because they know his voice" (John 10:4 NIV). Did you hear that? *He's already gone before you!*

***

AND WHEN YOU GET THERE, YOU'LL DISCOVER THAT EVERYTHING HAS BEEN WORKED OUT.

OCTOBER 20

Rational or Biblical Thinking?

For my thoughts are not your thoughts ... saith the Lord.

(Isaiah 55:8)

Just because you've always believed something, doesn't make it true! When God tells you to take off the old and put on the new (see Colossians 3:8), he's talking about old ways of thinking. Why? Because sincerity won't protect you from the consequences of poor judgment! Don't just be a *rational* thinker; become a *biblical* thinker. Here are a few examples of rational thinking:

1) *"God's not doing anything about it, so I must."* What's behind that? Fear? Pride? Paul says, "He worketh all things after the counsel of his own will" (Ephesians 1:11). God knows what He's doing; He's too good to do anything bad, and too wise to do anything foolish, so trust Him—and don't get ahead of Him!

2) *"The hurt will never go away until they apologize to me!"* What if they never do? Forgiveness is the key to inner healing, and that key is in your hand, not theirs! (Mark 11:25). You can't take hold of

your future until you let go of your past! Forgive, let it go, and move on!

3) *"It runs in my family so there's nothing I can do about it."* Wrong! "Old things have passed away; behold all things have become new" (2 Corinthians 5:17). Pass it back—don't pass it on! If God could give the children of Israel the 400 years "back pay" that Pharaoh had stolen from them, then He can restore everything the enemy has taken from you, and your family before you.

***

TODAY, MAKE YOUR PRAYER, LORD, LINE MY THOUGHTS UP WITH YOURS.

The Pulpit Search Committee

The Lord sees not as man sees.

(1 Samuel 16:7 AMP)

A pulpit search committee brought the following report to the congregation: "In our search for just the right pastor, only one was found to have the qualities we need. After interviewing each of the candidates, here are their names, along with our comments:

Noah: A failure as a preacher; 120 years experience, but no converts. **Moses:** Stutters and loses his temper. **Abraham:** Got into trouble with the authorities and lied his way out. **David:** Would make a good minister of music, if he had better morals. **Solomon:** A walking encyclopedia of wisdom, but doesn't practice what he preaches. **Elijah:** Prone to depression, folds under pressure. **Hosea:** Divorced, and remarried to a prostitute. **Jeremiah:** Too emotional and negative; a real alarmist. **Amos:** A farmer, better suited to picking figs and raising cattle. **John:** Says he's a Baptist, but lacks tact. Dresses like a hippie. **Peter:** Bad-tempered; denied Christ publicly. **Paul:** Not good media material; too long-winded. **Timothy:** Has potential, but much too young. **Jesus:** Offends church members with his preaching. Hangs out with questionable characters. Upset the pulpit search committee with His pointed questions! **Judas:** Practical, cooperative, good with money, cares for the poor, well-dressed. We all agree—he's the man to fill our pulpit!

***

AREN'T YOU GLAD THAT "...THE LORD LOOKS ON THE HEART"?

OCTOBER 22

Gentleness

I will lead on softly, according as the cattle that goeth before me and the children be able to endure, until I come unto my Lord (Esau) unto Seir. (Genesis 33:14)

Francis Ridley Havergall writes concerning this story:

"What a beautiful picture of Jacob's *thoughtfulness* for the cattle and the children! He would not allow them to be over driven even for one day. He would not lead on according to what a strong man like Esau could do, and expected them to do, but only according to what they were able to endure.

"He knew exactly how far they could go in a day; and he made that his only consideration in arranging the marches. He had gone the same wilderness journey years before, and knew all its roughness and heat and length, by personal experience. And so he said, 'I will lead on softly' (Genesis 33:14)." What a wonderful attitude. How Christ-like!

You can *always* choose to be gentle, no matter how busy or pressured you are! It's a choice!

In the midst of all your goal-setting and achieving, you'd do well to remember two things. (1) Gentleness is a fruit of the Spirit, without which you may be successful, but you'll never be truly spiritual. (2) Gentleness is a Christ-like quality that might just impress some people more than all your accomplishments put together!

Galileo said, "The sun, with all those planets revolving around it and dependent on it, can still ripen a bunch of grapes as if it had nothing else in the universe to do."

***

IT'S WORTH THINKING ABOUT TODAY, ISN'T IT?

OCTOBER 23

How's Your Testimony?

Enoch ... had this testimony, that he pleased God.

(Hebrews 11:5)

Enoch's testimony was that "he pleased God." How about you? Do you spend your life trying to please yourself? If you spend your days working for *things,* and protecting what you already have, the answer is obvious. Is your testimony that you try to please *others?* Many of us are caught in this trap. We're afraid to share our faith in case someone ridicules us. We pass up opportunities to witness for Christ out of fear of rejection. Jesus said, "But whosoever shall deny me before men, him will I also deny before my Father which is in heaven" (Matthew 10:33).

There are forces at work today that seek to pull you down and compromise your testimony. When the angels were ready to destroy Sodom and Gomorrah, they gave Lot a chance to get his children out. But when he warned them, they laughed at him. The Bible says, "He seemed as one that mocked" (Genesis 19:14). What happened? Were they aware of his shady business dealings? His off-color stories? His pastimes? One thing is sure, when he needed his testimony most, he didn't have it. God is looking for people to-day who will live clean in a dirty world.

***

YOU CAN HAVE A TESTIMONY LIKE LOT, OR ONE LIKE ENOCH—IT'S UP TO YOU.

OCTOBER 24

The O'Malley Factor

What right do you have to condemn your neighbor?

(James 4:11 NLT)

A reader writes: "We share our home with two siblings cats—or more accurately, they share their home with us! Delaney's a quiet, affectionate soul, while O'Malley's a predator—and a world-class backbiter! For reasons known only to God and himself, O'Malley waits until Delaney's back is turned, then he pounces on her and bites her rear end. Like all seasoned backbiters, he acts without warning ... his attacks are unprovoked ... his victims can't defend themselves ... and he does it to get attention."

Backbiting—how often have you engaged in it, and afterward wished you hadn't opened your mouth at all? When you backbite, others may listen to what you have to say, but they'll never trust you. Because they know whatever you say *to* them, you'll later say *about* them. You see, when you hurt someone by gossip and innuendo, it says much more about your character than it does theirs! Listen: "Who may enter your presence? Those who refuse to slander others ... or speak evil of their friends" (Psalm 15:1-5 NLT).

Do you want to pray with confidence? Do you want His presence and His approval on all that you do? If so, don't backbite!

***

IF YOU CAN'T FIND SOMETHING GOOD TO SAY—THEN SAY NOTHING!

OCTOBER 25

Making Every Moment Count

It's in Christ that we find out who we are and what we are

living for. (Ephesians 1:11 TM)

President Kennedy's epitaph reads, "John Fitzgerald Kennedy. 1917-1963." The first date records his entry, the second his exit. *Everything he accomplished in between is represented by the hyphen in the middle—just a gap between two appointments.* In that regard, welfare recipients and White House occupants are equal.

So maximize your time! Esteem it as precious, for life is fragile and fleeting. When Jesus said, "Watch out. A man's life does not consist in the abundance of his possessions" (Luke 12:15 NIV), he was simply saying that life is built on purpose found ... challenges met ... opportunities seized ... and the will of God accomplished. What else is there?

Don't reach the top of the ladder only to wish you had spent more time pursuing things that really matter. All the annuities and money markets in the world won't keep you warm in the winter of your life. *All that matters is how you filled in the blank between eternity past and eternity future.*

The most difficult questions in school were not the true-or-false ones; the fill-in-the-blank ones stumped me every time. What's the point? Simply this: If you don't know the right answer, you can't fill in the blank correctly, *and if you can't do that, you die having missed the mark.* Don't let that happen to you! Listen again: "It's in Christ that we find out who we are and what we are living for" (Ephesians 1:11 TM).

***

WHEN YOU SUBMIT YOUR LIFE TO HIM, YOU'LL DISCOVER WHO YOU REALLY ARE!

OCTOBER 26

Is He Your Savior or Your Obsession?

I want to know Christ and the power of his resurrection and the fellowship of sharing in his sufferings.

(Philippians 3:10 NIV)

You have an option: You can reach for God's hand and make Him your source, or you can reach for His heart and make Him your obsession. The men and women He has used most are those who have sought Him with a passion.

Abraham's trip up Mount Moriah to offer up his son Isaac was all about one question and one question only: Was there anything he loved more than God? The Bible doesn't tell us a thing about Abraham's emotions—but how would *you* have felt that day? Each step taking you closer to plunging a knife into the heart of your child. Wouldn't you have bargained? Not Abraham—there was *nothing* he held nearer or dearer than the Lord. There was no possession that could ever take the place of God in his life. Try weighing yourself on those scales!

Paul said, "That I might *know* him." The Bible tells us that Adam *knew* his wife, Eve, and she conceived. Nothing can be born unless it is first conceived; and nothing can be conceived unless there is first an act of intimacy between two people. Your destiny, your equipping, and your anointing can only be conceived and sustained in the place of *intimacy*.

***

TODAY, MAKE THE CRY OF YOUR HEART: "THAT I MIGHT KNOW YOU."

OCTOBER 27

How to Deal With the Flesh

Walk not after the flesh.

(Romans 8:1)

I smiled as a lady shared this testimony:

My carnal nature got up before me today. It waited for me at the breakfast table. It sat beside me in the car and whispered all sorts of things into my ear. Things like: resentment toward my husband for not being more loving; anger toward my boss for being insensitive; fear—the kind that says there won't be enough money this month to pay the bills. I thought, surely all this entitled me to a good dose of self-pity.

Next I thought, if the day has barely started and it's this bad, what will it be like by suppertime? Then I heard a familiar voice laughing in the background, and I knew exactly what was happening. I was letting the enemy do it to me again! So I called, "Time out!" The Word says, "Submit yourselves therefore to God. Resist the devil, and he will flee from you" (James 4:7). That was it! I hadn't taken time to submit to the Lord. I was operating in my flesh.

There is no sweeter sound than the footsteps of Jesus when you invite Him in and the footsteps of the enemy as he rushes to get out. You can't fight the flesh in the power of the flesh. You do it through the power of the Holy Spirit. And today that power is yours!

***

TRY IT—IT WILL WORK FOR YOU!

OCTOBER 28

When It's Hard to Forgive

First forgive anyone you are holding a grudge against, so that your father in heaven will forgive your sins, too.

(Mark 11:25 NLT)

Are you struggling to get over something? Are you having a hard time forgiving? If you are, here's a prayer for you to pray today:

"Lord, there is nothing harder than trying to forgive when you've been terribly wounded. And it's worse when the offenders show no remorse, and even seem to gloat over the pain they've brought into your life. That's where I am today, and I don't want to forgive.

"I know enough to understand that I must—no matter what. You have given me no option, but I'm struggling with it.

"Help me to realize that unforgiveness can kill; it can destroy my friendships, my joy, my peace, my potential, and even my life.

"Today I choose to forgive those who have taken so much from me, who have broken my heart and wounded me. For Your sake, I forgive.

"Thank You, Lord, for the strength to walk in love and forgiveness, especially when the memories return and 'the committee' in my head begins to speak."

***

"THANK YOU FOR THE GRACE TO FORGIVE MOMENT BY MOMENT, AS YOU HAVE FORGIVEN ME. AMEN."

OCTOBER 29

Cheap Cross

My people draweth nigh unto me with their mouth, and honoureth me with their lips; but their heart is far from me.

(Matthew 15:8)

In a small Mexican town where a religious festival was in progress, several street vendors were selling crosses. Some were gold, others were silver, but most were cheap wooden crosses. At the top of his voice, one man cried, "Cheap cross! Cheap cross!" Nobody bought a gold cross, nobody bought a silver cross, everybody bought a cheap wooden cross.

Isn't that just like us? We give God one dollar out of ten, or one day out of seven, and occasionally we might even make a sacrifice. But generally speaking, we live by this formula: just enough salvation to make us feel safe, just enough religion to make us feel right, just enough to get by. *It's called lip service.*

Today, if your love has grown cold, and other things have taken His place, stop whatever you're doing, and get back into His presence. Repent! Ask God to cleanse you and restore to you your "first love." (See Revelation 2:4.)

***

I PROMISE YOU, HE WILL—HE'S JUST WAITING TO
BE ASKED.

OCTOBER 30

Become an Early Riser

O God, thou art my God; early will I seek thee.

(Psalm 63:1)

Want a suggestion that's guaranteed to make things better? Become an early riser! That's right; spending time with God before your day starts is an incredible way to energize yourself. Some of the world's most successful people have done it.

Isaiah writes, "My soul wants to be with you at night, and my spirit ... at the dawn of every day" (Isaiah 26:9 NCV). David said, "Early will I seek thee..." (Psalm 63:1). Look at the life of Christ: "Very early in the morning, while it was still dark, Jesus got up ... and went off to a solitary place, where he prayed" (Mark 1:35 NIV).

If you want to enjoy that kind of communion, you'll have to exercise that kind of control. That means you'll have to turn off the TV, get to bed earlier, and rise earlier. If you do, it'll be one of the most rewarding changes you'll ever make. Here are three things that will happen:

(1) You'll experience a greater sense of peace, because you're no longer relying on your own resources. (2) Because you've opened yourself to God

at the beginning of the day, you'll sense His guidance all through it. (3) As you communicate with Him, you'll be instructed, empowered, refreshed, and more successful at whatever you do. Think about it!

***

TRY IT—YOU'LL BE AMAZED BY THE RESULTS!

OCTOBER 31

How God Feels About Indifference

"Curse Meroz," said the angel of the Lord ... because they did not come to help the Lord.

(Judges 5:23 NIV)

God has strong feelings, and even stronger words, for those who are callous and do nothing. The gentle Jesus, who loved the little children, took a *whip* and drove the money changers out of the Temple because they were taking advantage of the weak and the poor. (See John 2:14.) The Bible doesn't say you shouldn't be angry; it says, *"Be ye angry, and sin not"* (Ephesians 4:26). Don't be resentful! It's right to feel passionately about a lost generation being destroyed by schools without discipline and homes without parents. When God's people get angry enough, things will begin to change. *But as long as you can tolerate it, you will never change it!* You are called to be salt and light. *Salt cleanses and light reveals.*

When Martin Luther saw Tetzel selling *indulgences* (the right to sin freely and without consequences) in the Church, he rose up in righteous anger, and a reformation started that cleansed the Church and changed it forever. Maybe you can't change history, but how about working on your own little corner? Listen: "The people of Zebulun risked their very lives" (Judges 5:18 NIV). That's why God cursed Meroz—*because they did nothing!* Child of God, get back to your post. Put on your armor and take up your sword.

***

FOR THE BLESSING AND PROTECTION OF THE LORD BELONG ONLY TO THOSE WHO DO.

NOVEMBER 1

Dad—Be There

He will turn the hearts of the fathers to their children.

(Malachi 4:6 NIV)

Almost twenty million children in America grow up without a father. These children are five times more likely to commit suicide, ten times more likely to do drugs, and twenty times more likely to go to prison. Luther Burbank said, "If we paid as much attention to our plants as we do our children, we'd be living in a jungle of weeds!" Dad, answer these three questions:

1) *Are you giving your children things instead of yourself?* By the time they're twelve, they'll have learned 75 percent of all they'll ever know. The question is, from whom? Television? Some drugged-out rap artist? Their peers? As the twig is bent, so grows the tree!

2) *Are you giving your best to your career, or to them?* If you spend all your energy at work and leave none for your family, you'll pay a high price. Your children will grow up to either resent you and repeat your mistakes, or rejoice in the

memory of a home where love was spelled T-I-M-E.

3) *Are you setting the spiritual tone for your family?* Or does your wife run circles around you in this area? Listen: "Fathers ... bring them up in the training and instruction of the Lord" (Ephesians 6:4 NIV).

***

TEN OR TWENTY YEARS FROM NOW, WHAT ARE YOU GOING TO WISH YOU'D DONE TODAY?

NOVEMBER 2

The Someday Trap

Do not withhold good ... when it is in your power to act.

(Proverbs 3:27 NIV)

Have you fallen into the "someday trap"? You know, "Someday when I have the money, or someday when I have the time." Listen: "...Don't tell your neighbor, 'Try me tomorrow,' when the money's right there in your pocket" (Proverbs 3:27-28 TM). God will only give you more when you use what He's already given you. If you constantly dwell on what you don't have instead of what you do, you'll never feel like you have enough!

Forget the big things! Turn the clutter in your closet into the answer to somebody else's prayer. Better yet, give away new stuff—stuff you really want to keep. That'll develop character, crucify self-centered-ness, and help you to be more like Jesus. You did say you wanted to be like Him, didn't you?

If you want to measure your generosity, check out the Macedonian Church, the most impoverished in Europe. Listen: "Though desperately poor ... they gave ... far more than they could afford! Pleading for the privilege of helping out—this was totally spontaneous ... and caught us completely off guard. What explains it was that they had first given themselves unreservedly to God and to us. The other giving simply flowed out of the purposes of God working in their lives" (2 Corinthians 8:3-5 TM).

***

HOW'S THAT FOR GIVING—CAN YOU MEASURE UP?

NOVEMBER 3

Why Pray Anyway?

My prayer returned into mine own bosom.

(Psalm 35:13)

First, prayer makes us slow down. We run all over, talk to everybody, and finally when all options are exhausted, we turn to God. Then when we get quiet before Him, we start getting answers. His word to you today is, "Be still, and know that I am God" (Psalm 46:10).

Next, prayer makes us God-conscious. Until this point we have only been problem-conscious. The disciples were like that when Jesus told them to feed the multitude with five loaves and two fish. They said, "What good will this be among such a crowd?" But look at the results! When we realize the problem is too big for us, and we put it into His hands, things begin to happen.

Finally, prayer keeps us honest. When we're speaking to others, we often tell only our side of the story. But when we're in the presence of God, we realize He knows our very thoughts. Three times Jesus asked Peter, "Lovest thou me?" Peter finally looked at Him and said, "Lord, thou knowest all things; thou knowest that I love thee" (John 21:17). We can fool others, but we can't fool Him.

***

THERE YOU HAVE IT—THREE GOOD REASONS TO MAKE PRAYER A PRIORITY IN YOUR LIFE TODAY!

NOVEMBER 4

In Between

He said to his disciples, Let us go over to the other side.

(Mark 4:35 NIV)

To get from where you *are* to where you are *going,* you have to be willing to be *in between.* It's hard to let go of what's familiar and stand with your hands empty while you wait for God to fill them; especially in these three areas:

1) *Feelings.* When you've been hurt, you can actually become comfortable with feelings of anger and resentment. And when you finally face them and decide to let them go, you can feel empty for a time; this is normal. You're in between pain and the peace that comes from forgiving and accepting. Hang in there; it will pass!

2) *Relationships.* When you let someone go (even a bad relationship), it can be frightening, because now you're dealing with a sense of loss. Please don't rush into another one half-dressed and ill-prepared. Wait. Talk to God. You need this time to become whole and make healthy choices.

3) *Jobs, homes, or goals.* You've let go of the old and the familiar, but you're not sure yet whether you can handle the new.

Listen: "Weeping may endure for a night, but joy cometh in the morning" (Psalm 30:5). Joy is on the way! But until it gets here, you've got to hold steady and trust God to know what He's doing.

When Jesus said to His disciples, "Let us go over to the other side," the lessons they learned and the miracles they experienced in between changed them forever.

***

AND THEY'LL CHANGE YOU, TOO!

NOVEMBER 5

A Prisoner of Love

How great is the love the Father has lavished on us.

(1 John 3:1 NIV)

The difference between God and everybody else you know is—love! You may say, "I have a car," but you can never say, "I am a car." Similarly, you may say, "I have love," but you can never say, "I *am* love." But God can! He is love! It's His very essence!

Settle it once and for all. God loves you unconditionally! Get rid of your "daisy petal" mentality—"He loves me. He loves me not." God's decision to love you is based on Him—not you!

Paul writes, "God put his love on the line for us ... while we were of no use whatever to him" (Romans 5:8 TM). Think about that; you can't earn God's love, and you can't forfeit it. All you can do is accept it and pass it on to others.

One day a little girl asked her mother, "If Jesus lives in my heart, do you think if I wrote Him a note saying 'I love you,' and then swallowed it, that He'd read it?" Her mom smiled and said, "No, dear, the best way to show Jesus you love Him is to love others." Good answer!

***

AREN'T YOU GLAD TODAY THAT HIS LOVE COMES
WITH NO STRINGS ATTACHED?

NOVEMBER 6

Paul's Principles for Handling Temptation

Watch and pray, that ye enter not into temptation...

(Matthew 26:41)

Martin Luther once said, "You can't keep the birds from flying over your head, but you can keep them from building a nest in your hair." Temptation is inevitable; how you deal with it is a matter of personal choice. So, how *do* you keep temptation from leading you into sin? By putting these four principles from the Apostle Paul to work in your life each day:

1) *"Everything is permissible for me—but not everything is beneficial"* (1 Corinthians 6:12 NIV). Ask yourself, "Is it helpful spiritually, mentally, and physically?"

2) *"Everything is permissible for me—but I will not be mastered by anything"* (1 Corinthians 6:12 NIV). Ask yourself, "Is it habit-forming? Does it bring me under its power and control?" Look out—every stronghold begins with a thought, and every habit with a single act!

3) *"Therefore, if what I eat causes my brother to fall into sin, I will never eat meat again"* (1 Corinthians 8:13 NIV). Ask yourself, "Will my actions cause me to lose my influence and respect with others? Will it hurt or confuse them?"

4) *"Whatever you do, do it all for the glory of God"* (1 Corinthians 10:31 NIV). Ask yourself, "Am I doing this to honor the Lord, or to promote myself?"

Tough questions! But by asking them you'll always know what to do, and you'll always know how your conduct will affect you, others, and ultimately the Kingdom of God!

***

MAKE PAUL'S PRINCIPLES YOURS TODAY!

NOVEMBER 7

Take Another Look at Your Sowing

Whoever sows generously will also reap generously.

(2 Corinthians 9:6 NIV)

There are three principles you need to understand about sowing and reaping.

1) *Everything you have is a seed!* A boy's lunch became the seed that fed 5,000—when he put it into the Master's hands. Listen: "For God ... will give you more and more seed to [sow] and will make it grow so that you can give away more and more..." (2 Corinthians 9:10 TLB). Note: God gives seed to sowers—so keep sowing!

2) *The seed you sow will never leave your life!* It just moves from where you are today to where you'll be tomorrow. Consecutive sowing guarantees consecutive reaping; it's a law! Listen: "...whoever sows generously will also reap generously" (2 Corinthians 9:6 NIV).

3) *God will never ask you to give what you don't have, but He'll always ask you to give what you'd like to keep.* Why? Because giving proves you've

conquered self-interest! The Bible says, "...God loves a cheerful giver. And God is able to make all grace abound to you, so that in all things at all times, having all you need, you will abound in every good work" (2 Corinthians 9:7-8 NIV).

"How much can I believe God for?" you ask.

***

AS MUCH AS HE CAN TRUST YOU WITH, AND AS MUCH AS HIS WILL FOR YOUR LIFE REQUIRES!

NOVEMBER 8

The Formula

Be very careful, then, how you live.

(Ephesians 5:15 NIV)

In Ephesians 5, Paul gives us the formula for a happy, fulfilling life. Let's look at it today.

1) *"Walk circumspectly"* (verse 15). The word *circumspect* means "to be disciplined in your thoughts, speech, actions, and motives." Your wandering days are over! It's time to enter the Promised Land, drive out the enemy, and take what belongs to you.

2) *"Redeeming the time"* (verse 16). Get serious! Begin each day by praying, "Father, thank You for this day. Some were alive yesterday, who didn't live to see it. I accept it as a gift from You, and commit myself to maximizing every moment of it, for Your glory."

3) *"Understanding what the will of the Lord is"* (verse 17). The word *understanding* in this verse means "to make sense of." Sometimes people say, "Hey, what's happening?" That's because they don't know. But we do, for our steps are guarded, guided, and governed by the Lord (see Psalm 37:23).

4) *"Be filled with the Spirit"* (verse 18). You ask "How?" Listen: "Speaking to yourselves in psalms ... making melody in your heart to the Lord" (Ephesians 5:19). You can be Spirit-filled wherever you are. When it's not appropriate to sing, you can make melody in your heart! When there's no one around to talk to, you can speak to yourself in psalms!

***

THAT'S HOW TO ENJOY A SPIRIT-FILLED LIFE!

NOVEMBER 9

He's With You Today

Even when I walk through the dark valley of death ... you are close beside me.

(Psalm 23:4 NLT)

Have you suffered the loss of a loved one? Are you struggling to cope? If so, read this prayer and make it yours today:

"Lord, I have lived this day to bury one I love. My gratitude is as full as my grief, and my peace as deep as my pain—all because of You. I need You now as never before; shepherd my soul through these dark and painful days.

"You send us to this Earth for a season, and then You receive us again unto Yourself. I understand the cycle, but I wasn't quite as ready to let go as I thought I'd be. All my life I've known that someday this would happen, but the finality of it is crushing.

"One thing I know, death cannot kill love, and hands cannot bury it. So on this my loved one's coronation day, I give You praise for a life well-lived."

If you are grieving today, listen to these words of hope: "For the Lord himself shall descend from heaven with a shout, with the voice of the archangel, and with the trump of God: and the dead in Christ shall rise first: then we which are alive and remain shall be caught up together with them in the clouds to meet the Lord in the air: and so shall we ever be with the Lord. Wherefore comfort one another with these words" (1 Thessalonians 4:16-18).

***

TODAY, IF YOU'RE IN THE VALLEY, REMEMBER YOU'RE NOT ALONE!

NOVEMBER 10

One More Time

Please strengthen me one more time.

(Judges 16:28 TLB)

Samson's disobedience cost him his sight, his strength, his usefulness, his anointing, and his testimony. But don't count him out! God heard his cry for mercy, and his hair began to grow again. His supernatural strength returned, and God gave him an opportunity to accomplish even more in his death than he did in his life. Child of God, you may be hurting deeply today because of your failures. Legalistic Christians may have pointed their fingers and said you're not worthy to serve the Lord. Remember, that's *their* opinion, not *God's!* In spite of all that he had gone through, Samson finished his life victoriously, and he is named among the heroes of faith in Hebrews 11.

There are two things you need to know about God. *First, His love will never let you off;* "whom the Lord loveth he chasteneth" (Hebrews 12:6). Listen to these words: "Being punished isn't enjoyable while it is happening—it hurts! But afterwards we can see the result" (Hebrews 12:11 TLB). *Second, His love will never let you go.* When the Prodigal Son returned, his father was waiting for him.

You can experience that love in times of personal failure and despair. It's not just a theory; it's a reality!

***

DON'T GIVE UP. LOOK UP AND CRY LIKE SAMSON, "TOUCH ME ONE MORE TIME!" I PROMISE YOU, HE'LL DO IT.

NOVEMBER 11

Help With Your Prayers

Let's walk right up to him and get what he is so ready to give.

(Hebrews 4:16 TM)

Set aside time each day to spend with God—and discipline yourself to keep it! If you're diligent about keeping other appointments, but feel like you can change or cancel your appointment with God any time you feel like it, can you imagine how that makes Him feel? Be careful: God's Spirit can be grieved! You say, "But I'm so busy." That's the lamest excuse you can offer. How you spend your time reveals what's important to you. If you don't pray, it's because you don't realize its potential, or you don't think you need God's help. Change your schedule! Rearrange your priorities! Make time for prayer! You won't succeed (as God counts success) unless you do.

Martin Luther once said, "I have so much business to do today, that I'll never get it done unless I first spend the first few hours in prayer." John Wesley said, "God does nothing, except in answer to prayer." It's not optional. If you want to see anything accomplished, you must pray, and pray with confidence. Listen, "How bold and free we then become in his presence, freely asking according to his will, sure that he's listening. And if we're confident that he's listening, we know that what we ask for is as good as ours" (1 John 5:14-15 TM).

***

WHAT ASSURANCE!

NOVEMBER 12

God Has Everything Under Control!

...Fear not, neither be discouraged...

(Deuteronomy 1:21)

Listen to these words from the God who loves you beyond expression, protects you around the clock, and goes with you wherever you go.

When there seems to be no way out, He says to you: "...Fear not: stand still [firm, confident, undismayed] and see the salvation [deliverance] of the Lord, which He will work for you today..." (Exodus 14:13 AMP).

When the problem looks too big, He says to you: "Be strong, courageous, and firm; fear not nor be in terror before them, for it is the Lord your God who goes with you; He will not fail you or forsake you" (Deuteronomy 31:6 AMP).

When you feel like you just can't cope anymore, He says to you: "...do not look around in terror and be dismayed, for I am your God. I will strengthen and harden you to difficulties, yes, I will help you; yes, I will hold you up and retain you with my [victorious] right hand..." (Isaiah 41:10 AMP).

When you long for peace of mind, He says to you: "Do not fret or have any anxiety about anything, but in every circumstance ... continue to make your wants known to God. And God's peace ... which transcends all understanding, shall garrison and mount guard over your hearts and minds..." (Philippians 4:6-7 AMP).

***

AREN'T YOU GLAD HE HAS EVERYTHING UNDER CONTROL?

NOVEMBER 13

Accident or Design?

The heavens are telling the glory of God; they are a marvelous display of his craftsmanship.

(Psalm 19:1 TLB)

Whether you look through a telescope or a microscope, God is an awesome designer. Take a look at these three things.

1) *Temperature.* The sun is 12,000 degrees Fahrenheit, and we are 93 million miles away from it—just the right distance. If the Earth's temperature was even fifty degrees hotter or colder, all life would cease. Why was the Earth not placed twice as far away, or twice as close? Accident or design?

2) *Rotation.* We rotate 365 times a year around the sun. Suppose we only rotated thirty-six times instead? Well, our days and nights would be ten times as long; we'd be terribly hot on one side, unbearably cold on the other, and life as we know it would begin to disappear. Accident or design?

3) *Air.* Oxygen constitutes about 21 percent of our atmosphere—just the right amount. Why not 50 percent? Well, if it were 50 percent, the first time

someone lit a match we'd all be toast! Is it 21 percent by accident or by design?

Where there is a design, there must be a designer! Would you like to know Him?

***

THROUGH JESUS CHRIST, HIS SON, YOU CAN KNOW THE GREAT DESIGNER PERSONALLY AND RECEIVE ETERNAL LIFE.

NOVEMBER 14

His Ways and His Acts

He made known his ways unto Moses, his acts unto the children of Israel.

(Psalm 103:7)

God showed His acts to Israel, but He revealed His ways to Moses. There's a big difference. You already know the wonderful things God can do, but how well do you know His ways?

Have you ever heard something about someone, and thought, *That doesn't sound like her—there's more to this?* That's because you know their character and you know how they act. That's the kind of confidence God wants you to have in Him.

It's good to praise Him for the things He's done, but you only learn His ways by spending time with Him. At first you're like a child trying to keep pace with your father; it's hard because his legs are longer than yours, and His thoughts are far above yours.

Regardless of how hot the furnace gets, when you know God's ways, you know His hand is on the thermostat. When He increases the heat, you know it's because He wants to accomplish something in your life. David said, "Teach me your way ... that I may walk and live in your truth" (Psalm 89:11 AMP). Things that seemed chaotic suddenly begin to have purpose when you can pray:

"LORD, EVEN IF YOU DON'T ACT, I THANK YOU FOR YOUR WAYS. IF YOU DON'T DELIVER ME AND I HAVE TO FACE THIS, I'M GLAD YOU'RE IN CONTROL, AND THAT YOU'LL DO WHAT'S BEST. YOU DON'T EVEN HAVE TO EXPLAIN; I'M GOING TO TRUST THAT WHEN IT'S ALL OVER, EVERYTHING YOU PERMITTED WILL WORK TOGETHER FOR GOOD, BECAUSE I'M CALLED ACCORDING TO YOUR PURPOSE."

NOVEMBER 15

When Others Look at You

Let your light shine before men, that they may see your good deeds and praise your Father in heaven.

(Matthew 5:16 NIV)

Could people look at you today and wonder, *How come they live in basically the same circumstances as me, yet live such a different kind of life? Why is their love so deep and lasting, while mine is so shallow? How can they forgive and not hold a grudge? How can they have such integrity?*

Some of the nicest people you know (and some of the most successful) are wandering around in spiritual darkness. They don't have so much as a ray of light! When the truth of that hits you, you'll become impatient with Christians who just run around shining their lights on each other! Jesus said, "Let your light shine before men" (Matthew 5:16 NIV). Why? So that they can see the difference! So that they'll want what you've got!

When others look at you today, what do they see? Your love? Your consistency? A visible manifestation of Christ in you? People will only be attracted to God because you make Him attractive!

So when someone asks you today, "What's your secret?" say, "I'm glad you asked"—and then light their way home!

***

WHAT DO OTHERS SEE WHEN THEY LOOK AT YOU TODAY?

NOVEMBER 16

Have You Been Worrying Lately?

Do not be anxious about anything.

(Philippians 4:6 NIV)

If you want to test your memory, try remembering what you were worrying about a year ago. Paul said, "He who began a good work in you, will carry it on to completion" (Philippians 1:6 NIV). Notice, *we* didn't start this work—*He did!* He just gave us the privilege of being involved. He never put us in charge. *He's* the captain of our salvation, and He's never lost a passenger! Sure, there will be rough weather and times when you feel queasy. Jesus said, "In this world you will have trouble, but take heart! I have overcome the world" (John 16:33 NIV).

We're not hurt so much by what happens to us, as by our interpretation of what happens to us. You can't control what happens *to* you, but with God's help you can control what happens *in* you. Remember the words, "Rejoice in the Lord always" (Philippians 4:4)? They were written from the worst prison you've ever seen. The secret was, Paul was in prison, but prison wasn't in Paul—the Kingdom of God was, and that equals righteousness, peace, and joy in the Holy Ghost. Did you hear that? *A right relationship* with God gives you confidence; *a peace* that is not subject to your surroundings or other people's actions; and *a joy* that works from the inside out.

***

NOW, AREN'T YOU GLAD YOU'RE A CHRISTIAN?

NOVEMBER 17

A Mother's Influence

Her children arise up and call her blessed.

(Proverbs 31:28)

Helen Young writes:

"There will come a time when there'll be no more slamming of doors, no more toys to pick up on the stairs, no more childhood quarrels, and no more fingerprints on the wallpaper. Then may I look back with joy and not regret.

"May I have the wisdom to see that today is my day with my children; that there are no unimportant moments in their lives; that no career is more precious, no work more rewarding, and no task more urgent.

"May I not defer it, nor neglect it, but accept it gladly—and understand that my time is short and my time is now, for my children won't wait."

There would be no Samuel without a Hannah; no John Mark without a Mary; and no Timothy without a Eunice. These great men were what they were because of the mothers they had!

What was the secret of that winning combination? Mother with child—just that simple. So, please, mother ... stay at it! Don't ever forget the permanence of your imprint. At times your children may seem ungrateful and act irresponsibly; they may ignore your reminders and forget your advice.

***

BUT BELIEVE THIS: THEY CANNOT ERASE YOUR INFLUENCE!

NOVEMBER 18

You Have Permission to Enjoy Yourself Today!

I complained, and my spirit was overwhelmed.

(Psalm 77:3)

Your words are like photographs of your thoughts. The moment you express them, you empower them. You also create a climate that affects everything else around you.

Some of us can't give ourselves permission to enjoy life because we grew up "burden-conscious" instead of "blessing-conscious." We say things like, "Nobody understands me ... everybody expects too much of me. I get no appreciation." David said, "I complained and my spirit was overwhelmed." That's still how it works!

Who created your schedule anyway? Do you get your self-worth from carrying the world on your shoulders? Does the voice in your head say, *If you don't do everything perfectly and on time ... you're a failure ... others won't need you ... love you ... respect you?* Look out; that's the voice of pride! However humble and self-sacrificing it may sound, it's pride!

What's really important in your life? If you'd only a year to live, you'd figure it out in a hurry, wouldn't you? Three things would change right away: (1) you'd place more value on what you've got than on what you want; (2) you wouldn't be in such a hurry; (3) being right and perfect would lose their appeal.

***

SO, INSTEAD OF COMPLAINING AND BEING OVERWHELMED TODAY, WHY DON'T YOU COUNT YOUR BLESSINGS, AND FIGURE OUT WHAT'S REALLY IMPORTANT?

NOVEMBER 19

You First

Eat this scroll; then go and speak to the house of Israel.

(Ezekiel 3:1 NKJV)

The prophet was told to digest the message himself before he shared it with others. Until the Word is *part of you,* until it's been absorbed into your own life, it won't come out with power and authority, and it won't produce lasting fruit. What we feel compelled to share with others, is often what the Lord is trying to say to us. Again Paul says, "I obtained mercy, that *in me first* Jesus Christ might show forth all longsuffering, for a pattern to them" (1 Timothy 1:16). Did you hear that? "Me first."

In Rome there is a fountain where tourists throw coins into the water and make a wish. The water in the fountain pours from the mouths of two lions cast in stone. *They give it out—but they never taste it! It pours from their mouths, but they are not refreshed by it themselves.* Are you getting the idea? Jesus said, "Out of his innermost being shall flow rivers of living water" (John 7:38).

In ancient Israel they had to gather fresh manna each day. If it was kept overnight it spoiled. Jesus must be new to you every morning. He must become your *daily* bread.

∗∗∗

HAVE YOU EATEN OF THAT BREAD TODAY?

NOVEMBER 20

Building for Three Generations

Do not forget the things your eyes have seen or let them slip from your heart as long as you live. Teach them to your children and to their children after them.

(Deuteronomy 4:9 NIV)

Recently Chris Demetriou, who is building a great church in London, told me, *"I'm not building this for myself; I'm building for three generations—for that's where God has placed His blessing."* Your influence should outlast your lifespan and touch your children and your children's children. Whatever you're building is not just for you; *it's for them.* If this is the standard by which your life is measured, how are you doing today? The son of a well-known missionary once confided, "My parents sure loved the heathen, but I'm not sure they ever loved me." Tragically, because he rebelled against God and everything they ever preached, their vision died with them! Law without love can cost you your family!

Abraham *prayed* for everything he received, Isaac *inherited* it, and Jacob *schemed* and took shortcuts to it. But when trouble hit Isaac's life, he remembered and returned to his father's God. So did Jacob! (See Genesis 32:24-26.)

Cover your children and your grandchildren with prayer every day. Sow the Word of God into their hearts. Don't just *talk* about it—*show* them! By the time your child is twelve, he or she will have asked a half-million questions, and you'll have had a half-million opportunities to tell them what God has to say.

***

WHEN YOU GO, MAKE SURE YOU LEAVE THE LIGHTS ON FOR THEM!

NOVEMBER 21

Intimate Worship

I will love thee, O Lord, my strength.

(Psalm 18:1)

Sometimes you just run out of words. Your heart overflows with praise, but your lips struggle to find expression. Those are the times when you long to move beyond praise into the place of *intimate worship.* Is that how you feel? If so, here's a prayer and a song of praise—from your heart to His:

"God, You alone are King of my heart; my Hero, my Helper, my Confidant, my Friend. You are the great and only Lover of my soul; my Solace, my Listener, my Amazing One, Protector, Provider, Supreme Sacrifice, Source of life and love and all good gifts.

"You are the River that runs through me, the Rock of Ages beneath me, the God of glory above me, and the Spirit of life within me.

"My heart beats for You. Yours is the love I lean on. Yours is the hand I reach for. Yours is the breast my tears find their way to. You are my Counselor, my Comforter, and the Captain of all my ways.

"You are the Searcher of my heart, the Keeper of my secrets, and the Giver of my dreams. You are all the Wonder that is love to me—my most Intimate Companion and Dweller in the deepest parts of me.

"We walk together now and through all eternity—Savior and sinner, Master and servant, Father and child. The most natural conversation of my day is prayer. The constant beat of my heart is praise. I will love You, O Lord, my strength! Amen."

***

MAKE THIS YOUR PRAYER TODAY!

NOVEMBER 22

Trade Offs

The way to life—to God ... is vigorous and requires total attention.

(Matthew 7:14 TM)

Do you consider your life a success? Before you answer, listen carefully to these words: "Success is waking up in the morning and bounding out of bed, because there's something out there that you believe you're called to do and you love to do it. Something you believe in; that you're good at; that's bigger than you; and you can hardly wait to get at it again." To succeed at anything you have to make trade offs. Here are three of the biggest:

1) *Immediate pleasure for personal growth.* It takes decades to grow an oak tree, but days to grow a squash. Which do you want to be? Are you willing to discipline yourself?

2) *Everything for one thing.* The younger you are, the more experimenting you should do. But once you've found God's purpose for your life, stick with it, give it all you've got, and refuse to be sidetracked. (See Philippians 3:13.)

3) *Quantity for quality.* You don't really pay for things with money; you pay with time. For exam-

ple, you might say, "In five years I'll have enough to buy my dream home, then I'll slow down." Five years could be *one-tenth* of your adult life. *By translating the dollar value of something into time, you'll know whether it's a worthwhile investment.*

Remember to give God the first part of every day, the first day of every week, the first portion of every paycheck, and the first consideration in every decision.

***

THAT'S A FORMULA THAT CAN'T FAIL!

NOVEMBER 23

Take Your Stand

The righteous cannot be uprooted.

(Proverbs 12:3 NIV)

When Dr. Frances Kelsey joined the Food and Drug Administration in Washington, a pharmaceutical firm in Ohio applied for a license to market a new drug called Kevadon. It seemed to relieve nausea in early pregnancy, so it was given to millions of expectant women in Europe, Asia, and Africa. Although scientific studies revealed harmful side effects, the company exerted great pressure on Dr. Kelsey to give the drug approval. Repeatedly she said no; there were just too many unanswered questions, and even though the drug was popular and very profitable, she stood her ground.

After a fourteen-month struggle, the company suddenly withdrew its application. Kevadon was Thalidomide, and by that time, the horror of "Thalidomide babies" was shocking the world. A firm "no" from a courageous doctor who refused to give in spared agony to millions. Martin Luther King Jr. said, "Our lives begin to end the day we are silent about things that matter."

Joseph said to Potiphar's wife, "I cannot sin against the Lord." The three Hebrew children told the king, "We will not bow down to your idols." Solomon said, "The righteous cannot be uprooted."

***

ASK GOD FOR COURAGE TO TAKE A STAND FOR WHAT'S RIGHT. IF YOU'RE WILLING, GOD WILL ENABLE YOU TO DO IT.

NOVEMBER 24

Get Jonah Off Your Boat!

Pick me up and throw me into the sea ... and it will become calm.

(Jonah 1:12 NIV)

God hasn't authorized you to be somebody else's life-support system—especially if they're running from Him and using you to do it! When Jesus is on your boat, you'll make it through any storm, but when you allow Jonah on board, he'll turn your life into an episode of *The Jerry Springer Show!*

You can't fix Jonah! God has prepared "a great fish" to do that (Jonah 1:17). The kindest thing you can do is to wake him up and throw him overboard. *As long as you keep rescuing him, God can't deal with him.* Pride makes us think that we can do what only God can!

Look at Jonah: While the crew is desperately throwing stuff overboard, he's sleeping. He didn't want to be delivered; he wanted to be comfortable! Do you know someone like that? The reason they haven't changed is because they're not ready yet! Jonah was so set in his ways that he was in the belly of the whale for three days before he even prayed. (If that had been me, the moment I spotted "Jaws," I'd have been on my knees calling on God!)

***

THIS MAY BE HARD TO ACCEPT, BUT THE BEST THING YOU CAN DO FOR JONAH (AND YOURSELF), IS TO THROW HIM OVERBOARD AND LET GOD DEAL WITH HIM.

NOVEMBER 25

Get Real!

Handle me, and see.

(Luke 24:39)

Jesus could say to Thomas, "Handle me and see—I'm real!" Can you say that? Do you dare let people get close enough to you to see your strengths and your weaknesses—to know that you're real? If we are the Body of Christ, *then we must let people in!* Take off the mask! Get rid of the ridiculous religious facade that hides your struggles and shortcomings, and say to the world, "Come on, handle me and see—I'm real. I'm not perfect. I struggle with my kids. I battle with habits. I don't always read and pray as I should. But I'm a child of God. He has made a difference in my life, and He can do it for you, too!"

Ghandi once said, "If I could find Christians who were truly like Christ, I would be one, too." Imagine having Ghandi on our team! However, the Christians he knew preached love but practiced discrimination. They taught righteousness but perpetuated a system that reinforced poverty and despair.

It's time to "get real"! Jesus was called the "Good Shepherd." The word *good* is translated, "winsome." Are you winsome? When you arrive, what do you bring with you? Do you turn people *on* or *off?* Using Jesus to bore people should be a crime! When you've had all the spiritual experiences you can have in church, how is your influence and reputation in the market-place of life? Can you look at those you live and work with today and say, "Handle me and see"?

***

ULTIMATELY THAT'S THE SCALE ON WHICH WE ARE ALL WEIGHED!

NOVEMBER 26

Disclosure

I will love him, and will disclose Myself to him.

(John 14:21 NAS)

Too many of us only know God through *the experience of others.* Our relationship with Him is like the one we have with our dentist—we only call on Him when we're hurting. But Jesus said, "I will reveal Myself to you." This is an invitation to get personal with Him.

Yes, there's a price tag. Listen: "The one who obeys me is the one who loves me ... and I will reveal myself to him" (John 14:21 TLB). Are you walking in obedience? Have you forgiven that person who hurt you? Have you paid that debt yet? Are you still living in disobedience concerning that relationship?

Jesus said, "If you ask Me anything in My name, I will do it. If you love Me, you will keep My commandments" (John 14:14-15 NAS). Do you see the connection? *Jesus will spontaneously answer your requests when you instinctively obey Him.*

Has your obedience become mechanical and meaningless? If the answer is yes, you need to fall in love with Him all over again. Get into His presence and stay there until you've seen His face, heard His voice, and said yes to all He's asking.

***

TODAY HE LONGS TO DISCLOSE HIMSELF TO YOU.

NOVEMBER 27

Life Begins at Eighty

With long life I satisfy Him, and show Him my salvation.

(Psalm 91:16)

Listen to these wonderfully humorous words by the renowned Frank Laubach on his eightieth birthday.

"The first eighty years are the hardest; the second eighty are just a succession of birthday parties! Once you reach eighty, everybody wants to carry your bags and help you up the steps. If you forget your name, or anybody else's, or an appointment, or your telephone number, or promise to be three places at the same time, or you can't remember how many grand-children you have—all you have to do is say you're eighty.

"At sixty or seventy everybody gets mad at you for everything, but at eighty you have a perfect excuse no matter what you do. At sixty or seventy, they expect you to retire to a house in Florida and complain about your lumbago. I think they call it arthritis now. At sixty or seventy you ask everybody to speak up and stop mumbling because you can't understand them, when the truth is your hearing is about 50 percent gone. But if you make it to eighty, everybody is surprised and they treat you with respect just for having lived so long. So please, try to make it to eighty; for it's the best time of your life."

Now in a more serious vein, listen to these words: "If you walk in my ways and obey my statutes ... I will give you a long life" (1 Kings 3:14 NIV). Child of God, you have a scriptural right to two things: (1) more days in your life, and (2) more life in your days.

***

CLAIM THEM BOTH TODAY!

NOVEMBER 28

He Still Believes in You

Now go and give this message to his disciples including Peter.

(Mark 16:7 TLB)

In 1929 Georgia Tech played the University of California in the Rose Bowl. A California player named Roy Reigels recovered a fumble but made a mistake and ran *the wrong way.* One of his teammates tackled him just before he scored. Reigels was devastated!

During halftime the California players sat quietly waiting to hear what the coach had to say. Coach Pierce looked at the team and said, "Men, the same team that played the first half will start the second, *including Reigels."* Roy Reigels responded, "I couldn't face that crowd in the stadium to save my life. I'll never play again!" Coach Pierce put his hand on Roy's shoulder and said, "Son, you made a mistake; but the game is only half over, and I need you to go out there and give me the best you've got." His team won in the second half, and Roy played like a hero. Later he told a friend, *"When I realized that my coach still believed in me, I could do nothing less than give him my best."*

Have you fumbled the ball? Have you run in the wrong direction? Do you feel like quitting? *Don't give up! Your coach still believes in you!* The One who restored Peter after his weakness and denial wants to put you back on His team and make you a winner.

***

GIVE HIM A CHANCE TODAY—GET BACK IN THE GAME!

NOVEMBER 29

Childlike

Except ye ... become as little children, ye shall not enter into the kingdom of heaven.

(Matthew 18:3)

What did Jesus mean when He said, "Become as little children"? *He meant a child is teachable!* David cried, "Give me understanding, that I may know thy testimonies" (Psalm 119:125). *If you're teachable, you're reachable.* If you're hungry for God's Word, you have a future.

A child is dependent. Jesus said in John 15:5, "Without me, ye can do nothing." We speak those words glibly, and then go out and act like it all depends on us. If we succeed, we become drunk on a success we had nothing to do with. If we fail, we fall apart under the weight of an assignment He never gave us to begin with. The truth is, you couldn't even get out of bed in the morning without Him!

A child is trusting. It never occurs to him to wonder if his needs will be met. He's learned to trust. Sadly, it's only after we have exhausted our own efforts that we turn in desperation to God. Someone has said, "If we used God as a *first* resort, we wouldn't have to use Him as a last resort."

***

TODAY, YOU NEED TO BECOME AS A LITTLE CHILD—TEACHABLE, TRUSTING, DEPENDENT, AND OBEDIENT.

NOVEMBER 30

Silence in Strength

Even a fool, when he holdeth his peace, is counted wise.

(Proverbs 17:28)

President Calvin Coolidge was a reserved man of few words. One day a reporter attempted to interview him. The conversation went like this:

Reporter: "Do you wish to say anything about the war threat in Europe?"

Coolidge: "No."

Reporter: "About the strike in the clothing factories?"

Coolidge: "No."

Reporter: "About the farm production problem?"

Coolidge: "No."

As the reporter began to leave the room, Coolidge unexpectedly called him back and said, *"Don't quote me!"*

Never let yourself be pressured into saying something when you don't feel like talking or don't have an answer. Silence is not lack of communication; it's a very effective form of it. *What you don't say, you'll never have to explain.* Paul says, "Charity [love] suffereth long, and is kind" (1 Corinthians 13:4). All of us have people in our lives who irritate or provoke us, and the easy way is to react and tell them off. But what would Jesus do? The Bible says, "When he was reviled, he reviled not again" (1 Peter 2:23). *Make His way, your way!*

***

ASK GOD TODAY TO GIVE YOU THE GRACE TO SAY NOTHING.

DECEMBER 1

Called to Be a Parent

And whoever receives one such child in My name receives Me.

(Matthew 18:5 NAS)

Think about the constant needs and demands of a child. Yes, constant! They need to be loved ... to be listened to ... to be answered ... to be helped ... to be held ... to be corrected ... to be trained ... and always to be encouraged. The next time you see a mother with children, stop and salute; better yet, pray for her! She's one of life's unsung heroes!

I saw a mom the other day with a baby in her arms and a toddler at her feet. Was she ever busy! She had to cope with untied shoes, a runny nose, twelve questions a minute, a rattle dropped five times, a toddler who fell three times, loud crying, a bottle of juice spilled in her bag and mopped up with her last clean diaper—and finally, a baby who threw up all over her! Yet with love and incredible patience she hung in there, and handled it all.

I hope she knows that God noticed everything she did—and I hope, too, that she has a husband who appreciates her and helps out. There is no higher calling! If you're a parent, God's richest blessing is upon you today!

***

REMEMBER, BY SHOWING COMPASSION TO A LITTLE CHILD, YOU'RE SHOWING IT TO GOD!

DECEMBER 2

Self-Acceptance

May you be founded securely on love.

(Ephesians 3:17 AMP)

It's agony to be with people and feel deep down that they don't like you; or to want to do something, but not feel free enough to step out and try it. Sound familiar? My healing began when I read the Bible and discovered that God chose to love me—just as I am! Imagine that! I didn't have to earn it! That set me free to stop trying and trust what God said about me. It took a while, because I'd spent a lifetime putting myself down.

God had a special destiny for me, but I couldn't fulfill it as long as I was insecure and had a poor self-image. So I began confessing His Word over my life each day. One of the verses that helped me greatly was this: "Before I formed you in the womb I knew and approved of you [as my chosen instrument]" (Jeremiah 1:5 AMP).

Next, I learned the difference between my *who* and my *do.* God doesn't love everything I do, but He loves me! He sees my heart, not just my flesh. Now, if He can keep the two separate, then He can teach me to do the same, too. You see, His unconditional love enables you to accept yourself as you are and then see yourself as you're going to be.

***

WHAT ASSURANCE—ACCEPTED   IN THE BELOVED!

DECEMBER 3

It's Time to Get Up and Walk!

Do you want to get well?

(John 5:6 NIV)

What a question Jesus asked, "Do you want to get well?" Who wouldn't? Well, perhaps you'd be surprised! Kay Arthur tells of meeting a beggar one day on a street in Old Jerusalem. As he sat begging, his trouser leg was pulled up to reveal terrible sores. She says, "My nurse's heart brought my feet to a halt. I wanted to bend down and shield the open wound from the dirt. It should be washed, medicated, and dressed by someone who cared.

"Suddenly, a friend gently took my elbow and propelled me toward my destination. I was a tourist and I didn't know about these things. My friend then proceeded to tell me that this man *did not wish* to be well. He made his living from his wound! As I looked back sadly, I caught one last glimpse of a man who was less—much less—than he could have been."

Are you using your circumstances as an excuse to *stay* the way you are? Today if Jesus asked *you,* "Do you want to get well, emotionally, physically, or spiritually?" what would your answer be?

✳✳✳

TODAY, IT'S TIME TO GET UP—AND WALK!

DECEMBER 4

The Moment of Truth

Peter remembered the word of Jesus.... And he went out, and wept bitterly.

(Matthew 26:75)

As the cock crowed, Peter remembered his words to Jesus, "If I have to die with you, I'll never disown you" (Mark 14:31 NIV). The moment of truth had come for Peter, and it will come for you, too. Suddenly you'll see things in yourself you never thought were there. God permits the storm to blow away your cover and reveal your weakness, so you can begin to deal with it. Sometimes the very point at which you thought you were strongest is your point of hidden weakness. Sound familiar?

Maybe you were raised to always appear strong and look like you "have it together," but now God is permitting all that to be stripped away. Self-confidence is shattered! Ego is exposed! Paul says, "Have no confidence in the flesh" (Philippians 3:3). Only when we reach this point can we lay a sure foundation, not with our pride or ability, but His grace.

We know we can do *nothing* of eternal value in our own ability. That's easy to *say,* but having that truth deeply rooted in our being is another matter.

Peter was never the same after that night. He was humbled. He was now a candidate for the grace of God. "Be clothed with humility: for God resisteth the proud, and giveth grace to the humble" (1 Peter 5:5).

***

HAS GOD BEEN DOING THIS IN YOUR LIFE LATELY?

DECEMBER 5

We Need More Kings

And hath made us kings and priests unto God.

(Revelation 1:6)

Charles Neiman says, "Priests provide the *vision,* and kings provide the *provision.* The priests take care of things in God's house, while the kings go out to do battle, and bring back the spoils to finance and fulfill the purposes of God." What insight!

Christian businessperson, you're a king! You have a place in God's plan that's as important as that of any pastor or prophet. If religion has convinced you that God is against wealth, or against doing things with excellence, listen: "I am the Lord ... which tea-cheth thee to profit" (Isaiah 48:17). David said, "The Lord shall increase you more and more, you and your children" (Psalm 115:15). God has increase on His mind, and He wants *you* to be like-minded. New Testament believers were blamed for "turning the world upside down," but there's something we often over-look—those who owned houses and land, sold them, brought the money from the sales, and placed it at the apostles' feet. (See Acts 4:34-35.) It's time you started seeing God's purpose in your business and its success.

There is no shortage of money—it's just in the hands of the wrong people! In the next five years, history's greatest transfer of wealth from one generation to the next will take place—billions of dollars!

***

I'M PRAYING FOR AN ARMY OF KINGS TO GO GET IT AND BRING IT INTO THE KINGDOM OF GOD, SO THAT WE CAN LIFT UP THE NAME OF JESUS ON EVERY CONTINENT!

DECEMBER 6

It's Not Too Late!

Do not throw away your confidence; it will be richly rewarded.

(Hebrews 10:35 NIV)

Are you discouraged? Do you feel like giving up? If so, read the following words and make them your prayer today.

"God, I've done everything I know to see my dreams come true. I've had seasons of working hard and seasons of 'letting go and letting God'; still, the things I've believed for seem like they'll never happen.

"I feel like Sarah—I'll never hold the one thing I long for most. God, don't let me miss my destiny. Don't let me hope for things that are not part of Your plan for my life. Let me hear Your voice guiding me, reassuring me, and telling me You love me.

"Give me a fresh glimpse of Your promise to me, so that I can fight with faith and take hold of it. Help me also to understand the difference between what I must go after and what I must wait on You for. When it's up to me, give me the strength to demolish doubt and march fearlessly into the new day You've prepared for me. When it's up to You, give me grace and patience to wait; fill me with the joyful anticipation that accompanies a perfectly timed present.

"Lord, they say that You are never, ever late. So in these days of waiting, when time seems endless, keep me firm in my faith. Don't let me stop short of my blessing."

***

"REMIND ME AGAIN THAT I MUST NOT THROW AWAY MY CONFIDENCE, FOR IT WILL BE RICHLY REWARDED! AMEN."

DECEMBER 7

Are You Maturing?

Therefore let us ... go on to maturity.

(Hebrews 6:1 NIV)

Before you answer that question, read these words carefully:

Maturity is the ability to control your anger and settle your differences without violence or resentment.

Maturity is patience; it's the willingness to pass up immediate pleasure for long-term gain. It's the ability to "sweat it out," in spite of heavy opposition or discouraging setbacks. It's the capacity to face unpleasantness and frustration without complaining or collapsing.

Maturity is humility. It's being big enough to say "I was wrong," and when you're right, never needing to say, "I told you so."

Maturity is the ability to make a decision and follow through on it, instead of exploring endless possibilities and doing nothing about any of them.

Maturity means dependability, keeping your word and coming through in a crisis. The immature are masters of alibi; they are confused and disorganized. Their lives are a maze of broken promises, former friends, unfinished business, and good intentions.

Maturity is the art of being at peace with what you can't change, having the courage to change what you can, and having the wisdom to know the difference.

***

TODAY, IT'S TIME TO "...GO ON TO MATURITY."

DECEMBER 8

A Season in Dry Docks

Examine yourselves, whether ye be in the faith.

(2 Corinthians 13:5)

At the Belfast shipyard, where the famous *Titanic* was built, ocean liners often came to be serviced in dry dock. Ships that could do forty knots, carry tons of cargo, and make great profit would suddenly start losing power—and money. When this happened, the trouble was usually under the waterline where the eye couldn't see. The problem: *barnacles*—big outcroppings of coral and sludge clinging to the sides and robbing the ship of her power. So it had to be put in dry dock until the hindering barnacles were stripped off. (See Hebrews 12:1 TLB.)

Have you noticed a loss of power in your life lately? *The solution could be a season in dry dock!* All of us need it. David said, "Search me, O God, and know my heart" (Psalm 139:23). Paul says, "Examine yourselves" (2 Corinthians 13:5). It could be a critical spirit, an attitude of self-pity and blaming others, or a life that has become self-centered. One thing is certain, you will never know until you get into God's presence and let Him reveal what is under the waterline in your life. A little time now will save you a lot of time later!

***

WHEN HE REVEALS AND REMOVES, YOU CAN FINALLY BE EVERYTHING HE HAS CALLED YOU TO BE.

DECEMBER 9

Gut-Level Honesty

Thou shall not bear false witness.

(Matthew 19:18)

In a recent major survey, people were asked, "What would you be willing to do for ten million dollars?" (Are you sitting down?) Twenty-five percent of them said they'd abandon their families; 23 percent said they'd become a prostitute for a week; 7 percent said they'd even murder a stranger!

Are you shocked? Are you saying, "I'd never do that"? Don't be so quick—the survey also revealed that Christians were "almost as likely as non-Christians" to falsify their tax returns, call in sick when they were not, cheat on their mates, or tear down someone else's character to make themselves look better. Have you done any of those things recently?

Listen to these words: "Don't lie to each other, for you have stripped off your old evil nature and all its wicked deeds. In its place you have clothed yourselves with a brand new nature that is continually being renewed as you learn more and more about Christ" (Colossians 3:10 NLT). Note the words "you have clothed yourselves." It's a garment you have to put on every day!

Want a challenge? Start modeling the truth ... the whole truth and nothing but the truth, so help you God. Think the truth! Face the truth! Love the truth! Pursue the truth! Walk in the truth!

***

FROM THIS DAY FORWARD, PRACTICE "GUT-LEVEL HONESTY."

DECEMBER 10

Scaring Birds or Sowing Seeds

At the proper time we will reap a harvest if we do not give up.

(Galatians 6:9 NIV)

Jesus told the story of a farmer who sowed seed in four different kinds of ground, but only the first could produce anything. What happened to the seed in the other three? Weeds choked the second, the third was ruined by rocks, and the fourth was devoured by birds.

And that's still how it works! *You either spend your life pulling weeds, removing rocks, scaring birds—or sowing seeds.* Make the right choice and you prosper; make the wrong one, and it'll be a long, hard winter.

Here are your options today: (1) Quit because of the "weeds" that attempt to choke the life out of your dreams. (2) Get discouraged because of the "rocks" you have to climb over or go around on your way to your goals. (3) Exhaust yourself fighting off "birds" that constantly attack your values and try to rob you of your vision. (4) Go through life sowing "good seeds" and reaping good harvests. It's up to you!

Negative thinking will always empower your problem and keep you from reaching your destiny! It'll ensure that your harvest never makes it to the barn! So focus on the end game. When things go wrong, don't you go wrong with them! Remember, God has promised that when the time is right—you will reap!

***

WHEN YOU GET UP EACH DAY, TELL YOURSELF, IT'S TIME TO GO OUT AND DO SOME MORE SOWING.

DECEMBER 11

God Is Your Source

Everything we have has come from you, and we only give you what is yours already!

(1 Chronicles 29:14 TLB)

Sometimes we forget that, and we act like our employer or somebody else is our source. No! They may be the *instrument* God uses, but He alone is the *Source.* Listen: "Everything ... has come from you." He holds the deed and title to absolutely everything we have.

An old lady who hadn't eaten for days was praying for bread. Two boys heard her and ran to the store, bought a loaf of bread, then climbed up on the roof and dropped it down the chimney. The old woman was thrilled, gave thanks, and began to eat. Later, when the boys knocked on the door and asked her what had happened, she told them how she had been praying for bread and God had sent a loaf down the chimney. They laughed and said, "*We* heard you praying, we bought the bread, and we dropped it down the chimney. Now what do you think?" She replied, "*The devil may have delivered it, but God still sent it!*"

Even if God has to turn the devil into His errand boy, He will come through for you! David said, "I was young and now I am old, yet I have never seen the righteous forsaken or their children begging bread" (Psalm 37:25 NIV). Have you?

***

REMEMBER, GOD IS STILL YOUR SOURCE!

DECEMBER 12

Receiving – Searching – Believing

They received the word with all readiness of mind, and searched the scriptures daily, whether those things were so. Therefore many of them believed.

(Acts 17:11-12)

What a testimony! The new Berean Christians were so hungry for God that they received the Word with a *ready mind,* then took it home and studied it for themselves to see if the things they had heard were really so. What a contrast to the Athenians, who "spent their time in nothing else, but either to tell, or to hear some new thing" (Acts 17:21).

We are living in such an age today! Many are searching for *something* new to interest them, move them, and entertain them. Recently someone asked, "What has God been saying to you?" I replied, "The same thing He's been saying for a long time; and He's going to *keep* saying it until I do something about it."

Do you want to succeed? Listen to God's formula for a happy and successful life: "This book of the law shall not depart out of thy mouth; but thou shalt meditate therein day and night, that thou mayest observe to do according to all that is written therein: for then thou shalt make thy way prosperous, and then shalt thou have good success" (Joshua 1:8). This formula will work for you if you make it part of your daily life.

***

GET INTO THE WORD AND WATCH THE DIFFERENCE IT MAKES IN YOUR LIFE.

DECEMBER 13

Stress Fractures

Come unto me, all of you who are weary.

(Matthew 11:28 NLT)

A recent *Sports Illustrated* article says; "Stress fractures begin when the shocks and strains of playing game after game create tiny cracks in the outer layers of bone. When those cracks become large enough to cause severe pain, they're known as stress fractures." What a picture!

If you've ever had a "stress-fractured spirit" or an aching heart, you know what I'm talking about. It can eat at you all day and keep you awake all night. You can numb it with alcohol or drugs, an illicit affair, or a hyperactive lifestyle, but they just make it worse!

So what do you do? Two things: *First, change your focus!* Jesus said "Come unto me ... and I will give you rest ... let me teach you ... and you will find rest for your souls (Matthew 11:28 NLT).

Second, change your lifestyle! Stop making a big deal out of everything. Laugh more. (Can you even remember the last time you laughed?) Admit your imperfections. Let some stuff go. Stop trying to be Wonder Woman or Mr. Fix-It! Get away for some fun. Yes, Christians need fun, too! Cancel some of your "not so important" meetings. If you want things to change—you'll have to change them!

***

TALK TO GOD TODAY; HE'LL GIVE YOU THE STRENGTH TO DO IT.

DECEMBER 14

A Friend of Sinners

This man receiveth sinners, and eateth with them.

(Luke 15:2))

One of the greatest compliments His enemies ever paid Jesus was when they called Him "a friend of ... sinners!" (Luke 7:34). *Could you be accused of that?* In the story of the Good Samaritan, Jesus taught us how *religion* treats hurting people and how *He* treats them. Religion passed right by the injured man and refused to get involved. Why would a church turn its back on the very people who need it most? People with AIDS; people who've had abortions; people struggling with alcohol and drugs; people in prison. Could it be concern about their own *image?* Or about their *financial support?* Jesus ate with sinners, spent endless hours talking with them, and even accepted invitations to stay as a guest in their homes.

The Good Samaritan showed compassion, not contempt. He went out of his way to show the love of God to this man who had taken the wrong road, and he even paid the cost to restore him. Then Jesus said, *"Go, and do thou likewise"* (Luke 10:37). He's saying that to you, too! Most people think a good sermon is one that goes over their heads and hits their neighbor right between the eyes. Not so! You have been called to be His hand extended to those who've lost their way.

***

THE FRIEND OF SINNERS IS CALLING YOU TODAY TO SHOW HIS LOVE TO A HURTING WORLD. WILL YOU GO?

DECEMBER 15

The Old-Fashioned Way

Ask for the old paths, where is the good way.

(Jeremiah 6:16)

Jeremiah is speaking about qualities that never go out of date—like *loyalty!* Solomon says, "Never abandon a friend" (Proverbs 27:10 TLB). In the Book of Ruth, when famine and trouble came, Naomi's two daughters-in-law reacted in totally different ways. Orpah kissed her and left, but Ruth stood by her and said, *"Whither thou goest, I will go"* (Ruth 1:16). Thank God for the friend who stands by you.

How about old-fashioned *courtesy?* How you treat the elderly, for example, says a great deal about your character. The Word says, "Rise in the presence of the aged, show respect for the elderly" (Leviticus 19:32 NIV). This can lengthen or shorten your life. Listen: "Honour thy father and mother ... that it may be well with thee, and thou mayest live long on the earth" (Ephesians 6:2-3). That's serious stuff!

How about *honesty?* Do you remember when a man's word was his bond, and a good-faith handshake meant more than a roomful of lawyers? Listen to the Word: "In all things [be] willing to live honestly" (Hebrews 13:18). Whether you're a farmer putting your best apples on the top of the barrel, or a pastor exaggerating the size of your congregation, Paul says, "Provide things honest in the sight of all men" (Romans 12:17).

***

CHILD OF GOD, IT'S TIME TO GO BACK TO THE "OLD PATHS."

DECEMBER 16

Living for Others

He never thought of doing a kindness.

(Psalm 109:16 NIV)

Make sure that what you're most concerned about is what God's most concerned about. Otherwise you'll have eternity to wish you had done things differently! The King James Version says, "He remembered not to show mercy." Could that charge be laid at your door? You're ambitious, hard-working, and responsible, but have you forgotten to show mercy—especially to those who seem to deserve it least? David said, "With the merciful thou wilt show thyself merciful" (Psalm 18:25).

Listen to this moving illustration:

When the British government sought to reward General Gordon for his brilliant service in China, he declined all money and titles, but accepted a gold medal inscribed with the record of his thirty-three engagements. It was his most prized possession. But after his death the medal could not be found. Eventually it was learned that he had sent it to Manchester during a severe famine, directing that it should be melted down and used to buy bread for the poor. On the date he sent it, these words were found written in Gordon's diary: *"The last earthly thing in this world that I valued, I have given to the Lord Jesus Christ."*

***

THERE IS NO WAY TO LIVE FOR JESUS WITHOUT LIVING FOR OTHERS!

DECEMBER 17

God Will Use Whatever You've Got

What is that in thine hand?

(Exodus 4:2)

When God asked Moses, "What is that in thine hand?" you can almost hear the discouragement in his reply: "A rod." Just a walking stick. *But it was what came naturally to him!* Today, the Lord wants you to know that He'll use what comes naturally to you! The secret is to put what you've got into His hands. Make it available to Him. When Samson faced a thousand Philistines, he had nothing to fight with but the jaw bone of an ass. It was *what was available to him!* It was enough! Reverently speaking, God could have used a daffodil, if that was all Samson had had that day!

When Pastor Ray Bevin from Wales preached recently on this thought, a church secretary came to him in tears and said, "I see it! All my life I've felt inadequate and inferior because I wasn't talented like other people. I never thought God could use me, but today I see *God has been using me for years.* Every time I sit down at my word processor and type seventy words a minute, *that's God using my gift!"*

Stop trying to be someone else, and discover who you are. Instead of trying to compare yourself with others, or change what God has made you, recognize the gifts and strengths you've got, and start building on them.

***

YOU'LL BE AMAZED WHAT GOD CAN DO WITH THEM!

DECEMBER 18

Have You Discovered Your Gifts?

For God's gifts and his call are irrevocable.

(Romans 11:29)

If you've never discovered your gift, or if you've been running from it—it's still there! That means you can choose to do something with it, beginning right now. God's gifts are never loans; they are always deposits. They are never exhausted or depleted. The more you use them, the stronger they get. Paul told Timothy, "Stir up the gift that is within you" (2 Timothy 1:6).

Author John Mason says, *"You were born an original; don't die a copy!"* Discover your gift! In the time of famine, Elijah asked his servant to go and look at the horizon and come back and tell him what he saw. He said, "I see a little cloud the size of a man's hand" (1 Kings 18:44). But that little cloud was the beginning of a *downpour* and the *end of a drought.* Don't despise your small beginnings. Walt Disney told people, "This whole thing began with a mouse."

In the New Testament, they started with 120 believers against the might of pagan Rome, but they ended up changing the world. There are people waiting to be reached, saved, and blessed by what God has placed within you.

***

ASK HIM TO HELP YOU DISCOVER YOUR GIFT, UNLOCK IT, AND OFFER IT BACK TO HIM FOR HIS GLORY.

DECEMBER 19

"Bang, Bang! You're Dead!"

Except a corn of wheat fall into the ground and die, it abideth alone: but if it die, it bringeth forth much fruit.

(John 12:24)

A man once received a telephone call, and when he answered it a voice on the other end said, "Bang! Bang! You're dead!" Then he recognized the familiar voice of a friend saying, "John, I was just calling to remind you that we all need to die to ourselves every day." That's hard to remember! Paul says, "For we know that our old self was crucified with him, so that the body of sin might be rendered powerless" (Romans 6:5). Some days our "old man" is anything but dead. We're aware of him when someone steps on our toes; when we don't get the appreciation we think we deserve, self-pity rises to sit on the throne. I'm sure you know what I mean!

The Christian life is so opposite from the way of the world. You can't *rule* unless you're willing to *serve.* You can't *receive* unless you're willing to *give.* You can't *live* unless you're willing to *die* to self.

Jesus said unless you die to self and sow your life into the lives of others, you'll always be alone. Here's the answer to loneliness! *Find a need that no one else is meeting, and sow your life like a seed into it.* Jesus said, "He that is greatest among you shall be your servant" (Matthew 23:11).

***

REMEMBER, "THE WAY TO THE THRONE ROOM IS THROUGH THE SERVANTS' QUARTERS."

DECEMBER 20

Consider the Birds

Live in harmony with one another; be sympathetic, love as brothers, be compassionate and humble.

(1 Peter 3:8 NIV)

Have you ever seen a flock of geese flying in a "V" formation? What a lesson they provide for you and me! When one of them gets sick or wounded, it never falls from formation by itself. Two other birds fall out with it, and follow the ailing bird to the ground. One of them is usually the mate of the wounded bird, since geese mate for life and are extremely loyal. Once on the ground, the healthy birds protect and care for the sick one; even to the point of throwing themselves between it and any predator. They stay there until the wounded bird is either able to fly again, or until it dies. Only then do they leave and rejoin the flock.

That's what the family of God should be like. Listen again to these words: "Live in harmony; be sympathetic, love as brothers." Have you ever seen brotherly love in action? Brothers may fight among themselves, but if someone else touches one of them, he often ends up fighting *them all!*

When you don't agree with your brother, don't tear him down—pray for him; and if he fails, pick him up!

***

LET THE WORLD SEE HOW MUCH WE LOVE ONE ANOTHER. (SEE JOHN 13:35.)

DECEMBER 21

Don't Get Spread Out Too Thin

Little by little ... until you have increased enough to take possession of the land.

(Exodus 23:30 NIV)

Listen to what God told His people about possessing the land because He's saying the same thing to you today: "I will not drive them out in a single year, because the land will become desolate and the wild animals too numerous for you. Little by little I will drive them out before you, until you have increased enough to take possession of the land" (Exodus 23:29-30 NIV).

God knows when you're ready for something, and in His mercy, He won't give it to you before then. He'll give it to you "little by little," as you mature in character and discernment. He'll also check your relationship with Him, and if all these things line up correctly, He'll give you *more.* Ministries have failed and good people have finished up under a crushing yoke of debt and despair, because they failed to discern God's plan or to *wait* for His timing.

God knew there were too many enemies to handle at one time, and if His people tried to inhabit all the cities at once, they'd be spread out too thin and the enemy could easily defeat them. One of Satan's oldest strategies is getting you to reach for too much, too soon.

We want to go by leaps and bounds, but He's saying "little by little ... until you have increased enough to take possession of the land."

***

REMEMBER, THAT'S HIS WAY AND IT'S ALWAYS BEST!

DECEMBER 22

Three Kinds of People

A friend loveth at all times.

(Proverbs 17:17)

Experience teaches us that there are three kinds of people:

(1) *Critical people.* They're the *users* who reach for your strength, but run from your weakness. When you're in trouble, they hold you at arm's length in case they become tainted by association. Sadly, you'll find them in the Church as well as the world.

(2) *The cautious crowd.* They won't always criticize, but when you're in trouble they wait to see if you make it through the tunnel, and even when you do, they wait to see how others treat you. Only when it's safe will they reach for you again. They're *fair weather* friends.

(3) *The committed ones*— the friends who love at *all* times. Though they hear the *worst,* they still believe the *best.* When others leave, they stay! When the critics tear you down and the cautious crowd stands silently by, they'll speak up for you. Paul said about a true friend, "The Lord give mercy unto the house of Onesiphorus; for

he oft refreshed me, and was not ashamed of my chain" (2 Timothy 1:16). Jonathan loved David and stood by him, even when it could have easily cost him his life. Don't you think we need more people like this?

***

ASK GOD TO MAKE YOU THAT KIND OF FRIEND TODAY.

DECEMBER 23

Take the Brakes Off!

They ... would not put their shoulders to the work.

(Nehemiah 3:5 NIV)

Against all odds, God's people rebuilt the walls of Jerusalem, but sadly some of them refused to put their hearts into it. Could that be said of you?

Two men were riding a tandem bicycle up a hill. When they finally reached the top, exhausted, the one on the back seat said, "Man, you're lucky; if I hadn't kept the brakes on all the way, we'd have slid back down that hill again!" You may smile, but a lot of God's people live with the brakes on. They speak of being "balanced," or "prudent," or "not making waves," but the truth is, they don't make any impact at all!

On the summit of Mount Everest there's a marker placed in memory of one of the oldest climbers ever to attempt to scale the mountain. It reads simply: *"He died climbing!"* Make that your testimony!

Harold Kushner says, *"Our souls are not hungry for fame, comfort, wealth, or power. Those rewards create almost as many problems as they solve. Our souls are hungry for meaning, so that our lives matter, and the world will at least be a little bit better for our having passed through it."*

***

WHATEVER GOD'S CALLED YOU TO DO—BUILD CATHEDRALS OR SWEEP STREETS—TAKE THE BRAKES OFF AND GIVE IT EVERYTHING YOU'VE GOT!

DECEMBER 24

The Sculptor

I will pour my spirit upon thy seed, and my blessing upon thine offspring.

(Isaiah 44:3)

Listen: *I took a piece of living clay, and gently formed it day by day;*

And molded with my power and art, a young child's soft and yielding heart.

I came again when years were gone, it was a man I looked upon;

He still that early impress bore, and I could change it nevermore.

Nothing so totally changes your life as children. They'll keep you on your toes most of the time, and on your knees the rest of it. If you think having a baby will solve your problems, think again! If you think life will be easier when they reach their teens, you're dreaming! The first time they take the family car or go on a date, you'll pray that the values you taught them will guide them and bring them home safe.

If you were raised without words of love, make sure your children aren't! Tell them often that you love them—it's the basis of their self-worth. Plant the

Word deep in their hearts. Give them an anchor, because life will give them lots of storms. Cover them with prayer daily. Expect God to bless them, for He promised, "I will pour out my spirit upon thy seed."

***

THAT'S THE WORD FOR TODAY FOR YOU AND YOUR FAMILY.

DECEMBER 25

The Reason Why

Great is the mystery of godliness: God was manifest in the flesh.

(1 Timothy 3:16)

In his book, *The Reason Why,* Robert Laidlaw tells of two friends who attended law school. One became a judge, while the other squandered his life, broke the law, and one day finished up in court. Sitting on the judge's bench was his old friend, and everyone wondered what kind of sentence he would pass. To their surprise, he demanded the full penalty of the law. No sooner had he passed sentence, however, than he stepped from the seat of judgment, took off his robes, and walked over to the dock where his old friend stood. He put his arm around him and gently said, "Let it be recorded today that not only have I passed sentence upon him, *but I will stand chargeable with all his debts."* In that moment, his *judge* became his *redeemer.*

Christmas is the story of the day God took off the robes of deity and put on the garments of humanity. He left a palace to come to a stable because He *loved you.* Listen to the poet:

The Maker of the universe, As man for man was made a curse.

The claims of law that he had made, Unto the uttermost He paid.

Did you hear that? *He* paid! Had you been the only sinner who ever lived. He would have *come*. He would have *died,* and He would have *paid* the price just for you!

***

GREAT IS THE MYSTERY OF GODLINESS!

DECEMBER 26

Enough Is Enough!

Shamgar ... killed six hundred Philistines with an ox goad, thereby saving Israel.

(Judges 3:31 TLB)

The Philistines had been running roughshod through the land, bullying God's people, and Shamgar wasn't taking anymore. Maybe like we do, he had been waiting for God to do something about it. But God was waiting for him, because all He needs is someone He can use.

Shamgar discovered he had *rights.* The right to *own.* The right to *defend.* The right to *win.* Do you know your rights today? Listen: "Keep the charge of the Lord thy God, to walk in his ways, to keep his statutes ... that thou mayest prosper in all that thou doest" (1 Kings 2:3). You have the right to succeed! Look at who your Father is!

You also have the right to *defend* what God has given you. Don't surrender your family to the world. Remember, God keeps His promises: "All thy children shall be taught of the Lord; and great shall be the peace of thy children" (Isaiah 54:13). Shamgar wasn't talented; he was simply determined! And God honored that determination. He not only slew six hundred Philistines; he delivered an entire nation.

***

TODAY, IT'S TIME TO TELL THE ENEMY, "ENOUGH IS ENOUGH!"

DECEMBER 27

"Good Night, Gracie"

I am bringing all of my energies to bear on … forgetting the past and looking forward...

(Philippians 3:13 TLB)

Are you old enough to remember television's *The Burns and Allen Show?* At the end of each episode, George Burns would look at Gracie Allen and simply say, "Good night, Gracie." When those words were spoken, the show was over—finished!

And sometimes that's all it takes: a simple "good night." You lay it to rest, and you move on.

I've spent endless hours counseling people who've lost precious time constantly struggling with issues that should have been put to bed a long time ago. How much happier and more productive they could have been if they'd just faced them, and simply said, "Good night, Gracie."

More things are forgotten than are ever solved, so take stock of your life today and determine what's holding you back. Recognize your losses, and have the courage to write them off. That's what Paul did. Listen: "Forgetting the past and looking forward to what lies ahead." Until you get over the past, you'll keep sacrificing your future. Don't live that way another day!

If you're still obsessing over past failures, listen to this promise: "I've blotted out your sins; they are gone ... return to me, for I have paid the price to set you free" (Isaiah 44:22 TLB).

***

WHAT MORE DO YOU NEED?

DECEMBER 28

Rebuild Your Altar

Then he restored the altar of the Lord.

(2 Chronicles 33:16 NIV)

Just about anybody in the Bible who ever made a difference built an altar unto the Lord. Abraham built seven during his lifetime.

In this story Manasseh turned back to God. Listen: "In his distress he sought the favor of the Lord his God and humbled himself greatly before the God of his fathers (2 Chronicles 33:12 NIV). Few had fallen lower than this man. He promoted witchcraft, practiced human sacrifice, and even put a huge idol into the Temple. Yet in a Babylonian prison he turned to God. And the One whose "compassions fail not" reached him, restored him, and gave him another chance—*and He'll do it for you, too!* Nehemiah says, "Thou art a God ready to pardon" (Nehemiah 9:17). Did you hear that? God is ready when you are—all you have to do is come to Him.

Manasseh rebuilt his altar, and so must you. An altar is a place of *cleansing.* Today allow the blood of Jesus to cleanse you from the attitudes and actions that rob you of your fellowship with Him. It's also a place of *sacrifice.* Ask Abraham! It's here that God asks you for your *first,* your *only,* your *best,* and your *all.*

***

IF YOU'RE NOT GIVING IT TO HIM, THEN EXAMINE YOUR LIFE AND START PUTTING FIRST THINGS FIRST!

DECEMBER 29

Seize the Day

"This is the day that the Lord has made; we will rejoice and be glad in it."

(Psalm 118:24)

Listen to these words:

I cannot count the times I called my sister and asked, "How about going to lunch today?" She would gasp and stammer, "I can't ... I have clothes in the washer ... my hair is dirty ... I wish I'd known yesterday ... I had a late breakfast ... It looks like rain." And my personal favorite, "It's Monday." Well ... she died a few days ago, and we never did have lunch together!

We have so many excuses for postponing life ... We'll visit the grandparents when we get the baby potty-trained ... have friends over when we're able to replace the living room carpet ... go on a second honeymoon when we get the kids through college. Are you listening to yourself at all?

Life has a way of accelerating as you get older. The days get shorter and the list of promises gets longer. Then suddenly you wake up one day, and all you have to show is a list of "I'm going to's," or "I plan to's," or "someday when things are settled down a bit."

Seize the day! Live in the present! If it helps, think about all those people on the *Titanic* who passed up dessert! For what? David said, "This is the day that the Lord has made; we will rejoice and be glad in it."

***

TODAY'S A GIFT FROM GOD; GRAB IT AND SQUEEZE EVERY OUNCE OF JOY FROM IT!

DECEMBER 30

Breaking Addictions

The Lord is the strength of my life.

(Psalm 27:1)

What are you addicted to? Think before you answer! What controls you? What is it that you just can't live without? What is it that you constantly turn to, to relieve your pain, your loneliness, or your frustration?

Addictive behavior is usually just an attempt to hide from reality, or to put off dealing with areas where we're hurt, or angry, or afraid.

A well-known Christian author writes: "Except for cigarettes, most of my addictions did not fall under the heading of substance abuse. I was addicted to reasoning ... worry ... judgment ... compliments ... self-pity ... pouting ... controls ... and work. When I realized I was addicted to these things, I determined that in God's strength, I was going to be free and live a disciplined and productive life.

"Everything was great—until the pain started. If I had not had the inner strength to withstand it, I'd have given in, which would have temporarily relieved the pain but started the cycle all over again.

"Today God does not just want to *give* you strength—He wants to be your strength. Think about that! Through His indwelling power, He wants you to know that you can break every addiction in your life!"

***

WHEN YOU BECOME ADDICTED TO JESUS AND HIS PRECEPTS—YOU'LL WATCH YOUR OTHER ADDICTIONS VANISH!

DECEMBER 31

Come to Jesus

Are you tired? Worn out? Burned out on religion? Come to me, I won't lay anything heavy or ill fitting on you. Keep company with me and you'll learn to live.

(Matthew 11:28-29 TM)

Why do we continue preaching a God who cannot be approached to people who have spent most of their lives hiding from Him? Their concept of God is already distorted. Some have said to me, "God's too holy; I can't measure up." Listen, your acceptance is not based on His *holiness;* it's based on His *love. God* thinks you're worth saving, so He redeems you by His love. His *standards* never change, but neither does His *compassion.* Listen: "His compassions fail not. They are new every morning" (Lamentations 3:22-23). Without that none of us have hope!

The basis of any worthwhile relationship must be *trust.* We can talk to *anyone* about our successes, but we need someone we can talk to about our failures. We have to know for sure that they understand the *worst* about us and still believe the *best.* If you want someone to love you completely, then they must *know* you completely, because only then will their love satisfy you. That's why Jesus said, "Come to Me."

You have nothing to fear when you tell it to Jesus, for you're not telling Him anything He doesn't already know. Even before you approach Him today, He has already made up His mind about you.

$$* * *$$

YOU'RE LOVED. YOU'RE SECURE. YOU'RE HIS. WHAT MORE DO YOU NEED?

Everybody needs a new beginning and a fresh start for each day.

Find out why over one million people are regular readers of Bob Gass's devotional writings!

Other Inspiring Books From BOB GASS

The Life-Series

Overcome past hurts and disappointments, discover that failing in a situation doesn't make you a failure, and unlock your creativity to learn how to succeed at being yourself.

Back Cover Material

A JUMP-START FOR COLD MORNINGS

The lives of millions of people have been touched by the uplifting daily devotionals in the *Best of the Word for Today.* Many say, "It's just what I needed today."

This book is filled with spiritual insights and divine revelations from the Word of God. As you read, you will be challenged, inspired, led, and transformed. There is no better way to begin each day.

Bob Gass writes, "The only difference between what you are right now and what you'll be five years from now is in: (a) the books you read; (b) the relationships you build; (c) your ability to hear from God for yourself. This book is a jump-start for cold mornings. It contains 365 of our best days, One idea, just one, can change your entire life. Here are a year's worth of them-just for you."

BOB GASS was twelve years old when he opened his heart to the call of God. At that time he was living in war-torn Belfast, Northern Ireland. Five years later he came to the United States of America to follow the call of God and to share the light of God's Word. As a result, countless lives have been touched and changed. His devotional writings and his other books are read by millions of people around the world. His books include *A Fresh Word for Today, Forgetting Your Past, Discovering Your Destiny, and Starting Over.*

Books For ALL Kinds of Readers

At ReadHowYouWant we understand that one size does not fit all types of readers. Our innovative, patent pending technology allows us to design new formats to make reading easier and more enjoyable for you. This helps improve your speed of reading and your comprehension. Our EasyRead printed books have been optimized to improve word recognition, ease eye tracking by adjusting word and line spacing as well as minimizing hyphenation. Our EasyRead SuperLarge editions have been developed to make reading easier and more accessible for vision-impaired readers. We offer Braille and DAISY formats of our books and all popular E-Book formats.

We are continually introducing new formats based upon research and reader preferences. Visit our web-site to see all of our formats and learn how you can Personalize our books for yourself or as gifts. Sign up to Become A RHYW Registered Reader.

www.readhowyouwant.com

Printed in Great Britain
by Amazon